COMPELLING INTEREST

Compelling Interest

EXAMINING THE EVIDENCE

ON RACIAL DYNAMICS

IN COLLEGES AND UNIVERSITIES

Edited by
Mitchell J. Chang,
Daria Witt,
James Jones,
and Kenji Hakuta

STANFORD EDUCATION
An imprint of Stanford University Press

Stanford University Press
Stanford, California

Printed in the United States of America
on acid-free, archival-quality paper.

Library of Congress Cataloging-in-Publication Data

Compelling interest : examining the evidence on racial dynamics
in colleges and universities / edited by Mitchell J. Chang ... [et al.].
    p. cm.
  Includes bibliographical references and index.
   ISBN 0-8047-4034-8 (cloth : alk. paper) —
ISBN 0-8047-4035-6 (pbk. : alk. paper)
    1. Discrimination in higher education—United States.
2. Educational equalization—United States.   3. Affirmative
action programs—United States.   I. Chang, Mitchell J.
LC212.42 .C66   2003
378.1'9829—dc21   2002151608

Original Printing 2003
Last figure below indicates year of this printing:
12   11   10   09   08   07   06   05   04   03

Designed by James P. Brommer
Typeset in 10.5/14 Bembo

CONTENTS

MARYA BURKE is research associate of educational policy studies at the University of Illinois, Champaign-Urbana.

MITCHELL J. CHANG is assistant professor of higher education and organizational change at the University of California, Los Angeles.

JAMIE DAUGHERTY is research associate of educational policy studies at the University of Illinois, Champaign-Urbana.

TIMOTHY K. EATMAN is research associate of educational policy studies at the University of Illinois, Champaign-Urbana.

KENJI HAKUTA is Vida Jacks Professor of Education at Stanford University.

JAMES JONES is professor of psychology at the University of Delaware.

SHANA LEVIN is assistant professor of psychology at Claremont McKenna College.

JEFFREY F. MILEM is associate professor of education at the University of Maryland.

KATHY NORMAN is research associate of educational policy studies at the University of Illinois, Champaign-Urbana.

DAWN OWENS-NICHOLSON is research associate of educational policy studies at the University of Illinois, Champaign-Urbana.

WILLIAM TRENT is professor of educational policy studies and sociology at the University of Illinois, Champaign-Urbana.

LINDA F. WIGHTMAN recently retired from her appointment as professor of education at the University of North Carolina, Greensboro.

DARIA WITT was associate director of the American Educational Research Association's Presidential Panel on Racial Dynamics in Higher Education and a research associate for the Center for Comparative Studies in Race and Ethnicity at Stanford University.

American higher education in recent years has become the locus of high-profile debates about race-conscious social policy. This focus is fueled by the ever-increasing stakes associated with advanced degrees, a broad public recognition of demographic changes, and a general sense that these goods—whether in public or private institutions—need to be distributed in a fair and just manner. Not far below the surface of the policy debates lies a complex tangle of ideologies, histories, and blame that often interferes with rational analysis of the issues. Despite these complexities, many social scientists and educators believe that empirical research on the significance of race in American society can make an important contribution to this highly politicized and emotionally charged arena of public policy.

With these issues in mind, a project initiated by the American Educational Research Association and the Center for Comparative Studies in Race and Ethnicity at Stanford University was launched in the summer of 1997 to inform public policy by examining a broad array of the social science literature that addresses the intersection of race and higher education. For this project, a panel of race relations and diversity experts from across the country was convened to discuss and explore the knowledge base on race and intergroup relations in colleges and universities.

The panel members include Walter Allen, James Banks (ex officio), Shirley Brice-Heath, Willis Hawley, Sylvia Hurtado, James Jones (co-chair), Yolanda T. Moses, Daryl Smith, Claude Steele, William Taylor, Ewart Thomas, William Trent, Kenji Hakuta (co-chair and principal investigator), Mitchell Chang (executive director), Daria Witt (associate director), and Clara Shin (legal analyst). Through a series of meetings that helped sharpen the focus of the project, we deliberated over the cumulative knowledge of the social sciences. In the course of our deliberations, we discovered that the research related to race-conscious social policy is substantial and consistent. Scientists like to spend much of their time scrutinizing each other's theories and methodologies, something they are trained to do very well. But when one takes several steps back from these local skirmishes and examines the entirety of the work with the benefit of distance and synthesis, considerable agreement and consensus can be found.

After the panel reached this consensus, we then proceeded to consider how existing empirical findings could best inform public policy. We are not naive about the nature of public policy, but as responsible researchers, we are aware of our social obligation to state in as clear a manner as possible what we *do* know. Given our academic strengths, we decided to compile a research volume as a means to achieve our objectives. At the initial stages of putting this book together, the expertise of panel members was called on to determine the topics for each of the chapters and to recommend experts in the field who should be commissioned to write a chapter. Panelists then consulted with the writers on the outlines and drafts of each of the chapters. The writers presented earlier drafts at a national conference, Facing the Courts of Law and Public Opinion: Social Science Evidence on Diversity in Higher Education, held at Stanford University on May 20 and 21, 1999. There were more than 275 attendees at this conference, including Bill Lann Lee, acting assistant attorney general for civil rights, who delivered the keynote address. The conference proceedings are posted online (http://www.stanford.edu/hakuta/racial_dynamics/Proceedings.htm), and feedback generated from the conference was used to refine the chapters. All of these collaborative efforts over the course of two years have resulted in this book.

The conclusions from this work can be simply stated:

- There is clear evidence of continuing inequities in educational opportunity along racial categories.
- Test-based definitions of merit are incomplete.
- Race is a major social psychological factor that structures American consciousness and social behaviors.
- Racially diversified environments, when properly utilized, lead to quantitative as well as qualitative gains (otherwise unattainable in homogeneous environments) in educational outcomes for all parties.

The major policy implications deriving from these conclusions are equally clear:

- Interventions that specifically address past and current effects of racial discrimination are still needed to achieve equality of opportunity for all.
- University admissions must operate under an inclusive definition of merit that takes into account the relative intellectual and civic contributions an applicant will make to the university and the broader community, and that accurately addresses the detrimental effects of social and environmental factors on the test performance of members of racial and ethnic groups that continue to be targets of discrimination.
- To promote widespread democratic participation and to be truly equitable, admissions and campus diversity policies should not only consider the individual but also reflect the salience and negative consequences of race in American society.
- Colleges and universities that seek to realize the full benefits of diversity for all members of the university community and of the broader society must maximize and integrate all dimensions of diversity, which includes student, faculty, and administrative composition, a more inclusive curriculum, and structured and continuing dialogue across racial and ethnic lines, to name a few.

We hope the research presented in this book serves to increase the sophistication with which society addresses the key issues of fairness, merit, and the benefits of diversity as they pertain to higher education. This book was prepared with funding support from the American Educational Research Association (AERA) and the Center for Comparative Studies in Race and Ethnicity (CSRE) at Stanford University. We are especially grateful to James Banks, who initiated this project during his tenure as president of AERA, and Albert Camarillo, director of CSRE, who encouraged this project and provided supplemental funding. We also thank Mark Rosin for his extraordinary editorial assistance. Lastly, we thank our respective departments for making available the necessary time to complete this book.

Kenji Hakuta
Mitchell J. Chang
Daria Witt
James Jones

COMPELLING INTEREST

Chapter One

INTRODUCTION

Daria Witt, Mitchell J. Chang, and Kenji Hakuta

Next year will mark the fiftieth anniversary of the pioneering Supreme Court decision *Brown v. the Board of Education of Topeka, Kansas*, which reversed *Plessy v. Ferguson* and made racial segregation illegal. The lawyers arguing the case for Brown used social science evidence to disprove the many commonly held beliefs about race and racism that had been used to justify segregation. Now, nearly fifty years later, as success and prestige become increasingly associated with advanced degrees, and as the U.S. population grows more diverse, the debates surrounding the consideration of race in higher education admissions and hiring decisions are growing more contentious, and the courts of law and public opinion are once again struggling with issues in this area that social science evidence has the potential to address.

Many questions pervade public discussions and underlie current court cases and ballot initiatives: What would a fair admissions and hiring process look like? Are standardized tests such as the SAT the best way to measure academic worth and potential? For whom are they valid and in what conditions? Who benefits from racially diverse campuses and in what ways? Should individual students all be judged by the same criteria regardless of group membership? Has the educational playing field been leveled for students of different races? Is affirmative action inherently discriminatory? To what extent does racism still exist? Does affirmative action compromise the quality of the student body? Will using only test scores and high school grades enable universities to admit enough students of color or do universities need to use alternate criteria to admit sufficient numbers? What should the role of colleges and universities be in helping to improve race relations in this country and to diversify future cadres of leaders? The research literature has much to say about these pressing questions, yet it has not received sufficient public, governmental, or legal attention. This book examines the potential of existing social science evidence to inform these very complex issues and questions in the hope of engendering more informed policies and public discourse about what has mostly been an ideologically driven topic.

Legal arguments for diversity and affirmative action are predicated on the notion that diversity (racial, ethnic, gender, and class) in higher education serves a compelling interest both to the institutions and to the society into which students will enter. Until recently, there was an assumption in much of higher education that the benefits of diversity are self-evident. Ample anecdotal evidence existed that convinced most educators of the validity of the claim. During the past few years, however, there have been many attacks on affirmative action and diversity programs in selective colleges and universities around the country. The passage of ballot initiatives in California and Washington state to end affirmative action, and court cases such as those against the University of Georgia, the University of Michigan, and the University of Texas law school have threatened the ability of higher education institutions to preserve the diversity of their student bodies. These challenges essentially question the judgments of educators about the best way to provide their students with a quality education. Although the judgments of educators may be disputable, an examination of existing research can help raise the level of discussion.

What does empirical research have to say about the educational effects of diversity? To answer this question, we conducted an extensive review of the social science literature. The research we uncovered, which we present in the following chapters, is closely aligned with the judgments of educators. In short, the evidence consistently demonstrates that a diverse student body adds value to the educational process and to institutions of higher learning when colleges and universities are committed to implementing and sustaining initiatives that promote the unique benefits that diversity provides.

Despite the general public's appearing to espouse the ideals and benefits of diversity (Ford Foundation press release, September 6, 1998), people often believe that affirmative action is not the best means for achieving a racially diverse campus and that any policy that takes race into account when apportioning opportunity inevitably harms members of racial groups who are not awarded preferences. For the most part, people acknowledge that slavery, legalized segregation, discrimination, and racism have hurt members of minority groups, particularly African Americans, in the past. A good portion of the public discourse, however, proceeds as if the Civil Rights movement brought an end to the harmful effects of policies and laws that existed for centuries and to discrimination and racism themselves. The popular belief seems to be that if they have not ended, it is time they did, but there is little that higher education can do to stamp them out completely; therefore, it is better for colleges and universities to proceed without accounting for racial differences (D'Souza 1991; Thernstrom and Thernstrom 1997).

Because of such interpretations, when it comes to determining how to allocate prized positions in highly selective institutions of higher education, "fairness" and "justice" are accepted at face value and not in relation to broader social circumstances. In other words, instead of understanding affirmative action as a policy that affords opportunity to students who have demonstrated merit despite the many obstacles that have arisen largely as the result of the historical vestiges of racism, it is understood as denying opportunity to more "qualified" individuals who happen to be white. The ways in which being white has afforded privileges to many individuals and generations of their family are not acknowledged. Indeed, this view of fairness ignores the very segregated nature of our society in which the majority of racial groups continue to lead almost completely separate existences and the different opportunities that those separate existences afford or deny (Hacker 1992; Massey and Denton 1993; Schuman et al. 1997).

This book takes the arguments concerning affirmative action in higher education and places them within the frame of reference that the last twenty years of social science research provides. It synthesizes the rapidly expanding, cumulative body of evidence on these issues in order to bring both contemporary and historical context into the discussions taking place in the courts and in public discourse. Although this book brings evidence to bear on what the benefits of diversity are, such evidence cannot be disentangled from the larger issues of the role of higher education, fairness and merit, and the ways in which race continues to matter in the United States. A broader consideration of the arguments can help clarify the compelling interest that diversity serves to individuals, institutions, and society. Before addressing some of those larger issues, we first present an overview of the status of affirmative action in higher education.

Case Law and the Benefits of Diversity

The legal notion of diversity as a compelling interest of an institution of higher education was defined by Justice Lewis Powell's decision in the 1978 Supreme Court case *Regents of the University of California v. Bakke*. This case challenged the University of California at Davis (UC Davis) medical school's practice of reserving sixteen spots in each entering class of one hundred for African American, Latino, and Asian American students—students who, as a group, commonly experienced racial discrimination. Allan Bakke, a white applicant, sued UC Davis claiming that the admissions process violated the Equal Protection Clause as well as Title VI of the 1964 Civil Rights Act, which bars racial discrimination by federally assisted institutions.

Justice Powell, who supplied the pivotal vote on this decision, held that racial quotas were unconstitutional but that a university should be permitted to take into account an applicant's race as part of the admissions process. Applying the strict scrutiny standard, Powell stated that the plan was permissible if (1) its objective was compelling and (2) the racial classification was necessary to achieve the objective. Powell wrote that diversity could be achieved through a process in which all factors being equal, race could be considered as a "plus" factor. He rejected other proposed objectives, including the need to reduce the shortage of minority medical students and doctors, the need to cure the results of past discrimination by society, and the need to increase the number of doctors who will practice in currently underserved communities.

Powell identified the medical school's interest in providing the educational benefits of a diverse student body as a permissible basis for the consideration of race in student admissions. Explaining this decision, Powell stated that qualified students with a background that is diverse in some way, whether it be ethnic, geographic, or economic, may bring to a professional school experiences, outlooks, and ideas that enhance the training of the student body and better equip the institution's graduates. Powell maintained that in addition to producing leaders trained through wide exposure to a robust exchange of ideas, a diverse student body encourages speculation, experimenting, and creativity that is central to the mission and quality of higher education.

Although in this case Justice Powell was writing solely for himself and not the majority of a deeply divided Supreme Court, his opinion in *Bakke* is now regularly upheld to defend race-conscious admissions programs. The extent to which Powell's opinion represents the opinion of the Court and educational realities is now being challenged on legal, civic, and empirical grounds.

Current Status of Minority Student Admissions

Although *Bakke* is still the law of the land in most of the country, the 1996 *Hopwood* decision in the U.S. Fifth Circuit Court (affecting Texas, where the suit was filed, as well as Louisiana and Mississippi) and the passage of the ballot initiatives Proposition 209 in California and Initiative 200 in Washington have outlawed the consideration of race in higher education admissions and hiring decisions in these states. Other ballot initiatives in states such as Florida threaten to overturn *Bakke* as well. Without *Bakke* and the permissibility of considering race as a "plus factor," the numbers of non-Asian minority students at selective public institutions in those states have drastically decreased.[1] In 1998, the first year Proposition 209 was in effect in the undergraduate admissions process, there was a 66 percent decline in the number of black students and a 53 percent decline in the number of Latino students admitted to the University of California at Berkeley, one of the flagship campuses of the University of California system.

At Boalt, California's most selective public law school, when Proposition 209 went into effect in the fall of 1997, the entering class included only one African American and fourteen Latino students.[2] To counter this alarmingly small enrollment of African American and Latino students, Boalt administrators implemented a number of changes and efforts in 1998. Among those efforts were reducing the importance of minute differences in grade point averages and law school board scores, abolishing the practice of granting bonus points to Ivy League applicants, encouraging students to write about their experiences with overcoming adversity (including discrimination), and granting extra consideration to qualified applicants who came from low socioeconomic backgrounds. Moreover, University of California campuses in general have engaged in stronger outreach to recruit qualified minority students from around the state. Overall these efforts resulted in more than doubling the previous year's number of underrepresented minority students choosing to attend Boalt (Boalt Hall news release, August 17, 1998).[3] Nevertheless, the number of underrepresented minority students attending both Boalt and the University of California, Berkeley, as a whole is still less than 50 percent of what it was before the elimination of affirmative action.

The University of California has also implemented some of the above changes at the undergraduate level. In addition, Governor Gray Davis in 1999 approved a Four Percent Plan in which the top 4 percent of each high school class would be admitted to the University of California system regardless of SAT score. Deemphasizing standardized test scores may well increase the acceptance rate of underrepresented students into the University of California system because this strategy addresses the persistent test score disparities between different racial groups. However, it is unclear whether this plan will significantly increase the enrollment of underrepresented students at both Berkeley and the University of California, Los Angeles (UCLA), the state's public flagship institutions. The numbers and proportion of African American and Latino students on these two campuses have shrunk as a result of Proposition 209, whereas the enrollment figures for these two groups of students have increased at less selective universities in the University of California system (i.e., University of California at Riverside; see Traub 1999). Interestingly, Proposition 209 has not resulted in the absence of non-Asian minorities from the University of California system. It has, instead, seemingly produced a significantly more segregated system in which the flagship institutions are predominantly white and Asian and the least selective institutions are disproportionately black and Hispanic. If this trend continues, it will have serious implications for not only de facto racial segregation but also equal educational and postgraduate opportunities (Karabel 1999). An effective plan will need to take into account both the overall enrollment of underrepresented students in the University of California system as well as their enrollment in the two most prestigious institutions.

In Texas, after the *Hopwood* decision, the decline in minority admissions was equally dramatic. In 1996, before the decision, there had been 266 matriculating black undergraduate students in the state's flagship university, the University of Texas at Austin. In 1997, the number had dropped to 190. Alarmed by this precipitous drop, the Texas legislature passed a Ten Percent Plan in which the top 10 percent of students from every high school in the state would automatically qualify for admission regardless of their SAT scores. This plan did not, however, increase the number of African American students to the level hoped—in 1998, only 199 African American students matriculated. By comparison, Latino student enrollment was not set back as much: in the fall of 1996, 932 Latino students enrolled, compared with 892 in 1997, and 891 in 1998 (University of Texas, Austin Office of Institutional Studies, November 4 1998, personal communication).

More recently, the *Chronicle of Higher Education* (Hebel 2000) reported that debates over affirmative action at the University of Virginia, which triggered the elimination of a scoring system that gave "booster points" to black applicants, may account for the largest single-year drop in black applicants in the institution's history. The number of black students seeking undergraduate admission to the University of Virginia fell by more than 25 percent, dropping from 1,287 in 1999 to 961 in 2000. According to the *Chronicle*, this drop fueled more campus debates over admissions policies and the wisdom of retreating from more aggressive affirmative action practices.

The Significance of Attending a Selective Institution

As a wide range of strategies are developed and implemented to increase the enrollment of underrepresented students in the wake of regional bans on affirmative action, a competing perspective has recently gained wider public attention. This perspective, which is typified by a recent article by James Traub (1999) in the *New York Times Magazine*, argues that the "end" of affirmative action is actually the "beginning of something better." In the absence of affirmative action, according to this argument, more legitimate efforts such as enhanced outreach programs will eventually bring the numbers of minority students back (almost) to their original levels. In the mean time, students who are not accepted to the most selective institutions "cascade down" to the less selective ones. The result, Traub hypothesizes, is that everyone is better off because no students are asked to do work that is over their heads and no students feel undeserving of the spots awarded them by their institutions.

This rethinking of race-conscious policies appeals to popular sentiments about educational access and meritocracy. Critiquing this argument, which he refers to as the new "conventional wisdom," Jerome Karabel (1999) points out that today's situation with professional schools easily belies the notion that everyone will be accommodated somewhere so affirmative action is not necessary. For example, according to Karabel, 62 percent of those who apply to medical school each year are not accepted by a single one. Therefore, a student cannot necessarily "cascade down" to another school lower down the pecking order. As Karabel states: "if you cascade down, you cascade out," and you are prohibited from joining the future ranks of doctors. The new "conventional wisdom" also fails to acknowledge that attending a selective undergraduate institution dramatically increases minority students' chances of both graduating and being accepted into a graduate or professional school (Bowen and Bok 1998). The latter is especially significant at a time when advanced degrees are becoming increasingly necessary for obtaining high-ranking leadership positions in many fields.

If admission to selective universities were not seen as a gateway to other golden financial and social opportunities, then race-conscious policies that grant access to that gateway would draw little fire. But clearly, attending and graduating from an elite institution afford significant tangible benefits. The groundbreaking study by two former university presidents, William Bowen and Derek Bok (1998), offers strong evidence for sizable economic advantages (in addition to other benefits) that attending a selective institution brings to students of all races. Among their many findings is that on average, relative earnings for white male graduates who in 1976 entered one of the twenty-eight selective schools in their study were 61 percent higher than were the earnings of their counterparts—that is, others who had received a B.A.—nationwide. They also found that the salaries of white female graduates of these schools who had matriculated in 1976 were on average 55 percent higher than those of their national counterparts. Graduating from a selective institution improves earning prospects for blacks even more significantly than it does for whites. The findings of Bowen and Bok's study show that black male college graduates from the twenty-eight selective institutions in their sample were found to earn an average of 82 percent more than their counterparts with B.A.'s nationwide. Similarly, black female graduates of these selective institutions earned 73 percent more than did black female college graduates nationwide.

Significantly, Bowen and Bok's findings contrast sharply with the popular image of minority students who are "in over their heads" at the selective schools into which they were admitted through affirmative action. Their results show that by every measure of success (e.g., grade point average, graduate school admissions, higher earnings after college, and satisfaction with college experience), the more selective the college or university that African American students attended, the more they achieved, holding constant their initial test scores and grades. Despite this evidence, one of the most common arguments levied against affirmative action is that it is unfair to the students who are admitted when they are not "qualified" to do the work.

Given the many tangible short- and long-term benefits gained from attending a selective college or university, many fear that decreased access to those institutions will not only negatively affect educational opportunities but will also exacerbate occupational, residential, and social segregation. It is important to point out that university affirmative action programs, taken together, seek to ensure universal access to higher education by striving to provide broader access for underrepresented minority groups, particularly to the most selective institutions. The majority of colleges and universities in the United States are not selective and do not need to have policies of affirmative action.[4] Indeed, given the current demands of the United States workforce for international competitiveness and solvency, the basic tensions underlying affirmative action debates do not center on whether or not higher education should be available to all those qualified and willing to participate, but on what "merits" the small number of spots available at highly selective institutions should be granted. Therefore, affirmative action litigation and much of the recent diversity literature focus on the admissions practices of four-year selective institutions of higher education that have disproportionately high numbers of white students. For these reasons, nonselective universities, community colleges, or colleges specifically targeted to underrepresented minority student populations (e.g., historically black colleges and universities) are often ignored in these discussions, even though those institutions provide fundamental insights into how higher education can best use diversity to achieve widespread educational benefits.

An important objective of this book is to broaden the thinking about diversity in order to move beyond the legal controversy over affirmative action policies and the allocation of the small number of spots available at selective institutions. This interest is driven in part by our concerns about the myopic and misleading legal challenges that neglect the dynamics of race in American society. After careful examination of the research literature, it became clear to us that the charges against affirmative action contradict the social science evidence. As such, we are troubled by the litigation surrounding affirmative action not only because it endangers the potential for maximizing the educational benefits of diversity at institutions such as the University of Michigan and UCLA, but also because it perpetuates certain pernicious myths about the reality of racism in this country (that it has ended), about the nature of university curricula (that they are now more inclusive), about the potential for underrepresented minorities to succeed (that they are inherently inferior), and about what constitutes merit (grades and test scores only). Although the legal consequences of affirmative action litigation have a direct impact only on the selective institutions and their applicants, the underlying implications that arise from this litigation are central to related educational practices of all institutions, regardless of their degree of selectivity, and to the pursuit of civil rights in society at large. It is in this broader context, relevant to all institutions of higher education, that we wish to consider debates over affirmative action and the need for racial diversity. To broaden the discourse, in this introduction we briefly raise several pressing issues and concerns that underlie the discussions throughout this book and are addressed more substantively in other chapters.

The Role of Higher Education

Perhaps most disturbing about the current attacks on affirmative action is that they regularly ignore the fact that the mission of virtually every college and university extends beyond the needs and rights of the individual student and institution to include as well an aspiration to improve the communities and lives of people who live beyond the university walls. Arguably, before the introduction of the GI Bill, higher education was considered a privilege bestowed only on the select few who were typically wealthy, male, and white. As societal values came to reflect civil rights interests, and as technology and other innovations have heightened the need for a highly skilled, well-educated, and highly specialized workforce, the need to diversify access to higher education has grown commensurately. At the individual level, a four-year degree grows increasingly critical in determining life opportunities. According to Donald Kennedy, former president of Stanford University, the impact of postsecondary education on lifetime earnings grew during the 1980s to create the largest disparity in history between those with college education and those without. Higher education also has an increasing responsibility for our country's economic future. As Kennedy states, "Higher education today is challenged to fulfill a new and staggering burden. Always expected to make young people more skilled, more cultured, and more thoughtful, it now is seen as the motive power for regional economic improvement and even for international competitiveness" (Kennedy 1997, 3).

If formerly underrepresented minority students now have widespread access to college education, why do we need to be concerned with bolstering diversity at elite institutions? Again, tensions surrounding the answer to this question emerge from conflicting notions of higher education, and specifically, elite higher education, as a private or a public good. Opponents of affirmative action have framed the debate in terms of the unfairness that the race-conscious admissions policy inflicts on the nonbeneficiaries of the policy, who as individuals are bereft of the prospects for higher earnings and better education they allegedly would have been granted in the policy's absence. We believe that limiting the mission of higher education to only individual interests is too narrow. The purpose of education, according to Thomas Jefferson, is not just to serve the individual participant but to foster a society of educated people who will in turn contribute to the economic and civic life of the entire community. Institutions of higher education, particularly elite institutions, have become an important medium for developing future societal leaders and for the advancement of knowledge essential to engendering economic progress and democratic participation. For these and other reasons, most colleges and universities have implemented an array of what might be loosely termed diversity initiatives (Chang 2000; Hurtado et al. 1998; Smith et al. 1997).

In determining their diversity policies, both universities and the communities into which they send their students must grapple with the following questions: To what extent can students receive a meaningful education that prepares them to participate in an increasingly diverse society if the student body and faculty are not diverse? How can universities address the issues that are central to a diverse society if they do not have adequate representation of that diversity? What role should universities play in compensating students for the inequities present in our current K-12 education system (Orfield 1990, 1992; Valencia 1991; Trent 1991; U.S. Department of Education, National Center for Education Statistics 1992)? What do selective institutions and the communities into which they send their students lose if they lack diversity? In other words, what are the implications of excluding people of color from the cohorts of those being prepared for leadership in our society?

Individual answers to these questions depend in part on whether one believes that higher education should anticipate the public's needs before they arise or merely react to them after they are felt. If the former, then the "health, the progress—indeed the survival—of universities," using the words of Constantine Zurayk (1968, 22), are linked to whether institutions can anticipate and develop effective strategies for the needs of a rapidly changing society. To be sure, the role of the university has changed dramatically over the past century, reflecting the changing needs and interests of society. In contrast to the early days of higher education, when universities were seen more as ivory towers divorced from the everyday workings of general society, the past century has witnessed a greater reliance by government and policy makers on these institutions of higher education (Bok 1990). The growing influence of the university is particularly evident in the case of elite institutions, which are usually research institutions that have tremendous influence on society. If colleges and universities are to remain responsive and relevant to the needs of the broader society, diversity-related issues will surely take on even greater significance as our nation's population grows increasingly more diverse. The linkage between diversity and the societal relevance of the university is reflected in the following statement made by the University of Texas chancellor William H. Cunningham in reference to the decision by the University of Texas Regents to appeal the *Hopwood* case: "Texas will soon be a majority/minority state. The long-term social, cultural, and economic vitality of Texas is irrevocably linked to its ability to recruit and graduate minority students. While families and the public school system share the major role in the process of preparing students to enter college, institutions of higher education must recognize their responsibility to recruit and graduate Texans from all ethnic backgrounds" (University of Texas system, press release, May 13, 1998).

In our own experiences as college and university professors and administrators, we have witnessed firsthand the tremendous impact that the presence of diversity in the student body, faculty, and administration has had at the institutions in which we work and in academia in general. Entirely new curricula have evolved, along with the emergence of new ways of analyzing problems, new historical, literary, and political paradigms, innovative pedagogical approaches and areas of research, and enduring bonds with local communities, all of which have made universities more dynamic, relevant, and intellectually stimulating places to work and learn. Although one's skin color and ethnicity do not reflect a particular mindset, given the significance of race in American society, people of different racial and ethnic backgrounds are likely to bring different experiences, perspectives, interests, and analyses to a college campus.

The presence of diversity in colleges and universities may also have implications for adequately preparing students for citizenship. Dennis W. Brogan (1944) once observed that high schools are places where students "instruct" each other to live in America. As the next century approaches, this statement is even more applicable to American colleges and universities, which have come to be viewed as a rite of passage to adulthood and lives beyond the university walls. Judging from the empirical evidence discussed in this book and from our own observations, students who are exposed to diverse experiences, perspectives, and ways of thinking that truly reflect the multiracial and multiethnic society of the United States will be better prepared to participate meaningfully in it.

College and university campuses are also ideal settings for engaging students in diversity-related issues. Traditional-age college students, for example, are relatively more open to embracing new ideas and to exposing themselves to different experiences. Consequently, college students often undergo tremendous personal growth and changes in their attitudes and perspectives during their undergraduate years (Astin 1993). Moreover, unlike K–12 schools, the relative autonomy of institutions of higher education allows these institutions to be more deliberate about engaging students, research, and educational programs. Given these unique conditions, colleges and universities have a rare opportunity to challenge students' stereotypes and to engender a willingness in students to improve their understanding of and interactions with people of other racial and ethnic groups.

This opportunity should not be overlooked, because natural settings in which diverse individuals share common goals and relatively equal status are rare yet extremely important for improving racial dynamics. Given the persistent patterns of segregated housing and K–12 schooling, many college students will encounter their first substantial experience with diversity during their undergraduate years. As historian Thomas Sugrue (1999) states in his deposition on behalf of the University of Michigan in the lawsuit brought against it: "There are unfortunately few places in American society where people of different backgrounds interact, learn from each other and struggle to understand their differences and discover their commonality." Residential settings on campuses, for example, present a unique but often untapped opportunity for molding intergroup relations.

Unfortunately, many universities relegate their diversity initiatives to marginalized multicultural affairs offices or offices of affirmative action that are piecemeal, understaffed, and not central to the infrastructure of the university. Although diversity initiatives have begun to evolve on many campuses, diversity is still too often compartmentalized into admissions, curriculum, a few racial awareness workshops, and hiring (the addition of a small number of minority faculty and staff), each of which is considered beneficial mostly to the students who are members of groups traditionally denied access. By contrast, when diversity is viewed as central to the educational enterprise and there is a strong, integrated commitment at all levels of the institution, the research literature shows that all members of the university community benefit from the new ideas, perspectives, ways of approaching problems, teaching methods, and scholarship (Smith et al. 1997). Given these benefits, new curricular approaches that embrace diversity should not be viewed as benefiting only students of color (and implicitly harming white students by "dumbing down" the curriculum); instead, these approaches should be recognized as providing an intellectually enriching and relevant "world-class" education for *all* students.

Merit

Another important issue in the affirmative action debate surrounds the notion of merit. In the public discourse, equity and excellence in higher education are often pitted against each other. Merit is usually narrowly, and exclusively, equated with test scores, and because the scores of blacks, Latinos, and Native Americans are as a group approximately one standard deviation below those of whites and Asians, these minority students are considered to be less deserving. Court cases such as *Hopwood v. Texas* and *Gratz v. Bollinger* have presented the score differentials between non-Asian minority students and the plaintiffs as central components of their testimony.

Equating merit solely with test scores ignores the multifaceted dimensions of academic success. Those who have earned a college degree know quite well that this achievement requires more than just high test scores. Other individual characteristics such as perseverance, creativity, experiences outside the classroom, demonstrated commitment to different causes, resiliency, public-speaking skills, leadership capacity, and ability to overcome challenges, to name a few, contribute to academic success. Moreover, because colleges and universities are responsible for providing their students with the best education possible, the notion of success at the institutional level can also be legitimately broadened to include an applicant's capacity to educate others and to contribute to each campus's intellectual and cultural life. Indeed, most institutions look beyond standardized test scores. What is routinely ignored in court cases that allege unfair preferential treatment toward minorities when differences in test scores are apparent is the fact that many white students with lower test scores than those of the plaintiffs were also admitted because they possess certain qualities that the university seeks (e.g., *Gratz v. Bollinger*). Some of these qualities might also be immutable characteristics, such as geographical diversity or legacy status; others might be a student's experience working on a farm or playing a musical instrument, or a student's athletic ability or commitment to public service.

Like their opponents, supporters of affirmative action also uphold the importance of merit in determining which applicants are to be admitted. The two sides disagree, however, on what constitutes merit. Supporters argue that current definitions of merit are too narrow and still favor those with privileged upbringings and backgrounds. Thus, in the absence of broader and more accurate definitions of merit, supporters of affirmative action argue that it helps to ensure that employers and institutions of higher education look beyond their traditional applicant pools and consider all qualified applicants fairly. Providing equal access and opportunity to those who have been historically excluded from these institutions was, and continues to be, the primary goal of affirmative action. As Maphela Ramphele (1999) points out in her discussion of the need for affirmative action in South Africa, throwing all applicants into the same pool and asking them to sink or swim ignores the fact that some people have "life boats," that the swimming pool is typically constructed for certain body types, and that the standards for judging success or failure to swim are shaped by the cultural lens used to evaluate performance.

Taking Account of Race

Critics charge not only that affirmative action practices contradict notions of merit but also that they violate the American creed widely considered the foundation of our society and culture. They argue, for example, that governmental efforts to artificially impose equal opportunity through race-conscious policies counteract the "race-neutral" spirit of the fourteenth amendment. In response, James Jones (1997) stressed that the Civil Rights movement regularly advocated race-conscious policies in an attempt to remove race as a barrier to opportunity and to minimize its negative impact. By all historical accounts, the movement was *not* an effort to eradicate the consideration of race in public policy. This important distinction is often obscured in the media and public discussion, where the Civil Rights movement has often been misinterpreted as having advocated a color-blind society under the slogan of "equal opportunity for all," in which equality would be achieved by abandoning race. Jones argues that to implement a policy of color blindness after centuries of affirmative action for European Americans would merely "calcify the inequality of previous generations in contemporary culture" (524). Civil rights legislation could not erase the effects of the discrimination that has persisted for centuries in this country. It could also not destroy prejudices that existed, and continue to exist, in people's minds and hearts. The paradox inherent in facilitating equal treatment of individuals by recognizing persistent biases against groups is encapsulated by a famous statement by President Lyndon B. Johnson during a 1965 speech at Howard University in which he justified the need for affirmative action:

> You do not wipe away the scars of centuries by saying: Now you are free to go where you want, and do as you desire. . . . You do not take a person, who, for years, has been hobbled by chains and liberate him, bring him to the starting line of a race and then say, you are free to compete with all the others, and still justly believe that you have been completely fair. (Quoted from Citizens' Commission on Civil Rights 1984, 27)

Given that egregious race-conscious practices originally created disparities in access and opportunities for racial minorities in this country, alternative policies that only use proxies—such as class—for race will not be nearly as effective in remedying these disparities. The research presented in the following chapters shows that different racial groups experience race with varying degrees of immediacy, meaning, and importance and that to disregard race and pursue a color-blind approach is to ignore contemporary realities. The disparity in access and opportunity between whites and blacks exists across all class levels. There is a substantial body of evidence, particularly in the desegregation literature, showing that disadvantages suffered by the poor are tremendously exacerbated by race. Although it is true that many white people are poor, it is almost exclusively Hispanics and African Americans who live in *concentrated* poverty (Massey and Denton 1993). The urban ghettos into which most low-income Hispanics and blacks are isolated present fewer opportunities for educational and economic opportunity than the more economically integrated neighborhoods in which low-income whites tend to live (Wilson 1987). This type of evidence refutes the assumption that all low-income children, regardless of race, are equally disadvantaged—one of the major premises underlying arguments for replacing the use of race with class as a plus factor in admissions decisions. Instead, the evidence supports the contention that race cuts across class barriers and that discrimination is a powerful force that money does not easily overcome.

The centuries of racism in this country have left a powerful legacy that permeates all levels of American life and that cannot, and should not, be ignored. Social science evidence belies the idealistic perception of the post–Civil Rights era that Americans are able to judge people solely on the basis of character. More likely, we live our whole lives operating within the societal constraints of our gender, class, and race (Jones 1997). To accurately assess the efficacy of affirmative action, we must understand the true effects of racism on all sectors of society. This legacy cannot be clarified or dismantled by superficial discussions and media sound bites. Thus, this book documents how group membership characteristics play a defining role in determining the experiences and access to opportunities for an individual. Although we uncovered a great deal of relevant research, it became clear to us that there is still an urgent need for more focused study of what policies and efforts are necessary to eradicate the effects of discrimination and to create truly equal opportunity. There must be broader commitment to this sort of study in order both to understand better the significance of racism's legacy and to establish effective and sustainable remedies. We believe that higher education, in which there is a tradition of focused dialogue, debate, and research, is the ideal setting for initiating and sustaining work in this area.

Although affirmative action litigation centers on admissions policies at selective schools, the impact of the litigation and the ensuing public debate are more far-reaching, as are the effects of the tendency to ignore the connection between race and opportunity and to downplay arguments of justice for past and present discrimination. The current sound bites that surface from the debates, for example, seem to have effectively persuaded the public that race and group membership are irrelevant, that racism has ended, and that individual rights should prevail over group rights. These contentions, which drive much of the public discourse on this topic, jeopardize much more than the admission of individual minority students to selective institutions. Consequently, we address in this book specific attacks on affirmative action and also the broad meaning of the absence of diversity in higher education for the public consciousness, for notions of equity, and for the meaningful education of people of all races and ages.

Synopsis

This book addresses the three major parts of the diversity debate: fairness, merit, and the benefits of diversity.

1. *Fairness*. Affirmative action policies are often criticized as being unfair because they give advantages to *individuals* on the basis of *group* membership. Fairness arguments are examined in this book through both empirical and theoretical evidence of persisting inequalities in opportunity and access for different racial groups. In an effort to dispel the common notion that only color blindness will achieve true equality, chapters also look at the extent to which racism in various forms is still prevalent among individuals and institutions in the United States, and at how race-conscious policies address racial disparities more effectively than do race-neutral ones.

2. *Merit*. To enhance our discussion of fairness, we explore the need for a broader definition of merit that moves beyond using only test scores and grades as indicators of a student's capacity for academic success.

3. *Benefits*. This book pulls together tangible, empirical evidence on the benefits that diversity (in all its multiple forms and dimensions) brings to the individual, the institution, and the broader society.

Common Misconceptions Addressed

There are four commonly accepted misconceptions about the dynamics of race in higher education and in the broader society that create powerful attitudinal barriers to embracing the benefits and fairness arguments of the diversity debate, and that prevent acceptance of a more inclusive and accurate definition of merit. Despite their lack of substantiation, these popular misconceptions have formed the basis for policies that address racial dynamics in the universities and in the broader society. The topics for each of the chapters were chosen and developed with these misconceptions in mind.

Misconception 1: Past inequalities in access and opportunity that racial and ethnic minority groups have suffered have been sufficiently addressed and no longer require attention. William Trent and his associates, in their chapter titled "Justice, Equality of Educational Opportunity, and Affirmative Action in Higher Education," examine the trends in participation in higher education by race and sector in enrollment, segregation, and earned degree patterns for 1980–96. To place these participation trends into context, Trent also examines particular features of the early stages of the educational pipeline from K-12 that have been shown to influence educational attainment. Trent reveals the tremendous disparity in the quality of the early pipeline experiences provided to students of different races, ethnicities, and socioeconomic status. These data point to the fact that until the educational playing field has been leveled, ignoring race—or developing a "color-blind" approach—disregards reality.

Misconception 2: Merit can be defined by test scores. Linda F. Wightman, in her chapter titled "Standardized Testing and Equal Access: A Tutorial," looks at the history of standardized test use and the evolution of tests as the principal screening device in determining admission to higher education. Arguments against affirmative action and other race-conscious policies that are intended to diversify university campuses are predicated on the common public notion that there are ways of measuring merit that are fairly precise and scientific, and that departure from using these tests inevitably results in unfair discrimination against someone who is more deserving. Evidence presented in this book shows that although useful, tests are far from infallible and comprehensive measures of merit, yet test scores are regularly used for measurement purposes beyond those for which they have been designed. Although these tests are statistically sound to perform a specific function, policies based on such a narrow definition of merit inevitably exclude meritorious students whose qualifications are not consonant with this definition. Wightman concludes that universities should look beyond students' test scores and grades as indicators of their capacity for academic success and include in their definitions of merit the broader qualities of leadership, perseverance, and citizenship.

Misconception 3: Fairness is best achieved through race-neutral policy. The chapter by Shana Levin, "Social Psychological Evidence on Race and Racism," reviews the theoretical and empirical evidence from the field of social psychology to examine two central questions: (1) Does race matter in everyday life? and (2) Should race matter in institutional policies? Levin presents evidence showing that although blatant forms of racism are comparatively rare, many persons still demonstrate unconscious biases toward members of minority groups, and that these biases influence social perceptions, attitudes, and behaviors with deleterious effects on the opportunities afforded many students of color. Because unintentional racial biases persist, policies of "color blindness" perpetuate the status quo. Examining various theories of fairness, Levin concludes that using the same standards to judge individuals from majority and minority groups is unfair because differences in power in society prevent the different groups from having equal opportunity. Therefore, both individual and group characteristics need to be considered in selection and evaluation procedures.

Misconception 4: Diversity programs benefit only students of color. The chapter by Jeffrey F. Milem, "The Educational Benefits of Diversity: Evidence from Multiple Sectors," addresses the question put forth by Justice Powell in the *Bakke* decision—whether a race-conscious policy serves a "compelling interest." Using a multidisciplinary analysis, Milem synthesizes evidence on how diversity benefits the individual, the institution, and society. Contrary to the popular perception that diversity programs benefit only students of color, social science evidence consistently points to the tremendous benefits that diversity in higher education brings to all students, to the institutions, and to society. Among the many benefits that diverse campuses bring are growth in higher-order thinking skills, increased motivation, improved retention, less racial stereotyping, higher earning potential, and greater likelihood of living, working, and socializing comfortably in integrated settings throughout a student's adult life. On the basis of available evidence, Milem concludes that diversity does not lower standards (as opponents of affirmative action often contend); indeed, it raises them by helping to create an environment that is more intellectually engaging because it includes a broader range of perspectives, experiences, and backgrounds.

Conclusion

After examining the knowledge base on racial dynamics in higher education, we realized that the research evidence has substantive policy implications and widespread educational usefulness, yet such linkages have not yet reached a broader audience. Part of our purpose in offering this book is to make these linkages explicit. However, we are not just documenting the state of current research in this area. We also seek to make a compelling argument for why institutions of higher learning need to focus on issues of racial dynamics, to establish a blueprint for research on what we still need to know, and to suggest strategies and practices for institutions to realize the educational benefits that diversity presents.

Our conclusions in support of affirmative action were arrived at from a rigorous systematic examination of the research as well as from our experience as educators. As we analyzed and assembled the broad spectrum of research presented in this book, we were particularly troubled by public discourse about diversity and racial dynamics, which for the most part has been based on views unsubstantiated by empirical evidence. The chapters that follow demonstrate how empirical evidence creates a very different view of racial dynamics in this country than that shaped by popular misconceptions. Although the evidence in this area is still emerging, there are many lessons to be learned from social science research that have powerful, immediate implications for diversity-related policies in higher education. The research shows, for example, that to bring about the benefits that a diverse student body potentially offers, institutional efforts must extend beyond admissions policies. Diversity must be conceptualized broadly to encompass any aspect of the institution that affects education or campus life. In short, all levels of the university must undergo a meaningful and substantive transformation (Chang 2000; Hurtado et al. 1998). When this happens, the evidence reviewed in this book indicates that the benefits associated with diversity do not only have a high rate of return, but are necessary for creating truly equal opportunity and for effectively educating students to live in the twenty-first century.

Chapter Two

JUSTICE, EQUALITY OF EDUCATIONAL
OPPORTUNITY, AND AFFIRMATIVE
ACTION IN HIGHER EDUCATION

William Trent, Dawn Owens-Nicholson, Timothy K. Eatman,
Marya Burke, Jamie Daugherty, and Kathy Norman

Attaining the complementary goals of social justice and equality of educational opportunity has always required strong affirmative efforts. This is especially the case in higher education. This chapter examines the evidence of our nation's progress in pursuit of those goals. We begin by examining features of the early stages of the educational experience that have been shown to influence college access. Specifically, we present data on early-childhood education, children at risk, the changing demographics of the schools, average reading proficiency, racial/ethnic and socioeconomic status composition of school districts by district size, and tracking and ability grouping.

We then present data on the patterns and trends in participation in higher education by race and sector—using the Carnegie classification—for the period 1980–96.[1] We report enrollment and segregation patterns for selected years during this period, and we address several questions. First, what are the patterns—levels, trends, contrasts—of participation in higher education by race and sector? We examine this question with respect to enrollment at the undergraduate level, with mention of earned degrees. Second, what is the approximate amount of diversity that characterizes undergraduate education? To investigate this question, we measured the level of segregation within four sectors of higher education.

The overall intent of our analyses is to understand better relative participation levels and differences in and across various sectors by race. The use of race as a factor in admissions obviously affects members of each minority group, including African Americans, Latino/as, Native Americans, and Asian Americans. Although we address important differences, our principle focus is on African Americans because the history of legalized discrimination against this group has resulted in barriers that distinguish them in important ways.

Setting the Context

The current opposition to the use of race in higher education admissions decisions in order to implement campus programs designed to address underrepresentation or achieve a more diverse university community stands in sharp contrast to Justice Harry Blackmun's admonition (*Regents of the University of California v. Bakke* 438 U.S. 265, 1978) that "in order to get beyond racism, we must first take account of race. There is no other way." More recent decisions as seen in *Hopwood v. Texas* (78 F.3d 932, 5th Cir. 1996) and *Wessman v. Boston School Committee* (996 F. Supp. 120, U.S. Dist. 1998), along with the constitutional provisions of Proposition 209 in California and Initiative 200 in Washington, reflect the ascendancy of a policy perspective that would severely limit the role of race in public policy and especially in educational policy and practice. In higher education, the spread of this more limiting public policy perspective threatens to dismantle more than a quarter century of targeted assistance to groups historically denied full participation and access largely on the basis of race. It is tragic irony that the Civil Rights movement that sought to help us get beyond race is now challenged by the potential of not being able to take account of race. Critics of affirmative action are even citing the fervent words of Dr. Martin Luther King's "I Have a Dream" speech that "one day men will be judged by the content of their character rather than by the color of their skin" in their efforts to limit the use of race in constructing remedy and redress. The moral appeal of this color-blind conception underestimates the pervasiveness of the cumulative effects of legal and customary discrimination, especially against blacks, and threatens to dismantle substantial progress realized during the post-*Brown* era.

Many of the proponents of affirmative action have been concerned to show the harmful consequences of the impact of *Hopwood* and Proposition 209, providing detailed examinations of declines in minority applications and enrollment and estimates of the actual difference that race makes at selective institutions either at the undergraduate level (Kane 1998) or in admission to law school (Wightman 1998b). Most recently, Bowen and Bok (1998) have provided a major analysis of the matriculation of blacks at highly selective colleges and universities that shows important benefits of affirmative action admissions policies. In each of the above analyses, the authors have focused considerable attention on the admissions process and the importance of the use of race to offset the lower test scores of African Americans and Latino/a applicants. Each study demonstrates the centrality of using race as a factor in securing the admission of these students to selective colleges and universities.

Much of the current debate, however, proceeds without careful reflection on the very brief thirty-seven-year period during which we have been seriously pursuing greater participation in higher education for minorities under any policy model. The current higher education context is obviously different in multiple and complex ways from the 1965 context, when the higher education act of that year was passed. In that initial authorizing legislation, major initiatives, especially those most closely identified with access to and participation in higher education, were set forth. The Trio programs—Upward Bound Talent Search, Special Services, and the Basic Educational Opportunity Grants (BEOG, now PELL grants) all came to fruition during the 1965–69 period. Each of these programs had as a core part of its origin a fundamental understanding that race and poverty were critical factors to be taken into account when increasing access to higher education.

Evidence of the condition of black participation in higher education at that time is illustrated in the 1971 Newman Report on Higher Education (U.S. Department of Health, Education, and Welfare 1971). The report shows that from 1964 to 1968, black enrollment in colleges and universities increased 85 percent, from 234,000 to 435,000. As a percentage of total enrollment, the change represented a growth of 1.4 percent in black enrollment, from 5 percent to 6.4 percent. This 1971 report, sponsored by then Secretary of Health, Education, and Welfare Elliott Richardson, labeled the progress in this area "the unfinished experiment in minority education" (44).

It is important to note that discussions about race in this period were discussions largely about blacks and whites. The experiment that Richardson referenced were those efforts of traditionally white colleges and universities to increase the presence of black students on their campuses. The success of these efforts was researched by Crossland (1971), who reported that by 1970,

nearly two-thirds of all black students were enrolled in other than traditionally black colleges and universities, whereas in 1964 more than half were enrolled in traditionally black colleges and universities.

The dominant public policy understanding of affirmative action in the
mid-1960s was one of support, which grew in part out of the leadership of
then President Lyndon B. Johnson.[2] In 1967, President Johnson issued Executive Order 11375, which included gender along with race as an illegitimate
basis of discrimination. In 1967 this order was perceived as a necessary way of
preventing harm to the legitimate educational aspirations of blacks and
women. Ironically, the same language of the Civil Rights movement, as noted
earlier, is now used by critics of affirmative action to dismantle the programs
that emerged in response to overcoming barriers.

In some ways the precursor of the public policy opposition to an affirmative use of race today may well have been the "benign neglect" statement of
the Nixon presidency.[3] Certainly *Bakke, Weber, Hopwood* (see Appendix A for
a description of each case), and the state constitutional amendments in California and Washington are the crystallization of a fundamental disagreement
with the prevailing views of the past forty years. Whereas race has traditionally been viewed as a legitimate basis for redress, even under *de facto* circumstances, it has now come to be painted with the brush of the "victimization
hypothesis." This hypothesis argues that "racial minorities" use their racial status to make illegitimate claims on scarce resources and opportunities.

Of course many vital aspects of the context have changed since the Johnson era. One of the arguments that emerged from these changes is that we
have managed to transcend race in most ways and that poverty or class is the
main cause of inequality.[4] For example, when it was first published in 1978,
William Julius Wilson's *The Declining Significance of Race* was widely cited by
members of the social science and public policy communities as empirical
evidence for the view that race is no longer the principal factor shaping inequality. Although the importance of class should not be understated, much
empirical evidence continues to support the significance of race. Fordham
and Ogbu's (1986) ethnographic work about urban black schools, for example, highlighted an oppositional attitude among students who were said to associate academic excellence with "acting white," which has been received as
evidence of how race shapes academic achievement for the "underclass." Wilson himself emphasized class along with race in his subsequent book, *The
Truly Disadvantaged* (1987).

The demographic transformation under way in the United States has complicated civil rights issues. As we have already observed, the debate about race in higher education in the United States has largely been a black–white discussion. That framework, although still providing a central focus for the discussion of race, is no longer sufficient. On the one hand, the diversity of the U.S. population makes it necessary that we recognize common barriers to full participation for all minority citizens. On the other hand, recent demographic shifts, as well as past patterns of access and opportunity, which varied from minority group to minority group, necessitate that we also recognize differentiated barriers to full participation. For example, there are critical reasons that the situation of blacks is very different from those of other communities of color. The legacy and stigma of slavery and Jim Crow laws as they impact African Americans stand in stark contrast to the "model minority" image (Nakanishi 1989; Chan and Wang 1991) of Asian/Pacific Americans. In addition, although the distinction is often made in higher education between those colleges and universities in the South, where segregation was legally enforced, and those outside the South, where the focus is now on achieving parity, examination of the long-term record of black participation in higher education in the United States shows that, simply put, the vast majority of all schools of higher education could be described as having denied access to blacks (Ballard 1973; Cobb 1998). In effect, custom was virtually as powerful as law. The plight of Native Americans is different still, given the history of U.S. management of the Bureau of Indian Affairs and Indian education. The diversity within both the Hispanic and Asian categories, along with the language issues associated with each, further complicates any discussion of an effective "common" response to the removal of barriers to full and equitable participation in higher education.

Economic factors are also central to the current debate. Some analysts have pointed to the earlier era of civil rights legislation as one in which heightened expectations and a sense of widespread prosperity formed the basis for a more generous consensus about social policies emphasizing access and opportunity. It is safe to say that some of these arguments were offered before the upturn in the U.S. economy of the late 1990s. It seems clear now that economic prosperity in and of itself is not sufficient to sustain public policies that foster access and opportunity. At the same time, it also appears that a sense of heightened expectations for unlimited opportunity and growth is necessary for public support of the traditional affirmative strategies. The current press of global competition for available work appears to encourage a zero-sum-game orientation to opportunity. Under this framework, the public is less generous, fearing a reduction of choice as well as a limitation of the chances for success for their children and themselves.

Today, there is also far more intense competition for the public dollar. Health care for the elderly, health care for the young and indigent, increased incarceration under a get-tough mentality, and a broad array of infrastructure repair costs compete with education for support. The programmatic interventions of the past thirty-seven years, which employ an affirmative use of race, are competing for funding with a set of issues that have very strong advocates. By contrast, education, especially higher education, continues to be viewed as a privilege, and there has been a substantial shift to a public sentiment that says those who benefit most have to be willing to cover more, if not all, of the costs. In addition, those who are assisted must merit any assistance that is provided. Hence the growth in loan assistance as the principle form of government financial assistance to students in higher education and the growing reliance on tests scores in the admissions process to determine merit. Merit per se is not being challenged by supporters of affirmative action; rather, what is being challenged, as discussed in Chapter 3 of this book, is a narrowing definition of merit that relies too heavily or nearly entirely on test scores. For those colleges and universities where selection of a student body is the challenge, the pressure to make admissions more objective usually increases the reliance on tests.[5] Public universities feel this pressure most intensely.

The above attributes of the current context make it more important that we take stock of progress—and the lack thereof—in the expansion of participation in higher education for different racial groups in the United States. Before addressing questions about the patterns of participation in higher education, it is important to look first at what research tells us about how race influences the early years of education in America.

Patterns, Trends, and Contrasts of Educational Opportunities

Perhaps one of the most enduring metaphors in all of education is that of the educational pipeline. It seems intended to evoke an image of the passage of

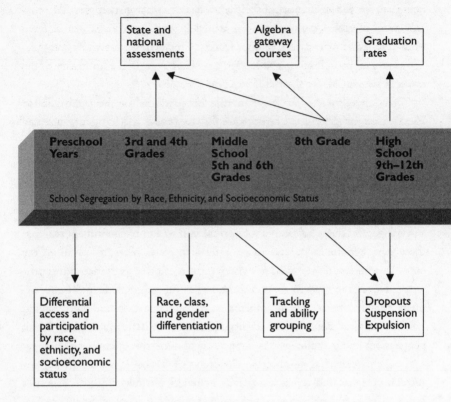

FIGURE 2.1   Critical Stages of Schooling

students from school entry to school exit as a "flow" along what might naively be seen as a relatively straight or predictably curving pipe. The difficulty with the metaphor occurs when we try to account for the numbers of students who exit the pipeline in inappropriate places and at inappropriate times. For the most part we tend to view the pipeline as largely intact and accommodating the relatively smooth and uninterrupted flow of the majority of students from school entry to school completion. Leakage in the pipeline or inappropriate early exits have mainly been explained as individual failure.

Several scholars have challenged this prevailing view by suggesting that we might reject the pipeline metaphor in favor of one that is more consistent with the experiences of black, Latino/a, Native American, and many poor children. Michael Olivas (1986) reasons that thinking of a stream or a river would be

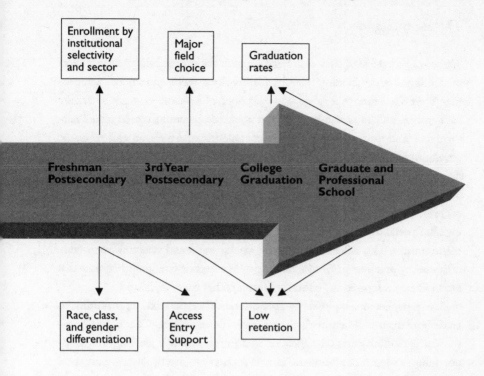

more appropriate, because there would be a greater possibility of addressing the occurrence of blockages in the river or stream, which could slow or divert the flow and/or redirect it. This alternate imagery seems especially fitting for many students of color because their participation in higher education is often fraught with barriers that obstruct their educational progress.

This section seeks to report on both the success and deficiencies in the pursuit of equal educational access and opportunity for minorities by describing the participation of students of color in higher education since 1980, examining both enrollment and degree attainment patterns. Figure 2.1 presents one illustration of how we might envision critical stages of the pre-K through graduate and professional school educational structure. At the bottom of the figure, we have indicated selected limiting conditions and practices that shape the relative presence of different populations of students at various points in this structure. The discussion of specific limiting factors follows.

The Early Stages

There is a broad-based consensus regarding the critical roles that the early years of childhood and schooling play in shaping long-term educational achievements. At the same time, a growing number of researchers point to family background, and, in particular, family structure, to account for poor school performance and low levels of achievement in African American and Hispanic communities. Coleman (1964) and others provided the initial empirical evidence for this latter argument when the Equality of Educational Opportunity Survey failed to confirm the conventional wisdom that school-to-school differences in quality of educational resources were the primary cause of differences in educational attainment between rich and poor, and minority and white communities. This debate about family background and structure versus discriminatory practices in K-12 schooling fuels a tension over policy choices that are too often discussed in "either/or" terms rather than "both/and."

The perspective employed in this discussion centers on "opportunity to learn" and examines factors that shape such opportunities. Clearly, family resources, including parental education and family stability, are important opportunity-to-learn conditioners. In this section we briefly discuss particular features of the early stages of the educational pipeline that have been shown to influence educational attainment. This discussion necessarily precedes the discussion of higher education patterns and trends because the early stages have enormous implications for college access. Specifically, we present data on early-childhood education, children at risk, the changing demographics of the schools, average reading proficiency, racial/ethnic and socioeconomic status composition of school districts by district size, and tracking and ability grouping.

We begin by first discussing the demographic realities of the nation's public elementary and secondary schools. Hodgkinson (1985) described the demographic imperative, the forces of population growth and change that yield our school population, and its implication for education. As minorities have become an increasingly large part of the nation's population, there has been an even greater rate of change in the school population. More importantly, the demographic shifts have been such that the schools have gotten greater numbers of students for whom school has not been a successful experience. There are greater numbers of economically disadvantaged students, greater numbers of students for whom English is a second language, and greater numbers of students from single-parent households. For example, during the period 1976–95, there was an 11 percent increase in minority students (U.S. Department of Education, Office for Civil Rights 1976, 1984, 1988, and 1990; U.S. Department of Education, National Center for Education Statistics 1992, 1995, 1996, and 1997). The percentage of Hispanic students has more than doubled, from 6.4 percent to 13.5 percent. The percentage of Asian/Pacific Island students increased from 1.25 percent to 3.7 percent. These data highlight racial and ethnic differences in opportunity to learn and in educational performance.

Early Intervention

Research results underscoring the need for intervention as early as the age of three years and the benefits of preschool, especially for minority and poor youngsters, have alerted the policy community to the need to redouble efforts focused on the early years (Campbell and Ramey 1994; Schweinhart, Barnes, and Weikart 1993). School readiness and the beginning of the schooling experience are greatly influenced by the early training and exposure that families and communities can provide. Early intervention provides a mechanism for counteracting the limitations of economically disadvantaged communities and helping students have a more equal starting point. Such opportunities are not evenly distributed across racial and income categories. Table 2.1 shows the prekindergarten participation rates of three- to four-year-olds by family income and race/ethnicity.

The data in Table 2.1 are from the 1990 census, and they show that generally, irrespective of race, participation in prekindergarten is greater for those families with higher incomes. Race, however, influences early intervention. Hispanic participation rates are consistently lower than are those of other groups at each income level. White and Asian participation rates are highest among the high-income groups. One of the key policy strategies for improving the number of students of all racial/ethnic categories who perform better early on in school is overcoming the financial constraints that limit early participation. Research by the National Assessment of Educational Progress (NAEP) shows that the gap in minority–white scores at age seventeen is

TABLE 2.1

*Prekindergarten Participation Rates of Three- to Four-Year-Olds by
Family Income and Race/Ethnicity, 1990*

Family Income	White	Black	Hispanic	Asian/ Pacific Islander	American Indian/Alaskan Native
$100,000 or more	59.7	49.7	43.6	53.0	51.2
$75,000–$99,999	50.9	45.9	34.9	44.8	37.2
$50,000–$74,999	44.5	42.5	28.6	40.2	35.8
$35,000–$49,999	35.8	36.2	23.8	33.5	29.5
$25,000–$34,999	28.5	32.6	19.5	26.6	29.0
$15,000–$24,999	23.4	29.0	17.0	22.5	26.5
$10,000–$14,999	22.3	27.8	16.7	22.1	28.9
$5,000–$9,999	23.4	26.8	17.5	22.1	28.3
Less than $5,000	22.6	24.1	16.9	21.8	25.0

SOURCE: U.S. Bureau of the Census 1990.

about the size of the gap at age nine. Early intervention may substantially reduce the size of the early gap and thereby preserve later school opportunity
and performance.

A number of factors conspire to place students at risk of educational failure. Among these are poverty, living in a single-female-headed household, residing in an urban area, and attending an urban school. The likelihood of experiencing each of these risks differs significantly by race. For example, in
1990, nearly half—44 percent—of the children identified as "at risk" were
African American. By contrast, only one percent were Asian. Roughly the
same percentage of children at risk were Latino/a (26 percent) and white (27
percent). Students at risk are more likely to drop out of school and more likely
to experience poor academic performance. Each of these outcomes dramatically reduces the numbers available for graduation and college enrollment.

One indicator of low academic performance is reading proficiency. Table
2.2 presents the average NAEP reading proficiency scores for students ages
nine, thirteen, and seventeen by race and ethnicity for selected years from
1971 to 1996. Black and Hispanic average reading proficiency scores are substantially below those of whites at each age and for each year. The gap, however, has narrowed slightly between blacks and whites and between Hispanics and whites during this twenty-five-year period.

TABLE 2.2

*Average NAEP Reading Proficiency (Scale) Scores for Students Ages
Nine, Thirteen, and Seventeen by Race/Ethnicity
for Selected Years, 1971–96*

Year	White			Black			Hispanic		
	Age 9	Age 13	Age 17	Age 9	Age 13	Age 17	Age 9	Age 13	Age 17
1971	214	261	291	170	222	239	—	—	—
1975	217	262	293	181	226	241	183	232	252
1980	221	264	293	189	233	243	190	237	261
1984	218	263	295	186	236	264	187	240	268
1988	218	261	295	189	243	247	194	240	271
1990	217	262	297	182	242	267	189	238	275
1992	218	266	297	185	238	261	192	239	271
1994	218	265	296	185	234	266	186	235	263
1996	220	267	294	190	236	265	194	240	265

SOURCE: U.S. Department of Education, National Center for Education Statistics 1997b.
NOTE: The key for interpreting scores is as follows: 150, simple, discrete reading tasks, generalizations; 200, partial skills and understanding materials; 250, interrelates ideas and makes; 300, understands complicated information; and 350, learns from specialized reading.

Racial and Poverty Composition of Schools

Student performance in schools is shaped by a variety of factors that tend to undermine the performance of minorities. Research has shown that the concentration of African American and Latino/a students in schools and the concentration of poverty in schools are highly correlated—they tend to occur together. The schools in which these two factors occur together are typically in large, urban districts. They are almost always more poorly resourced as measured by pupil-teacher ratios, teachers with advanced credentials, more experienced teachers, or an enriched curricula. Massey and Denton (1993), in their examination of racial segregation, describe the phenomenon of hyper-segregation, whereby race, ethnicity, and income converge to produce high levels of persistent segregation. The authors show that hyper-segregation has enormous implications for educational outcomes. In their simulations, Massey and Denton manipulated average school test scores by varying the levels of racial and poverty concentration. In general, they found that the greater the intensity of racial and income segregation, the lower the average test scores.

Table 2.3 shows the racial/ethnic composition of regular school districts by

TABLE 2.3

*Racial/Ethnic Composition of Regular Districts,
by District Size, 1987–88 to 1990–91*

Years	No. of Students	Native American (%)	Asian (%)	Hispanic (%)	Black (%)	White (%)
Overall						
1987–88	39,963,281	1.0	3.0	10.2	16.5	69.3
1988–89	40,120,672	1.0	3.1	10.7	16.4	68.8
1989–90	40,408,326	1.0	3.2	11.2	16.3	68.4
1990–91	40,911,261	1.0	3.3	11.6	16.2	67.9
By Size						
0–999						
1987–88	2,975,906	2.9	0.9	5.4	3.7	87.2
1988–89	2,975,605	2.9	0.8	5.4	3.8	87.0
1989–90	2,927,104	2.9	0.8	5.5	3.5	87.3
1990–91	2,917,080	3.0	0.8	5.5	3.3	87.5
1,000–4,999						
1987–88	12,539,341	1.1	1.4	5.2	9.3	82.9
1988–89	12,513,543	1.1	1.5	5.5	9.4	82.6
1989–90	12,544,546	1.1	1.5	5.7	9.3	82.4
1990–91	12,523,715	1.1	1.5	5.8	9.1	82.4
5,000–9,999						
1987–88	6,533,712	0.7	2.6	7.9	12.8	75.9
1988–89	6,433,060	0.7	2.7	8.2	12.9	75.6
1989–90	6,422,276	0.7	2.8	8.8	12.7	75.0
1990–91	6,477,862	0.8	3.0	9.2	12.8	74.3
10,000 and over						
1987–88	17,914,312	0.6	4.7	15.4	25.0	54.3
1988–89	18,199,464	0.6	4.8	16.0	24.6	54.0
1989–90	18,514,400	0.7	4.9	16.6	24.3	53.5
1990–91	18,992,604	0.7	5.0	17.2	24.0	53.2

SOURCE: U.S. Department of Education, National Center for Education Statistics 1986–87 to 1990–91.

NOTE: Percentages may not add to 100 percent as a result of rounding.

TABLE 2.4

Racial/Ethnic Composition of Regular Districts, by Socioeconomic Status (% of Population in Poverty), 1987–88 to 1990–91

Years	No. of Students	Native American (%)	Asian (%)	Hispanic (%)	Black (%)	White (%)
Overall						
1987–88	39,963,281	1.0	3.0	10.2	16.5	69.3
1988–89	40,120,672	1.0	3.1	10.7	16.4	68.8
1989–90	40,408,326	1.0	3.2	11.2	16.3	68.4
1990–91	40,911,261	1.0	3.3	11.6	16.2	67.9
By % of School-Age Children in Poverty						
<5%						
1987–88	4,243,231	0.3	3.6	4.2	3.7	88.2
1988–89	4,300,465	0.3	3.8	4.4	3.8	87.8
1989–90	4,349,079	0.3	4.0	4.7	3.9	87.1
1990–91	4,427,781	0.3	4.2	4.9	3.8	86.8
5%–<15%						
1987–88	13,645,900	0.7	2.6	5.4	7.4	83.9
1988–89	13,797,186	0.7	2.7	5.7	7.5	83.4
1989–90	13,998,850	0.7	2.8	6.1	7.5	82.8
1990–91	14,269,556	0.7	3.0	6.5	7.6	82.2
15%–<25%						
1987–88	10,932,698	1.0	3.5	8.8	14.2	72.4
1988–89	11,025,089	1.0	3.6	9.4	14.4	71.7
1989–90	11,144,517	1.0	3.6	10.0	14.3	71.1
1990–91	11,322,823	1.0	3.7	10.5	14.4	70.4
25% and over						
1987–88	10,984,196	1.5	2.9	20.0	35.2	40.4
1988–89	10,954,566	1.5	2.9	20.6	34.7	40.2
1989–90	10,915,880	1.6	3.0	21.5	34.5	39.5
1990–91	10,878,202	1.6	3.0	22.1	34.4	38.9

SOURCE: U.S. Department of Education, National Center for Education Statistics 1986–87 to 1990–91, 1994.

NOTE: Percentages may not add to 100 percent as a result of rounding. Only districts for which socioeconomic status data were available are included in these analyses.

district size. The data are for school years 1987–88 through 1990–91. Table 2.4
gives the racial/ethnic composition for regular school districts by poverty level.
The two tables together provide clear evidence that the largest school districts
and the districts with the greatest concentration of poverty are substantially
minority. In Table 2.3, the largest districts, those with 10,000 students and
over, were about 47 percent minority in 1990–91. More than 41 percent of
the enrollment in districts this size was black and Hispanic. This is in contrast
to an overall average of about 32 percent minority students in all schools for
that year. By contrast, in smaller districts of, say, 1,000 to 4,999 students, the
percentage of minority students was about 17.5 for 1990–91. Only 14.9 percent of the enrollment in districts this size was composed of African American and Hispanic students.

Table 2.4 shows an even more dramatic difference in racial composition
across school districts differing by levels of poverty concentration. In districts
in which the percentage of school children living in poverty was 25 percent
or more, the percentage of minority students was 61 percent in 1990–91.
Black and Hispanic enrollment averaged just over 56 percent. By contrast, in
the districts with the lowest level of poverty (under 5 percent), the minority
percentage in 1990–91 was 13.2 percent and blacks and Hispanics together
averaged just 8.7 percent.

The preceding discussion focuses primarily on examples emphasizing the
educational disadvantages that result from poverty and the highly correlated
factor of high levels of racial segregation. These contextual factors have been
shown to have an impact on opportunity to learn by limiting the educational
resources in these environments. In addition to these contextual factors, a variety of school-related practices have been shown to negatively impact opportunity to learn. Chief among these has been the use of ability grouping
and tracking in schools.

A substantial body of research has shown how grouping practices have
been used in ways that reassemble students along racial and social class lines,
with disproportionately higher concentrations of minority and poor youngsters in the lower ability groups (Oakes 1988; Slavin 1990). These studies report that the quality of instruction in the lower groups works to disadvantage
students in these groups in a cumulative way. In other words, students in these
groups learn less as a consequence of group membership, and this deficit is
cumulative as the placement continues. In this manner, poor and minority
students become increasingly less competitive in the classroom.

Tracking, the process of assigning students to academic tracks or streams as early as the middle school years, based on previous academic performance and measured ability, magnifies and compounds the effects of ability grouping in classrooms in the earlier grades. First, decisions about track placement are based on a combination of test scores, grades, and recommendations. Students who have been receiving lesser-quality instruction cannot compete well on these criteria and are seldom selected for the more challenging academic tracks, thereby magnifying the effects of earlier ability grouping. These effects are then compounded when, in the lower tracks, students receive a further comparative disadvantage by being placed—locked—in a less rigorous curriculum. Research by Heyns (1974), employing a status attainment approach, showed how tracking actually was associated with contributing to inequality between students over and above their existing student stratification. Subsequent research by Gamoran (1998) and Braddock (1993) showed that tracking, as a feature of school organization, is a principal way in which students are organized for instruction and that, depending on where in the organizational structure of the school curriculum one falls, tracking determines the quality of the learning experience. Student race is deeply implicated in track assignment. School desegregation research and research on tracking, such as the studies cited earlier, show that African American students have a much greater likelihood of being in the lower tracks of their schools.

The culmination of the harmful effects of tracking on minority and poor students' academic careers is seen in testing. Because tracking organizes students for instruction, it shapes course access. Taking the right courses—exposure to content and opportunity to learn—is a necessary, if not sufficient, prerequisite to performing well on achievement tests. Jencks and Phillips (1998) have provided compelling evidence on this point. They report that black students who take advanced placement courses score about as well as their white counterparts on the SAT. The problem is that very few African American students take these courses.

We can now assemble the list of accumulating disadvantages for African-American and Latino/a students:

- A high proportion of black and Latino/a students are at risk for reasons associated with poverty.
- Household and community poverty translates into poor school funding and a lower concentration of quality educational resources in those schools.

- Black and Latino/a students and their families are more likely to live in racially segregated communities and attend schools with high concentrations of other minority students.
- Schools characterized as having a high minority population have been shown to score lower on most educational quality indicators, including measures of teacher credentials and teacher experience.
- Communities characterized as having a high minority population and a high poverty rate are more often in large urban areas and must support large school districts with a weaker tax base.
- Exposure to educational practices such as ability grouping and tracking works disproportionately to the detriment of African American and Latino/a students.
- This limited opportunity to learn for African American and Latino/a students and a consequent reduction in educational choices and options are further constrained by performance on standardized tests.

The results of this set of accumulated experiences suggest persistent limitations on educational opportunity associated with race. As indicated by the research evidence, the strong association of these early pipeline experiences with race and ethnicity as well as socioeconomic status makes it difficult to entertain the idea that the playing field has been made level, thereby eliminating the need for race-sensitive policies and practices. If race still plays a significant role in educational access, then we should expect to see the effects of how it obstructs the movement for minorities toward higher levels of educational attainment. That restricted flow should be observable both in overall levels of access and in differentiated participation across different sectors of higher education.

Enrollment and Segregation in Higher Education

In this section we identify the differences in levels of overall participation and enrollment by sector for each racial category. We also document the changes in levels of participation that have occurred for each of those categories since about 1980. The data used for the enrollment, segregation, and degree attainment examination, unless stated otherwise, are from the Integrated Postsecondary Education Data System (IPEDS) for the years 1982, 1988, and 1996. The year 1996 is the most recent for which the IPEDS data have been completed.[6]

Despite the claims of critics regarding targeted admissions goals as racial

TABLE 2.5

Total Full-Time Undergraduate Enrollment by Race and Year

Race	1982		1988		1996	
	N	%	N	%	N	%
Black	567,388	9.5	630,318	9.2	800,450	10.9
Latino	314,987	5.2	442,560	6.5	528,157	7.2
Native American	36,700	0.6	47,465	0.7	70,066	1.0
Asian	157,054	2.6	264,655	3.9	422,212	5.7
White	4,770,129	79.4	5,318,505	77.5	5,137,470	69.9
Total	6,004,445[a]		6,859,547[a]		7,351,972[a]	

NOTE: *N*, number.
[a] Nonresident aliens are included in the totals.

quotas, there is an inherent difficulty in assessing progress without some baseline measure as a standard. The tradition in higher education has been to rely on a measure of parity. Researchers and policy makers have looked to see the extent to which representation for a group is occurring at a rate commensurate with that group's availability in a specified population category, usually referred to as an availability pool.[7] In doing this, it is important to differentiate between an availability pool and an eligibility pool. The latter is composed of those members of the category who have satisfied the basic criteria required to participate. High school completion, for example, would be a basic prerequisite for college or university enrollment. Having earned a bachelor's degree would be an expected prerequisite for graduate/professional school enrollment. This chapter follows that custom.

Table 2.5 provides the framing data for the discussion of overall accomplishments for participation in higher education for the years included in this study. The percentage data in Table 2.5 also provide the relevant data for a discussion of parity. To begin with, these data show that the level of full-time undergraduate participation in higher education increased by about 1.3 million students from 1982 to 1996. The share of full-time enrollment by each racial category also changed during this period. The share of full-time enrollment held by whites decreased from 79.4 percent in 1982 to 69.9 percent in 1996. The share of full-time enrollment held by blacks, Hispanics, Native Americans, and Asians each increased. The increase for blacks was 1.4 percent; for Latino/as, 2 percent; for Native Americans, 0.4 percent; and for

TABLE 2.6

*Enrolled Full-Time Undergraduates Compared with Those of College Age
and Those in the Eligibility Pool, by Race and Gender, 1988*

Race	College Age (in 1000s) March 1988			Eligible Pool (in 1000s) March 1988			Enrolled Full-Time Undergraduates Fall 1988		
	M	F	Total	M	F	Total	M	F	Total
Black	12.9%	14.3%	13.7%	11.6%	12.9%	12.3%	8.1%	10.6%	9.4%
	1,627	1,895	3,522	1,103	1,379	2,482	260,756	369,562	630,318
Hispanic	10.8%	9.7%	10.2%	7.9%	7.4%	7.6%	6.2%	7.0%	6.6%
	1,360	1,276	2,636	749	791	1,540	196,986	245,574	442,560
Native American	0.5%	0.5%	0.5%	0.5%	0.4%	0.4%	0.7%	0.7%	0.7%
	62	71	133	46	44	90	21,298	26,167	47,465
Asian/Pacific Islander	2.8%	2.6%	2.7%	3.1%	2.6%	2.8%	4.4%	3.6%	3.9%
	350	345	695	292	282	574	139,781	124,874	264,655
White	72.9%	72.9%	72.9%	77.0%	76.6%	76.8%	80.7%	78.1%	79.3%
	9,165	9,636	18,801	7,345	8,181	15,526	2,583,961	2,734,544	5,318,505
Total	99.9%	100.0%	100.0%	100.1%	99.9%	99.9%	100.1%	100.0%	99.9%
	12,564	13,223	25,786	9,535	10,677	20,212	3,202,782	3,500,721	6,703,503

NOTE: College age is defined as those aged eighteen to twenty-four; the eligibility pool is composed of high school graduates aged eighteen to twenty-four.

Asians, 3.1 percent. The Asian American share of full-time undergraduate enrollment actually more than doubled, increasing from 2.6 percent in 1982 to 5.7 percent in 1996. The answer to the general question about overall enrollment patterns is clear: actual increases in full-time enrollment occurred for each racial category, and the increases for African American, Latino/a, Native American, and Asian students resulted in a percentage decrease for whites, even though in actual numbers, white enrollment increased.

Tables 2.6 and 2.7 allow a comparison of the numbers and percentages of full-time enrolled undergraduates with percentages of college-age peers and those in the eligibility pool (high school graduates), by race and gender. In 1988, blacks were 13.7 percent of the college-age population and 12.3 percent of the eligibility pool, but they held just a 9.4 percent share of full-time enrollment. By 1996, blacks were 14.3 percent of the college-age population and 13.3 percent of the eligibility pool but held an 11.5 percent share of the

TABLE 2.7

*Enrolled Full-Time Undergraduates Compared with Those of College Age
and Those in the Eligibility Pool, by Race and Gender, 1996*

Race	College Age (in 1000s) March 1996			Eligible Pool (in 1000s) March 1996			Enrolled Full-Time Undergraduates Fall 1996		
	M	F	Total	M	F	Total	M	F	Total
Black	13.4%	15.3%	14.3%	12.3%	14.1%	13.3%	9.9%	12.9%	11.5%
	1,637	1,900	3,538	1,127	1,375	2,503	311,134	489,316	800,450
Hispanic	14.9%	13.7%	14.3%	11.1%	9.9%	10.5%	7.3%	7.9%	7.6%
	1,822	1,704	3,525	1,017	963	1,980	229,454	298,703	528,157
Native American	0.9%	1.0%	0.9%	0.9%	0.8%	0.9%	0.9%	1.1%	1.0%
	110	119	229	80	81	162	29,872	40,194	70,066
Asian/Pacific Islander	4.1%	4.2%	4.1%	4.6%	4.5%	4.5%	6.6%	5.6%	6.1%
	498	518	1,016	46	440	856	208,071	214,141	422,212
White	66.8%	65.9%	66.3%	71.1%	70.6%	70.8%	75.3%	72.6%	73.8%
	8,173	8,198	16,370	6,489	6,871	13,360	2,375,940	2,761,530	5,137,470
Total	100.1%	100.1%	99.9%	100.0%	99.9%	100.0%	100.0%	100.1%	100.0%
	12,239	12,439	24,678	9,130	9,730	18,860	3,154,471	3,803,884	6,958,355

NOTE: College age is defined as those aged eighteen to twenty-four; the eligibility pool is composed of high school graduates aged eighteen to twenty-four.

full-time college enrollment. The change from 1988 to 1996 shows that black full-time undergraduate participation in higher education increased by about 2.1 percent. Blacks as a percentage of the eligibility pool increased by 1 percent, from 12.3 percent to 13.3 percent, yielding only a slight change in progress toward parity based on eligibility during this eight-year period.

The disparity for Latino/a students is still greater because, on the basis of either measure, they are losing progress toward parity. Latino/a students were 10.2 percent of the population pool and 7.6 percent of the eligibility pool in 1988. By 1996, the comparable figures are 14.35 percent and 10.55 percent, respectively. This shows that the Latino/a college-age population has grown substantially over the eight-year period. Moreover, relative to that growth, there has been a comparable gain in the Latino/a eligibility pool, from 7.6 percent in 1988 to 10.5 percent in 1996. Full-time enrollment, however, has increased from 6.6 percent in 1988 to 7.6 percent (7.2 percent) in 1996, only a 1 percent change. Clearly, Latino/a students, despite substantial growth in enrollment and in both their population share and eligibility share, have lost ground toward parity. On the one hand, the progress that has been made in participation in higher education for blacks and Latino/as is substantial, and growth in Latino/a participation approaches that for Asian Americans. On the other hand, parity remains a distant goal for both African Americans and Latino/as. The current challenges to admissions practices that use race as a factor in admissions threaten what progress toward parity we find here. Even more troubling is the fact that the progress in participation that has been made is not equally distributed across all sectors of higher education. Because the educational opportunities differ by sector, it is important to examine the rates of enrollment in selected sectors.

Like earlier analyses conducted by Bowen and Bok (1998) and Kane (1998), the following analysis differentiates between unique sectors of higher education. It has been customary in the current debate to treat colleges and universities as sectors on the basis of their selectivity. Another way of differentiating sectors is by referring to Carnegie categories. Simply put, Carnegie categories group together colleges and universities that share similar or common attributes. In substantial ways, Carnegie categories constitute the reference categories that colleges and universities use in setting policies in order to remain on par within their tier or segment, which is what we mean here by sector.

The first Carnegie category, research I universities, are a special resource within the overall framework of higher education. They stand at the top of a hierarchically structured system of American higher education. Their faculties, physical plants, and material and intellectual resources distinguish them as a group. They have at the core of their mission both research and teaching, but some of their critics charge that research is the driving force of these institutions and that this is what gives them their advantage.

In the late 1960s and early part of the 1970s, activists targeted the research I universities for increased access for minorities in some part because it was reasoned that the undergraduate environment on these campuses would be more encouraging of aspirations for graduate study by minority students. In short, students attending these universities would be socialized in an environment in which the expectation for further study was the norm (Gumport 1994).

Additionally, research I universities are a critical resource because of the organizational network they comprise and in which they are embedded.

TABLE 2.8

Overall Full-Time Undergraduate Enrollment by Carnegie Category and Year

	1982		1988			1996		
Carnegie Category	N	%	N	% Enroll-ment	% Increase	N	% Enroll-ment	% Increase
Research I	1,047,330	17.4	1,193,375	17.4	13.9	1,201,500	15.5	1.0
Research II	379,569	6.3	395,658	5.8	4.2	396,710	5.1	0.3
Doctoral	629,046	10.5	687,382	10.0	9.3	685,657	8.8	−0.3
Master's/bachelor's	2,234,931	37.2	2,450,997	35.7	9.7	2,587,284	33.3	5.6
Associates of arts	1,517,683	25.3	1,741,810	25.4	14.8	1,990,171	25.6	14.3
Tribal	1,723	0.03	3,973	0.1	231.0	7,714	0.1	194.2
Other	165,887	2.8	206,365	3.0	124.4	192,626	2.5	−6.7
Uncategorized	28,276	0.5	179,987	2.6		706,732	9.1	
Total	6,004,445		6,859,547		12.5	7,351,972		13.3

Bowen and Bok (1998) show an aspect of this in their examination of the career results for graduates of the elite colleges and universities. Their evidence is compelling and shows the importance of elite linkages.

The use of the Carnegie classification system thus provides us with a vehicle for examining relative participation across sectors, with special attention given to research I universities. We now address questions about the patterns of participation in higher education by sector and race for selected years.

We begin by examining the distribution of this participation across four sectors of higher education: research I universities, research II universities, doctoral universities, and master's and bachelor's colleges and universities.[8] Table 2.8 gives the distribution for full-time undergraduate enrollment by sector and year.

The overall distribution across the sectors establishes the contribution that each sector makes to overall full-time undergraduate enrollment and provides a benchmark against which each of the racial category enrollment percentages can be compared for each year.

As might be expected because of the their large numbers, master's and bachelor's institutions have the greatest share of enrollment for each of the three years reported here. The next greatest share of enrollment is in two-year colleges (associate category), followed in order of magnitude by research

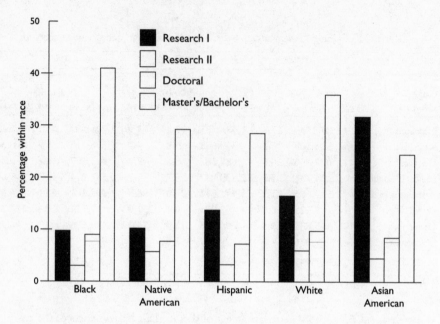

FIGURE 2.2 Enrollment distribution of Carnegie classification by race, 1996.

I, doctoral, and research II institutions. Fully one-third of all full-time students were in the master's and bachelor's sector for 1996, and this was actually a smaller percentage than was true for 1982 or 1988. The actual share increased by one-quarter million in this sector from 1982 to 1996. The second highest enrollment level in four-year college and university sectors is found for research I universities. The net change in this category from 1982 to 1996 is 154,170. The greater part of this change in undergraduate enrollment in the research I sector occurred between 1982 and 1988. Growth in this sector was only about 8,000 from 1988 to 1996.

Figure 2.2 presents full-time undergraduate enrollment participation levels by sector and race for 1996 (parallel analyses were conducted with 1982 and 1988 data, and revealed the same pattern). The graph shows the percentage of each racial group enrolled in the different Carnegie classification sectors across both public and private institutions.

Generally, the pattern for each racial group's distribution across the four sectors parallels that of the overall pattern shown in Table 2.8. The exception is for Asian American students, who have their highest full-time undergraduate enrollment in the research I sector. A major finding is that blacks, Native Americans, and—to a slightly lesser extent—Hispanics are underrepresented in the research I sector compared with whites and Asian students, as can be seen by the heights of the darkest bar in Figure 2.2.

In addition to the relative participation of each racial category in the institutions representing the Carnegie classifications, we also inspected the absolute frequencies in enrollment for the groups to look at changes over the 1982–96 time period. There was a pattern of substantial full-time enrollment growth for Asian American and Latino/a students in each of the four sectors. The actual student counts for Asian American and Latino/a students increased nearly by a factor of three in research I and research II universities. Increases in the two other sectors shown in the figure doubled for these two groups between 1982 and 1996. Asian American enrollment also nearly tripled in doctoral universities.

For Native American students and African American students, there were also enrollment increases in all sectors, but they were not as dramatic. Native American enrollment counts in the research I and research II sectors were twice as large in 1996 as they were in 1982.

African Americans experienced the lowest rate of change of any minority group in any sector. For example, the increase in their share of enrollment in the research I sector from 1982 to 1996 was just 28 percent (from 61,287 in 1982 to 78,373 in 1996). By contrast, their percentage of change in the doctoral sector was 44 percent, and in the master's and bachelor's sector the increase was 35 percent. In short, the increases for African American enrollment shares were larger in the somewhat less selective sectors.

These results demonstrate the diversity of enrollment patterns and especially the different levels of representation found for each racial group in each sector. It is clear in these data that the fourteen-year period from 1982 to 1996 provided dramatic enrollment increases for students of color. These changes, however, were experienced quite differently for African Americans than they were for the other groups. For African Americans, the rate of increased access has been lower, and this lower rate of change underscores the challenge of achieving parity either with respect to the population pool or the eligibility pool. Undoubtedly, the lower rates are linked to those factors discussed earlier in this chapter that conspire to obstruct educational progress.

Although we do not discuss in detail our analyses of degree attainment here, it should be noted that not surprisingly, the overall patterns of earned degrees awarded tend to mirror the patterns of enrollment. In general, African American and Latino/a students remain at just over 50 percent of parity on the basis of their eligibility status for the B.A. degree, whereas white and Asian American students exceed parity in degree attainment. Also noteworthy is that African Americans earned the smallest share of their degrees from the research I sector.

To conclude, despite more than a decade of progress in enrollment and degree attainment, the results show a very uneven pattern of participation and success by higher education sector for different racial groups. It appears that African American students have not enjoyed the same degree of progress as have Asian, Latino/a, and Native American students. The result is that African American students are enrolling at an increasingly lower rate in research I institutions, the most preferred sector in higher education. For African American students, progress toward parity with respect to either their population share or eligibility share is at a snail's pace, if it occurs at all.

Discussion and Conclusion

This chapter has sought to establish a basis for a clearer dialogue about the state of equity and opportunity in higher education. We began with a brief discussion of critical restricting conditions early in the education pipeline. We then examined enrollment and segregation for each racial category and for selected sectors of higher education. Now, we turn to the implications of our findings for the continuing debate.

First, there is considerable and mounting evidence that opportunity to learn is a central condition shaping the early short-term and subsequent long-term educational experiences of today's youth, especially African American and Latino/a youth. Moreover, there continues to be a broad-based public consensus that opportunity to learn ought to be fairly and equitably distributed. At the same time, there is substantial evidence that opportunity to learn is inequitably distributed and is shaped in part by students' race and economic circumstance. The available research further shows that often the confluence of these two factors is especially limiting.

Our review of that research and the tabular data presented here on race, poverty, risk status, and schooling underscores the need for continued and intensified attention to the role of these factors early in the educational careers of students. This will be essential if we are going to improve the rate at which we increase access to and participation in higher education for African American and Latino/a students. To increase their participation in the research I sector, early and consistent intervention is a necessity. As one example, we show the effect of school racial composition on going to college, and we show the very different racial and poverty composition of schools attended by students differing by race and ethnicity. As still another example, we cite the research on ability grouping, tracking, and retention in grade as further widespread schooling practices that are known to have a disproportionately negative impact on the educational careers of African American and Latino/a students. We must continue the development and implementation of schooling practices that detrack, including the increased use of appropriate instructional practices.

The results of our analysis of enrollment show persistent disparities that have a negative impact on African American and Latino/a students. Although there has been continuing progress in increasing participation for those students, our results show very little, if any, progress toward parity in enrollment commensurate with their eligibility. This is particularly the case for African American students who have increased their rate of graduation from high school, but in relative terms African Americans are actually falling behind. This is especially the case in the research I sector. Even with what has been shown to be the affirmative use of race in this sector (Kane 1998), it is clear that the benefit has not accrued to African American students at a rate that would place their increased participation anywhere close to the participation rates experienced by Asian American students, who have reached parity, or even Latino/a students. In short, the reality is that for African Americans, much remains to be accomplished in order to make real progress.

Equally important, the substantial increases in enrollment have occurred in the less selective sectors, where there are higher rates of segregation especially for blacks and Latino/as. Contrary to popular belief, special attention to race for the purpose of admission is not ubiquitous but instead is limited and typically conservatively applied. The enrollment patterns of the different racial groups in the master's and bachelor's sector provide limited indirect evidence of this. In each of the more selective sectors—research I and research II—the highest levels of segregation appear to be less than half that for the remaining sectors. Policies that would further limit the use of race will inevitably have the effect of increasing segregation in higher education. The same policies may also have a detrimental effect on the degree of attainment by minority students. Bowen and Bok's (1998) findings raise the policy suggestion that because the retention rates for African American and Latino/a students in the elite/selective schools are so high, it makes sense to make greater investments for minority students' attendance at those institutions. Bowen and Bok also found that the same students are more likely to pursue graduate degrees. Applying that logic here suggests that we will attend to both decreasing segregation and increasing minority student degree attainment by increasing minority student participation in the research I sector.

The data presented in this chapter provide evidence leading to the conclusion that the "unfinished experiment" to which the 1971 Newman Report referred in describing minorities' participation in higher education is still very much a work in progress. The nearly thirty-five-year-old effort to increase African American and other minority and poor students' participation in higher education that was mandated by the 1965 Higher Education Act has produced meaningful change, but the job is not complete. Both African American and Latino/a students continue to face serious challenges in securing admission to the research I sector. At the same time, there are models of practices that work—the now altered Banneker Scholarship program at the University of Maryland and the University of Michigan Rackam Scholars program, for example—and further application of these models is needed.

Failure to pursue these and similar initiatives will seriously restrict access and success for African Americans in the research I sector. As we have already begun to see, the elimination of the use of race as one of many admissions criteria will dramatically alter the overall level of participation of African American and Latino/a students, as in Texas, and/or dramatically reshape the distribution of African American and Latino/a students across the different sectors. Failure to pursue these and similar initiatives is to "turn back" and to turn away from the unfinished effort to correct the known injustices of the past. Efforts to substitute other factors, such as class, that are less objectionable have been demonstrated to be inadequate to sustain the rates of increase in minority participation across sectors that are needed to achieve the goal of parity. As the late Justice Blackmun stated: "In order to get beyond race, we must first take account of race. There is no other way." It is only because we have been able to take account of race in fashioning education policies since *Brown* that we have been able to achieve some of the gains reported here for underrepresented minority groups.

Chapter Three

STANDARDIZED TESTING AND
EQUAL ACCESS: A TUTORIAL

Linda F. Wightman

Standardized testing has played an increasingly prominent role in higher education admission decisions, particularly during the latter half of the twentieth century. Simultaneously, it has played an increasingly prominent role in the threat to diversity in higher education in an era of rising opposition to affirmation action policies and practices. This latter role for admission testing is primarily a result of the way that test scores are used and interpreted; it is not the tests themselves that create the problem.

Substantial research evidence supports the validity of standardized admission tests as one factor in the admission process. Evidence of test score misuse also exists. One example of score misuse is overreliance on standardized test scores for higher education admission decisions, ignoring a solid research base demonstrating their limitations. Related problems include viewing a test score as a comprehensive and objective measure of merit in selecting applicants and using scores of admitted applicants to assess the quality of an academic institution. Such misuses of admission test scores result in systematic adverse impact on minority applicants to higher education; they also mask the value of these instruments when they are used for the purposes for which they were intended. Yet, despite the available data, there has been an increasing call, particularly among the media and politicians most recently, to use test scores beyond the purposes for which they were validated.

Adding to the problem of inappropriate use of standardized tests in the complex admission process are several assumptions and suppositions about those tests for which little or no research support exists. This chapter identifies critical issues that must be evaluated when test scores are included among the factors considered in higher education admission decisions. It also brings to bear on those issues a compilation of relevant research and identifies critical areas in which supporting research is outdated, insufficient, or nonexistent.

A Historical Perspective on the Use of Standardized Tests in the Higher Education Admission Process

The enthusiasm with which standardized tests were embraced in the era following World War II was partly an expedient response to the substantial increase in the number of college applications that needed to be reviewed and partly a consequence of the perception of tests as neutral arbiters of academic credentials. The college opportunities afforded through the GI Bill resulted in an influx of college applicants who were not products of the socially elite private education system. Standardized test scores were viewed as a mechanism for admission committees to evaluate grades and courses from schools with which they were not familiar. Thus, an anticipated consequence of the early employment of standardized higher education admission tests was to open the doors of educational opportunity to a broad range of students who were not part of the traditional, privileged college-going population.

Over the years, the perception of standardized admission tests has changed from one of inclusion to one of exclusion; often they are viewed as a mechanism to deny access to increasingly scarce educational opportunities, especially at the most selective institutions, where the number of applicants substantially exceeds the number of available places. This section provides a perspective on where we are and how we got here by exploring the history of standardized testing in higher education admissions and tracing changes in the demographics of the college applicant population.

The Development and Growth of Admission Tests

A common admission test that could be used as part of the admission criteria across multiple colleges was first introduced in the United States in 1900.

Before that time, each college that chose to use an entrance examination administered its own. Such exams, used primarily by private colleges in the Northeast, were designed by each college to ensure that its admittees had acquired an adequate foundation in core academic courses and that they were prepared to undertake rigorous college work. The content of the examinations varied from one college to the next. From the perspective of secondary school headmasters, one problem with these examinations was that the secondary school needed to prepare multiple curricula for their students in order to ensure that they would receive instruction in the subject areas deemed important by the college(s) to which they applied. A second problem was that students applying to several colleges needed to prepare for and sit for several examinations. The urging from secondary school headmasters prompted the consideration of a common examination by a small group of colleges in the Northeast. During the first half of the twentieth century, that initial consideration evolved into formal, extensive nationwide testing of undergraduate, graduate, and professional school applicants as part of the higher education application and admission process. The chronology of key events in the development of the major standardized admission tests used by higher education is summarized in Table 3.1. Hanford (1991) provides a comprehensive and detailed history of the development of college admission testing programs. The following descriptions of the development of the Scholastic Aptitude Test (SAT) and the founding of Educational Testing Service are summaries of selected highlights from that history.

In 1900, a small group of influential colleges in the Northeast first agreed on core subject areas that would be included in the entrance examination process and then agreed to administer a common examination to all their applicants. This group of colleges established the College Entrance Examination Board (CEEB) to prepare and administer the new examinations on their behalf. The CEEB was initially located on the Columbia University campus in New York City. The first examinations developed by the CEEB were composed of essay questions, not multiple choice, and they were subject matter specific. Preparatory school headmasters welcomed the new examinations, primarily because their content provided a detailed description of the secondary school curriculum that was valued by the group of colleges to which their students aspired. This common essay examination system worked efficiently during the period in which the original participating colleges obtained their new

TABLE 3.1

Key Events in the Development of Standardized Admission Tests as Part of the Higher Education Application and Selection Process

Date	Event
November 17, 1900	Formation of the College Entrance Examination Board (CEEB) formally announced.
June 17, 1901	First CEEB tests administered to 973 students at 69 test centers (Donlon 1984).
June 23, 1926	First SAT, made up primarily of multiple-choice questions, was administered.
1929	SAT was divided into two sections—verbal aptitude and mathematical aptitude.
1930	AAMC first sponsored an objective test for applicants to medical school (called the Scholastic Aptitude Test for Medical School until 1946).
April 1, 1937	Wholly multiple-choice achievement tests were introduced for undergraduate admission.
October 1, 1937	The first GREs, known at that time as the Cooperative Graduate Testing program, were administered to first-year graduate students at Columbia, Harvard, Princeton, and Yale.
Fall 1939	The sixteen GRE Advanced Tests were administered for the first time.
1946	The admission test for medical school was renamed the Professional Aptitude Test; it was renamed the MCAT in 1948.
November 10, 1947	Representatives of nine law schools met with members of the CEEB to request an admission test analagous to the SAT but at the appropriate level and content for use in law school admission.
December 19, 1947	CEEB, ACE, and the Carnegie Foundation for the Advancement of Teaching agree to separate the testing operations and form a new enterprise—Educational Testing Service (ETS).
January 1, 1948	ETS started operations in Princeton, N.J.
February 1948	The LSAT was administered for the first time.
March 1953	Twelve graduate schools of business agreed that a nationwide testing program for business school admissions would be useful.
February 1954	The GMAT (called the Admission Test for Graduate Study in Business until 1976) was administered for the first time.
1957	The American College Testing Program was founded.

students from the narrow pool of U.S. preparatory schools in the Northeast. Shortly after World War I, several of those colleges began expanding the geographic area from which they recruited their potential students, with thoughts of becoming national rather than local colleges and universities. When their recruitment goals incorporated attracting academically able applicants from beyond the confines of the elite northeastern preparatory schools with which they were familiar, the colleges requested that the CEEB revise the test content to make it more comprehensive and less prescriptive. Simultaneous with (and at least partly a consequence of) the request for a shift in the examination's emphasis from the highly specific to a more general content, the CEEB began its first experimentation with the use of the multiple-choice item format. Because multiple-choice questions could be answered so much more quickly than essay questions, they were seen as a vehicle for more broadly sampling applicants' abilities and knowledge.

At the request of the CEEB, Carl Brigham, a psychology professor from Princeton University, developed a battery of multiple-choice questions to be used as an alternative to the original College Board essay examinations. He used the Army Alpha Test of general abilities, developed during World War I by the U.S. army to sort recruits into appropriate assignments, as a model. CEEB administered the first multiple-choice SAT in June 1926. Brigham also developed a multiple-choice version of examinations designed to assess subject-specific knowledge to be used in conjunction with the general aptitude assessment of the SAT. Initially, the participating colleges were uncertain about the utility and the validity of the multiple-choice format, but it was not long before they accepted that the new item format provided them with useful information about the academic preparation and potential of their applicants. Even so, it wasn't until the start of World War II that the multiple-choice examination fully replaced the essay examinations. The replacement was primarily a practical consequence of the travel restrictions related to the war. That is, the professors and secondary school teachers who traditionally graded the essays were unable to travel to New York City to grade the essays. By the time the war ended and the travel restrictions were lifted, new college applicants resulting from the GI Bill made it impractical to return to the old free-response essay examinations. In addition, colleges had become comfortable with the new test content and scoring, and so the multiple-choice format of the SAT became firmly entrenched.

The CEEB's success with the SAT aroused the interest of both graduate and professional schools. By the end of World War II, the CEEB was also administering the Medical College Admission Test (MCAT) and the Graduate Record Examinations (GRE) and developing the Law School Admission Test (LSAT). The expanding testing activities required expanding resources— resources beyond those anticipated and available under the then-current structure. In response, the College Board, along with two other enterprises that were engaged in testing activities (the American Council on Education and the Carnegie Foundation for the Advancement of Teaching) decided to consolidate test development, test administration, and test-related research into an independent organization. In 1947, the New York Board of Regents granted a charter to the newly formed Educational Testing Service (ETS). From its inception, ETS was an organization separate from CEEB, with ETS serving as the test maker but with CEEB owning the SAT and maintaining policy control over it. The College Board, first alone and then with ETS, held a monopoly in the college admission testing business from its establishment in 1900 until 1959, when the American College Testing Program (ACT) was founded by E. F. Lindquist.

ACT was founded in response to Lindquist's concept that the purpose of a college entrance examination should be different from that of ETS and the College Board. Specifically, Lindquist argued that a college entrance examination should predict college success but should also serve other educational purposes. The test envisioned by Lindquist would be "useful to high school counselors in advising students on their educational and vocational careers, or on their choice of type of college" (Lindquist 1958, 106.) It also would be useful to high school teachers in "adapting instruction to individual differences, and to high school administrators in evaluating the entire educational offering of the school. Likewise, the same test battery might be useful to the college authorities for placement purposes, or for purposes of counseling and guidance, or to help them better define the college's task by more adequately describing the status and needs of their entering student body" (106–7). The first ACT was administered in the fall of 1959.

The differences in purpose between the ACT and the SAT articulated by Lindquist more than forty years ago continue to define the primary distinctions between the two testing programs today. When the ACT was first introduced, it was used primarily in the Midwest, whereas the SAT was the examination of choice on the East and West Coasts. Over the years, partly as a consequence of national marketing efforts by both organizations and partly as a consequence of changing needs among colleges, many colleges and universities have come to accept either ACT or SAT scores from their applicants.

The Changing Face of the Applicant Pool

During the period in which the new tests where taking their place in the college admissions process, both the number and the demographic characteristics of students entering higher education were undergoing change. The changes in the applicant pool were very instrumental in establishing the place of the SAT and ACT at the undergraduate level and the GRE, LSAT, Graduate Management Admissions Test (GMAT), and MCAT at the graduate and professional school level. The search for applicants from a more national pool beginning around 1930 initiated the increase in the applicant population; the number of college aspirants increased more significantly after World War II, primarily as a consequence of new government support for education. Even so, the ethnic diversity of those seeking college admission did not increase noticeably until the late sixties and early seventies.

Ethnic and Gender Diversity in the Applicant Pool

In 1954 a statement defining the right of minorities to have access to higher education was clearly articulated by the U.S. Supreme Court in the important civil rights case *Brown v. the Board of Education of Topeka, Kansas*. One of the most noteworthy outcomes of *Brown* was the Supreme Court's explicit position that admission to publicly supported colleges and universities could not be denied on the basis of race. This decision also struck down the practice of "separate but equal" in education. Several earlier cases had paved the way for this landmark decision, including *Missouri ex rel. Gaines v. Canada* (305 U.S. 337, 1938), *Sipeil v. the Board of Regents of the University of Oklahoma* (332 U.S. 631, 1948), *Sweatt v. Painter* (339 U.S. 629, 1950), and *McLaurin v. Oklahoma State Regents for Higher Education* (339 U.S. 637, 1950).[1] Despite the clear position of the Supreme Court in *Brown*, states resisted. Thus, the rulings by themselves failed to produce a large influx of minority students into higher education. Both the Civil Rights Act of 1964 and subsequent efforts by civil rights groups to ensure that the act was enforced were required before evidence of increased access was seen in enrollment statistics. A variety of additional factors contributed to the change in the demographic makeup of the higher education population. These included "the infusion of federal funds into institutions of higher education" and the resulting "greater autonomy in decision on admissions" (Karen 1990, 230); the implementation of "need-blind" admission practices in the mid-1960s by most elite colleges, ensuring that no applicants would be denied admission because of financial need or denied financial aid after they were admitted; and the introduction of affirmative action programs for women and minorities in the late 1960s.

Availability of Data

Data about minority enrollment in higher education before the early 1970s are both scarce and constrained. Information about changes in minority enrollment from the mid-1950s to the mid-1970s is limited by the lack of systematic data collection during that period. The U.S. Census Bureau was the primary source of data about minority enrollment during much of that period, and the accuracy of some of that data, which was extrapolated from interviews of only 50,000 households, is questionable (Abramowitz 1976). Another source of data was the Office of Civil Rights, which collected data through biennial surveys. Its early surveys lacked continuity, omitted certain ethnic groups, and covered only full-time students (National Advisory Committee on Black Higher Education and Black Colleges and Universities 1979, 10). In 1976, the Office of Civil Rights and the National Center for Education Statistics (NCES) began collaborating on data collection and compilation, resulting in increased quality and consistency of data. Despite their limitations, the available data provide some indication of the shifting demographics during a critical time period in higher education. These data are especially important because they demonstrate how small the presence of minority college applicants and students was in higher education during the development and norming of standardized tests used for admission to undergraduate, graduate, and professional schools.

Trends in the Data

The available data demonstrate gains in enrollment for ethnic minority groups over the past thirty years, particularly in the early years after passage of the Civil Rights Act. Information about black students was recorded earlier than

TABLE 3.2

*Ethnic Background of ATP College-Bound Seniors for Selected Years,
from 1973 to 1998, Expressed as a Percentage of
Total Student Descriptive Questionnaire Respondents*

Response Option	1973	1978	1983	1990	1995	1998
American Indian	0.0	0.4	0.5	1.1	0.9	1.0
Black/African American	7.0	9.0	8.8	10.0	10.7	10.9
Mexican American or Chicano	1.0	1.7	1.9	2.8	3.7	3.9
Oriental or Asian American	2.0	2.6	4.2	7.6	8.4	9.0
Puerto Rican	0.0	1.0	1.2	1.2	1.3	1.3
White or Caucasian	87.0	83.0	81.1	73.4	69.2	67.1
Other	1.0	2.3	2.2	4.0	5.7	6.8
Number responding	784,848	893,767	875,475	947,258	973,870	1,049,773
Percentage of minority	11.0	17.0	18.9	26.6	30.8	32.9

SOURCES: The data for 1973, 1978, and 1983 are from Donlon 1984, 181; data for 1990, 1995, and 1998 are from College Entrance Examination Board 1998.

was information about other minority groups. Those data contribute to an understanding of minority enrollment trends in the latter half of the twentieth century. For example, the data show that the number of black college students increased by more than 275-fold in the ten-year period from 1966 to 1976. Of the total number of students enrolled, the number of blacks increased from 4.6 percent of the student population to 10.7 percent during that period (U.S. Department of Education, National Center for Education Statistics 1978, 120–21). The number of black students enrolled was reported by the Census Bureau to be 282,000 in 1966 and 1.062 million in 1978 (U.S. Bureau of the Census 1980, 2). These data include both two-year and four-year institutions. Because black students have traditionally been overrepresented in two-year institutions, which typically do not require admission tests, the proportional representation of black students among admission-test takers during that period most likely was somewhat lower. The College Board did not begin to collect descriptive statistics on its test-taking populations until 1972. The proportional representation of different ethnic groups among SAT takers for selected years, beginning 1973, is presented in Table 3.2. These data show a substantial increase in the percentage of minority test takers during the twenty-five-year period from 1973 to 1998. The percentage increased for each minority group, with the largest relative increase among Asian American test takers. It is note-

TABLE 3.3

*Total Enrollment in Four-Year Institutions of Higher Education,
by Race/Ethnicity of Student, for Selected Years from
Fall 1976 to Fall 1995 (Numbers in Thousands)*

Race/Ethnicity	1976	1980	1990	1993	1995
Total	7,107	7,565	8,579	8,739	8,760
White	5,999	6,275	6,768	6,639	6,517
Total minority	931	1,050	1,486	1,734	1,886
American Indian/					
Alaskan Native	35	37	48	59	66
Asian American	119	162	357	429	482
Black	604	634	723	814	852
Hispanic	173	217	358	432	486

SOURCE: U.S. Department of Education, National Center for Education Statistics, 1997b.

worthy that the total number of respondents increased by more than a quarter million between 1973 and 1998, so the percentage increases among minority test takers also represent increases in their absolute numbers.

Enrollment data by ethnic groups for four-year institutions alone are available from the NCES beginning in 1976. Data for selected years are shown separately by ethnic group in Table 3.3 for the period 1976–95. These data show that the number of ethnic minority students in all four-year institutions increased from about 931,000 (approximately 13 percent of the total) in 1976 to nearly 1,886,000 (approximately 21.5 percent) in 1995 (U.S. Department of Education, National Center for Education Statistics 1997a). All ethnic minority groups showed some increase in proportion to the enrollment distribution during that period, and as was shown for SAT takers, the largest increase was reported for Asian/Pacific Islanders. Their participation more than tripled from 1.7 percent of the total in 1976 to 5.5 percent in 1995. In absolute numbers, the total enrollment in all four-year institutions increased during that time period from 7.107 million to 8.76 million. These data are consistent with the rise in the proportion of minority SAT takers from 11 percent in 1973 to almost 31 percent in 1995, as shown in Table 3.2.

Similar trends are found with respect to minority enrollment in graduate and professional schools, as presented in Table 3.4. Less than 10 percent of each of the graduate school and professional school populations were com-

TABLE 3.4

*Graduate and Professional School Enrollment by Race/Ethnicity
for Selected Years from Fall 1978 to Fall 1994 (Numbers in Thousands)*

Race/Ethnicity	1976	1982	1988	1994
Graduate School Enrollment				
Total	1,219	1,235	1,472	1,722
White, non–Hispanic	1,019	1,022	1,153	1,287
Total minority	120	123	167	256
Asian American	24	30	46	73
Black, non–Hispanic	68	61	76	111
Hispanic	24	27	39	64
Professional School Enrollment				
Total	255	278	267	295
White, non–Hispanic	229	246	223	224
Total minority	22	29	39	64
Asian American	5	8	14	28
Black, non–Hispanic	11	13	14	21
Hispanic	5	7	9	13

SOURCES: U.S. Department of Education, National Center for Education Statistics, 1997;
U.S. Bureau of the Census, 1997.

posed of minority students in 1978. Those percentages increased to 14.9 and
21.7, respectively, by 1994. Law school enrollment data made available from
the American Bar Association (ABA) are consistent with the general trend
observed in professional school enrollment data shown in Table 3.4. The ABA
reported that approximately 9 percent of the first-year class were minorities
in 1977–78, compared with nearly 18 percent in the fall 1991 class (American Bar Association 1993).

The Role of Admission Test Scores in Litigation
about Special Admission Policies and Practice

Colleges and universities repeatedly warn applicants that test scores are only
one of many factors they use when deciding whom among their many applicants to admit. Most schools do not provide explicit information about how
test scores are used in the admission process, particularly the amount of weight

allocated to test scores relative to the other factors that are part of the decision to admit or reject. However, it is not unusual for some applicants who were denied admission, particularly to more highly competitive schools, to have higher test scores than many applicants who were admitted. Yet denial of admission to white applicants who earned higher standardized test scores than did applicants of color who gained admission has repeatedly served as the trigger to litigation in the area of affirmative action admissions in higher education. This section explores the past, present, and future of affirmative action litigation from the narrow perspective of the role of test scores in shaping the complaints, the defenses, and the rulings.

Affirmative action programs were introduced into the higher education system in the late 1960s with a stated goal of increasing and encouraging minority participation in higher education. The ways in which colleges implemented those programs have been the subject of litigation over the past twenty years. Most legal challenges to affirmative action admission practice have been predicated on interpretation of the fourteenth amendment to the U.S. Constitution, which provides that "No State shall make or enforce any law which shall . . . deny to any person within its jurisdiction the equal protection of the laws." The amendment's original purpose was to ensure that newly freed slaves were treated fairly by state law. In affirmative action litigation, the clause has been subject to varying interpretations. Thus far, the Supreme Court has been supportive of programs developed by colleges and universities designed to remedy past discrimination or to achieve diversity, but it also has imposed limits on those programs to prevent misuse or abuse. Key among those limits are that race-based affirmative action programs must be subjected to strict scrutiny and that the use of inflexible quotas, especially using race as the only factor for selection, is prohibited. The Supreme Court's most extensive explication of the limitations of race-conscious admission practices came in its ruling on a landmark case, the *Regents of the University of California v. Bakke*, in 1978, in which differential use of test scores was challenged under the fourteenth amendment.

An Overview of *Bakke*

Alan Bakke applied for admission to the University of California at Davis medical school during two different admission cycles and was denied both times. At the time he applied, the medical school used two separate admission standards—one for regular admissions and the other for a special program. The special admission program was designed to provide applicants from economically or educationally disadvantaged backgrounds the opportunity to be admitted when they otherwise would not because their applications did not meet traditional academic requirements. The school reserved sixteen of its hundred seats exclusively for applicants accepted under that program. Applicants checked a box on their application if they wanted to be considered under the special program. The practice at the medical school at the time Bakke was an applicant was to automatically reject applicants to the regular admission program if their test scores and grades were below a certain cutoff point. In contrast, applicants to the special program were not automatically rejected because of low test scores or low grades. Further, the admission committee did not rank their test scores against those of applicants in the regular admission pool.

White applicants were eligible to request consideration under the special admission program, but at the time of Bakke's complaint, none had ever been admitted under it. In fact, several of the sixteen seats reserved for the special admission program remained unfilled in each of the years that Bakke was denied, and he was not considered for any of them. A primary factor in his complaint was that he had presented higher test scores and grades than did applicants who were admitted under the special program. The basis of his suit was that he was excluded from consideration for admission under the special admission program exclusively because of his race, thus violating his constitutional right to equal protection under the fourteenth amendment. Even though the school argued that he did not meet the criteria of educational or economic disadvantage, the Court agreed with Bakke that race was the only factor that determined who would be admitted under the special program. On that basis, the Supreme Court found that UC Davis's special admission program violated the U.S. Constitution. From the perspective of affirmative action practices, the importance of *Bakke* was not in the Court's finding with respect to the special program at UC Davis. Rather, it was in the opinion of a majority of justices that although race could not be used as the sole factor for admission, race could be considered as a factor in order to advance students' educational experiences and learning. This endorsement is found in Justice Lewis Powell's declaration that "race or ethnic background may be deemed a 'plus' in a particular applicant's file, [so long as the applicant's race] does not insulate the individual from comparison with all other candidates for the available seats."

Since the *Bakke* ruling, higher education has acted under the proposition that when the goal of its admission practice is to establish or maintain diversity, race could be a factor in the admission process under two provisos. One proviso is that diversity is not defined exclusively in racial terms; the other is that race is only one of many factors used to admit a diverse class. The court did not define what those other factors should be, but neither did it suggest that having test scores and grades that were higher than those of other applicants who were admitted should in itself constitute grounds for a legal complaint against an institution by an applicant who was denied. Even so, subsequent challenges to affirmative action practices in higher education admissions have been raised, triggered by evidence or perception of differential use of test scores in the admission process.

An Overview of *Hopwood*

Approximately fifteen years after *Bakke,* four white applicants to the University of Texas law school instigated *Hopwood v. Texas.* In 1994, Cheryl Hopwood and the three other plaintiffs claimed that they were denied admission to the law school, although black and Mexican American applicants with lower LSAT scores and lower undergraduate grade point averages (UGPAs) were accepted. At the time the plaintiffs applied for admission, the University of Texas law school had an affirmative action admission program in place that did not differ in several respects from the UC Davis medical school program that the Supreme Court had rejected. That is, the school reserved approximately 10 percent of its places for Mexican American applicants and 5 percent for black applicants. In addition, separate admission committees were used to review minority and nonminority applicants. Thus, minority applicants were not compared directly with white applicants. Of relevance to the current discussion, the University of Texas relied heavily on LSAT scores and UGPAs in making all its admission decisions. The university claimed to use other factors, including undergraduate major, increasing or decreasing grade trends, grade inflation, personal perspective, life experiences, and state of residency, but it admitted to using a gross quantitative index, based only on test scores and grades, to initially sort its large volume of applications. Specifically, the school created an index score by weighting the LSAT score 60 percent and the UGPA 40 percent. The index score was used to sort applicants into three categories: presumptive admit, discretionary zone, and presumptive deny. The law school offered admissions to most but not all applicants in the presumptive admit category and denied admission to most but not all applicants in the presumptive deny category. Under the affirmative action admission program in place at the time, an index value of 199 was required for nonpreferred applicants to be presumptively admitted, whereas a value of 189 was required for black and Mexican American applicants. At the other end of the scale, an index score of 192 or lower placed nonpreferred applicants in the presumptive deny category, whereas a 179 or lower placed black or Mexican American applicants in that category. Striking in these figures is the fact that a black or Mexican American applicant was placed in the presumptive admit category with an index value that was three points lower than the value at which other applicants were placed in the presumptive deny category. These are the kinds of test and grade data that can lead opponents of affirmative action programs to conclude that a necessary consequence of these programs is a compromise of merit and academic standards.

When *Hopwood* was heard, the district court found that the school's affirmative action practice was in violation of the constitution because it used separate admission committees for minority and majority applicants. However, the court did not object to the lower index score requirement for black and Mexican American applicants. The court also used information about test scores and grades to determine that the plaintiffs were not denied admission as a consequence of the school's affirmative action program. The data showed that 109 resident white applicants with index scores lower than Cheryl Hopwood's had been admitted to the school. Further, 67 resident white applicants with index scores lower than the other three plaintiffs had been admitted (*Hopwood* 861, F. Supp. at 581). The plaintiffs appealed the district court's decision and the Fifth Circuit Court disagreed with the district court about the use of index scores. More important, the Fifth Circuit Court held that diversity could never be a compelling governmental interest in a public school of higher education. In other words, contrary to the *Bakke* ruling that race could not be used as the *sole* factor for admission, the Fifth Circuit ruled that the government could *never* consider race as a factor in college admission decisions. The Fifth Circuit ruling applies in the states under its jurisdiction—Texas, Louisiana, and Mississippi. The Supreme Court denied a petition by the University of Texas to review the case.

Further Litigation Issues

Because the Supreme Court refused to hear an appeal of the Fifth Circuit's ruling in *Hopwood*, its long-term implications remain unresolved. In the meantime, challenges based on similar premises, that is, that one or more white applicants were denied admission although minority applicants with lower test scores and/or grades were accepted, continue to mount. Two lawsuits filed against the University of Michigan—one by white students rejected for admission to its undergraduate program and the other by white students rejected by its law school—are still unresolved at the time of this writing.

A common theme across these cases is the use of the quantifiable variables of test scores and previous grades in making admission decisions. The complaints, alleging violations of the fourteenth amendment, arose from actual or perceived differential treatment of scores and grades between white applicants and minority applicants. Courts have found that using race as a determinative criterion in college admissions is a violation of the fourteenth amendment. Unfortunately, in the emotions of the debate, test scores and previous grades have taken on meaning and significance beyond their actual value or intended use. Among opponents of affirmative action, test scores and grades have become a surrogate for merit, whereas among proponents, they represent a barrier to equal opportunity.

Some admission programs aimed at increasing diversity in their schools have become vulnerable to legal challenges, at least partly as a consequence of overreliance on test scores and grades. This overreliance has also fueled the efforts of the popular press to turn the debate from one of equal opportunity to one of abandoning merit and academic standards. Test scores and grades are portrayed as seemingly objective measures that reflect some combination of hard work and achievement. Their limitations for such use are either misunderstood or purposely ignored. Changing societal perspectives made the time right in 1954 for both the courts and the public to reexamine the doctrine of separate but equal (which it did in response to *Brown v. Board of Education*). Similarly, the mood of society in the 1990s reflects near obsession with the concept that meritocracy, academic standards, and fairness are compromised when race becomes a factor in admission decisions. Additional research and scholarly analysis would be helpful in refuting the notion that tests alone provide a reliable and precise measure of either merit or academic standards. Such work would include, but not be limited to, gathering and communicating data for the purpose of demonstrating (1) the legitimate uses of tests, (2) the limitations of tests even when used legitimately, and (3) the deleterious consequences of using them for purposes for which they are not valid. It also should include broader definitions of merit as well as empirical links between those definitions and outcome measures such as academic success, professional contributions, and societal benefits.

Technical Issues in Equity and Assessment

Large differences in average performance on standardized admission tests between white test takers and test takers from some minority groups, especially those from black, Hispanic, and American Indian groups, have been widely documented across the spectrum of undergraduate and graduate admission testing programs. The largest differences tend to be between black and white test takers. Those differences are of a magnitude of approximately one standard deviation in each of the admission testing programs. The average score differences between white students and minority students have led to heated debates about the validity and utility of the tests, particularly with regard to admission decisions for minority group applicants. Other key technical testing issues related to the general questions about test validity are questions about test bias and about susceptibility of test scores to coaching.

Concerns about these issues are often articulated by critics, as in the following three statements about the role of testing in the higher education admission process.

- Standardized admission test scores do not add any useful information to the higher education admission process.
- Admission tests are biased against test takers who are not white and not male.
- Admission tests are highly susceptible to coaching, thus undermining their validity and adding to the test bias issue because test preparation is not as available to economically disadvantaged test takers as it is to others.

Empirical research generally does not support these statements. The extensive base of research on test validity typically concludes that the major higher education admission tests are valid for the limited purposes for which they were developed. The primary purpose of those tests is to measure selected "developed reasoning abilities" that are important to achieving academic success.

Research findings generally refute suppositions both that test bias provides the primary explanation for the observed performance differences among test takers from different ethnic groups and that the tests systematically disadvantage minority applicants to higher education institutions by underpredicting their subsequent academic performance. The data also show that the gains realized from test preparation are modest; they fail to show that test taker participation in test preparation activities lowers the predictive validity of the tests. This section summarizes the existing body of research in the area of test validity and its related issues; it also points to limitations in that research and suggests important issues in need of further research.

Predictive Validity

The application requirements of the vast majority of undergraduate, graduate, and first professional school programs include scores on one or more of the standardized admission tests previously described. Admission committees typically use those scores to draw inferences about applicants' future academic performance, usually first-year grades. The usefulness of test scores for that purpose is at the heart of the debate about test score validity. The term *validity* is used to describe the accumulated evidence to support the inferences that are made from the test score(s). One form of that evidence, referred to as predictive validity, is demonstrated when a statistical relationship between test scores and subsequent academic performance is established. The measure of academic success most often employed in predictive validity studies is first-year grades. First-year grades are not the only criteria that could be used to establish predictive validity evidence, but they are a popular choice for several reasons. First-year grades become available within a year of the start of school, whereas other criteria may require two or more years before a study could be conducted. In addition, first-year grades are based on a composite of academic performance accumulated over a year of school, thus allowing differences in course difficulty and grader stringency to average out. Finally, because many core courses are taken during the first year of school, the content on which the grade point average is based tends to be more consistent across students than it is at any later time.

Evidence to support the validity of the frequently used higher education admission tests has been fairly well established. Most major testing programs provide a free validity study service for schools using their tests, and hundreds of schools participate each year. The data analysis options vary somewhat from program to program, but all provide at least a correlation between first-year grades as the criterion and each of the following: test scores, previous academic grades (either high school grades or undergraduate grades, depending on whether the criterion grades are for undergraduate or for graduate or professional school), and the combination of the two. The results of those studies are relatively consistent across testing programs. The mean of the correlations obtained across hundreds of studies conducted for individual colleges is approximately 0.42 for verbal and mathematical SAT scores used together to predict first-year grades in college (Donlon 1984, 142). Among 685 colleges predicting freshman GPA using SAT verbal and SAT mathematics scores during the period 1964–81, 75 percent of the correlations exceeded 0.34 and 90 percent exceeded 0.27 (Donlon 1984). Among more than five hundred colleges using the ACT during 1989–90, the median correlation between first-year grades in college and the four ACT scores is 0.45 (American College Testing Program 1991, 17). Similarly, the 1993–94 data, based on 361 participating institutions, produced a median multiple correlation between college grade average and the four ACT assessment scores of 0.43 (American College Testing Program 1997, 56).

The outcome of correlating test scores with first-year grades in graduate and professional schools tends to show results that are as high or higher. Median correlations between 0.21 and 0.41 have been reported for the GMAT, LSAT, MCAT, and GRE general test (Livingston and Turner 1982; Wightman 1993; Wightman and Leary 1985). In addition to the routine testing-program-sponsored validity studies, many independent studies validating the tests used in admission decisions have been reported in the literature (see, e.g., Kramer and Johnston 1997; Pharr, Bailey, and Dangerfield 1993; Zwick 1993). The results from independent studies are consistent with those reported by the testing programs.

The correlation coefficients provide evidence of the validity of the tests, but the meaning of the correlation coefficient is sometimes misunderstood by consumers and test score users who have no training in basic statistics. That misunderstanding at least partly explains why some continue to raise questions about the predictive validity of admission tests, despite the extensive research supporting it. It may also explain why others respond to claims of substantial validity evidence by calling on test scores to do more than they were ever intended to do. A brief explanation and illustration of correlation coefficients as they are used to evaluate the predictive validity of admission tests follow in order to help explicate their use and interpretation.

When a test score is used to predict subsequent academic performance (e.g., first-year grades), a prediction equation that quantifies the relationship between test score and first-year average (FYA) is developed. The prediction equation can be represented by a straight line on a graph that shows for every student a single point that is determined by the student's (1) score on the predictor (e.g., the test score) and (2) score on the criterion (e.g., FYA). The exact position of the line on the graph is calculated so as to minimize the (squared) distance of every test/FYA point from the line. The correlation coefficient is an indicator of how well the line represents the points on the graph. Correlations can take on values from 0—meaning that there is no relationship between two variables—to 1—meaning there is a perfect one-to-one correspondence between the two variables. That is, when the correlation coefficient is 0, there is no relationship between the two variables depicted on the graph. The closer the correlation is to 1, the closer the points are to the line. And the closer the points are to the line, the more accurately the predictor (e.g., test scores) predicts the criterion score (e.g., FYA). Figure 3.1 demonstrates the relative meaning of correlations of different magnitudes. It presents three examples of data points and best-fitting prediction lines for hypothetical samples of a hundred students who have both test score data and first-year grades. In each example, test score is the predictor and FYA is the criterion. The test scores are reported on a scale of 200 to 800, with a mean of 500 and a standard deviation of 100. First-year grades are reported on a scale of 1 to 4, with a mean of 3.0 and a standard deviation of 0.45. Three different correlation coefficients (r) are represented in the illustrations—0.0, 0.4, and 0.6. A correlation value of 0.4 was selected for illustration because it is close to the median correlation reported by most higher education admission testing programs. A value of 0.6 is included because it represents the upper end of individual school correlations reported among the different testing programs. A value of 0.0 provides a baseline against which to examine the other relationships.

Notice that when the correlation is equal to zero, the prediction line is parallel to the x-axis (the axis on which the test scores are denoted) and crosses

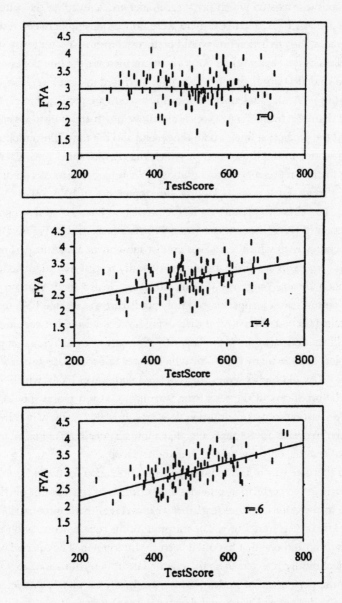

FIGURE 3.1 Scatter of points representing test scores and first-year averages (FYA) around the best regression line for selected correlation values.

the y-axis (the axis on which first-year grades are denoted) at the value equal to the average FYA. That is, if there were no relationship between test scores and grades, the prediction line would predict the mean FYA for every student, regardless of test score. When the correlations increase, the line slopes upward, so that students with higher test scores are predicted to earn FYAs higher than the mean FYA, and students with lower test scores are predicted to earn FYAs lower than the mean FYA. Notice also how much the points are scattered around the prediction line in both the second and the third illustration relative to the scatter in the illustration in which the correlation is zero. Each point above the line represents a student whose FYA is higher than was predicted by her test score. Each point below the line represents an FYA lower than predicted. The closer the points are to the prediction line, the more accurate the prediction of FYA based on test score. The data presented in Figure 3.1 show the accuracy with which test scores predict subsequent academic performance when correlations are of the magnitude typically reported by higher education admission testing programs. The illustrations clearly show that prediction based on test scores is superior to simply predicting the average FYA for every applicant (the best alternative if there were no relationship between the two). The illustrations also show the lack of precision for an individual applicant. The plots include many points for which lower test scores are associated with higher FYAs and higher scores are associated with lower FYAs, which is partly why the producers of the tests issue warnings that test scores should not be used in isolation to make admission decisions. It is also partly why college application materials advise applicants that admission decisions are based on a variety of criteria, only one of which is the test score.

An alternate way to use and interpret the correlation coefficient is to square it. Squaring the correlation provides a description of the amount of the variability in the criterion score (e.g., first-year average) that can be attributed to the predictor (e.g., test score). The meaning of the squared correlation is difficult to grasp and one that has often been misinterpreted. The squared correlation (technically referred to as the coefficient of determination) *does not* describe the percentage of students whose grades are accurately predicted. The Nairn/Nader report (Nairn and Associates 1980) is one example of this type of misinterpretation of the squared correlation. The following example may help clarify this concept. If the correlation between SAT scores and FYA (or ACT scores and FYA) is 0.4, then 16 percent (i.e., 0.4 squared) of the variance in FYA is accounted for by the variance in SAT (or ACT) scores. A way to interpret the meaning of the squared correlation coefficient is to imagine a situation in which there was no variability in the test score. For example, if a sample of students who all had the same test score were selected from the total population of students, the variance in FYA for that sample would be expected to be 16 percent smaller than the variance for the total population of students.

Testing specialists have long agreed that the squared correlation is of limited value in interpreting the usefulness of admission tests for selection purposes (see, e.g., Brogden 1946; Cronbach and Gleser 1965). This is because the correlations need to be interpreted within the framework of the limitations of the data from which they were computed. Thus, even though from a purely statistical perspective, correlations of the magnitude found between test scores and first-year grades are somewhat modest, they should not be dismissed offhandedly. The correlations reported in typical predictive validity studies are actually a reduced estimate of the true relationship between test scores and subsequent academic performance. The reduction is a statistical consequence of using the test score as a predictor when it also was a factor on which selection of the students was based. This phenomenon is known as *range restriction*. The correlation coefficient is related to the amount of variability (or roughly, the *range* of test scores) among students in the validity study sample. When test scores are used to help select applicants for admission, the range of test scores among first-year students (those who have attended the school and earned a GPA to be correlated with the test score) is less than the range among all of the applicants. The more selective the school is and the greater the emphasis on test scores in the admission process, the larger the underestimate of the correlation.

Critics of the use of test scores in the admission process often note that even though the median correlation between test score and subsequent grades is positive across all the testing programs, there is a substantial amount of variability from school to school. In fact, a handful of schools in almost every testing program's summary report show zero or slightly negative correlations. Those critics use the variation in correlations among different schools to question the accuracy of the claims of test validity. However, an alternate explanation for the observed variability in validity estimates is statistical artifact. The variability is at least partly attributable to the range restriction found within different schools. A second statistical artifact, sampling fluctuation, also accounts for a substantial proportion of the variability in validity estimates obtained

among different schools (Linn, Harnisch, and Dunbar 1981). Another statistical artifact contributing to low and negative correlations is the use of a com-
pensatory model in selection (i.e., allowing either high test scores to compensate for low grades or high grades to compensate for low test scores). See, for
example, Wightman's work (1993) demonstrating the impact of the compen-
satory model on the validity of LSAT scores.

Despite the existence of literally thousands of studies of the nature described earlier, which support the *validity* of standardized admission tests as predictive measures of first-year grades, their *utility* should not simply be accepted
without question. The technical question of whether test scores are statistically
related to an outcome of interest (e.g., first-year grades) is not sufficient to
determine *how* the test should be used in the admission process. Individual
schools need to evaluate (1) the importance of the validity study criterion in
their selection process; (2) whether there are other factors that predict the criterion as well or better than test scores; and (3) what impact using the test score
might have on their ability to attract the kinds of students they seek as well as
to fairly select among those who apply. Consider some examples.

Bowen and Bok (1998) recently examined the utility of SAT scores to
predict rank in class based on students' cumulative four-year GPAs. They estimated the relationship separately for black and for white students attending
the twenty-eight academically selective colleges or universities that are part
of the *College and Beyond* database (see Bowen and Bok 1998, xxvii–xxix, for
a listing of participating schools). Like other studies cited previously, their
analysis provided clear support for the validity of the test. Further, they determined that the relationship (i.e., higher test scores associated with higher
class rank) was found for both white and black students, again refuting the
claim that test scores are not valid predictors for black applicants to higher
education. Importantly, they also noted that the relationship "remains after
we control for gender, high school grades, socioeconomic status, school selectivity, and major as well as race" (74). Their graphical illustration of that relationship (Bowen and Bok 1998, fig. 3.10) not only shows the validity of the
test but also helps demonstrate the distinction between utility and statistical
significance. Specifically, despite the statistical significance between SAT score
and class rank, Bowen and Bok (1998, 74–75) found that for white students,
"an additional 100 points of combined SAT score is associated, on average,
with an improvement of only 5.9 percentile points in class rank." The same

amount of score gain "is associated with a class rank improvement of only 5.0 points for black students."

Other studies demonstrate that previous grades correlate as higher or higher than test scores with subsequent grades in undergraduate school. For example, studies based on both SAT and ACT data showed that high school record is typically the strongest single predictor (see, e.g., Donlon 1984; Linn 1982a). There is more of a tendency for test scores to be the stronger predictor in graduate and professional schools (e.g., Wightman and Leary 1985; Wightman 1993) when first-year grades are used as the criterion. Regardless, it is important to note that test scores and grades are not completely redundant predictors. All of the studies show that test scores and previous grades used in combination are more highly correlated with subsequent academic performance than is either predictor alone. Further, limited data suggest that even in testing programs in which test scores were stronger predictors of first-year grades than were previous grades, when the criterion is academic performance beyond the first year, the contribution of previous grades is greater than that of test scores (Powers 1982).

Finally, some researchers hold that although the data generally show that higher education admission tests are valid predictors of later academic performance, the amount of additional information provided by the scores pales when evaluated relative to the various costs of requiring the test of all applicants. Most notably, Crouse and Trusheim (1988, 6) posited that "SAT scores can provide important information only when they lead admissions officers to make admission decisions they would not have made without SAT scores." To support their position that admission test scores are of negligible utility, they calculated predicted GPA based on high school rank alone, then on high school rank and SAT score combined. They reported the correlation between the two predicted first-year undergraduate grades to be 0.88. Their analyses also demonstrated that using high school grades alone would change the admission decisions for only a very small proportion (approximately 10 percent) of the applicants.

Bias

Questions about test validity are often raised in response to concerns about whether admission test scores can be used to evaluate minority applicants in the same way they are used to evaluate white applicants. The various components of those questions usually are all related to the issue of bias. According to Scheuneman and Slaughter (1991, 1), "Bias is defined as the systematic over- or under-estimation of the true abilities of a group of examinees formed according to some demographic variable such as sex or ethnicity." Questions about bias are most often raised and debated in reaction to the large observed differences in average performance among test takers from different ethnic groups. But, importantly, the definition of bias is more than a definition about the magnitude of observed average score differences. That is, although large between-group score differences could be symptomatic of test bias, score differences are not sufficient by themselves to establish the existence of test bias.

Research on bias in testing has occupied substantial space in the testing literature in recent years. This research generally takes two foci. One focus is on individual test questions; the other is on differential validity of the test when used to predict future performance among test takers from different ethnic groups. Research efforts targeting individual test questions typically seek both statistical and nonstatistical procedures to identify and eliminate questions on which test takers from different subgroups who have similar ability on the skill being measured have different probabilities of answering them correctly. In the current testing jargon, this phenomenon is referred to as differential item functioning (DIF). Subsumed in item-level bias analyses is the concept of sensitivity review. That is, each test item is reviewed by a panel representative of the diversity of the test takers to screen items for insensitive or offensive subject matter or treatment. A primary goal of sensitivity review is to eliminate items that might disadvantage individual test takers by eliciting emotional reactions or responses. In contrast to the sensitivity review, the statistical detection methods identify differentially functioning items independent of any external characteristics of the items. Incorporating a combination of the two procedures in routine test development activities has resulted in considerable improvement, from the perspective of item bias, in the overall makeup of standardized test forms. The most egregious test questions, for example, those that dealt with subject matter such as slavery, abortion, and stereotypes of particular ethnic groups, are no longer found on standardized admission tests that routinely undergo DIF analysis and sensitivity review. Critics who cite examples of flagrant item bias or insensitivity problems typically use items from test forms developed and assembled before the introduction of bias detection methods in the 1980s (e.g., Espanoza 1993).

The second focus of the bias research is on questions about differential validity and differential prediction. These questions take two related forms:

- Are test scores less valid when used to predict subsequent academic performance of nonmajority applicants than they are for majority applicants? For example, is the correlation between test scores and first-year performance in undergraduate or graduate/first professional school different for different identifiable groups of students?
- Are test scores systematically unfair to nonmajority applicants? That is, do some groups systematically perform better than they are predicted to by the tests?

The literature on this topic is extensive, although some of the work is dated and needs to be updated or at least replicated. Overall, the research in this area suggests that test scores and previous grades are valid for black and Hispanic test takers. But there also is some evidence of differences in the magnitude of those validities both across testing programs and across different types of schools within testing programs.

Research in the area of differential validity and differential prediction often reports that the admission test overpredicts for minority test takers. *Overprediction* refers to the comparison of the FYA predicted by the test compared with the observed FYA. That is, when the test overpredicts, actual first-year grades earned by the test takers are lower than the FYAs predicted by their test scores. If the relatively lower average test scores earned by minority examinees were simply a result of test bias, then underprediction, that is, actual FYAs that were higher than the FYAs predicted by the test scores, would be an expected outcome. Explanations of the findings of overprediction must not mask the important distinction between *average* results and *individual* results. Specifically, although most research shows that on average test scores tend to overpredict future FYAs for black test takers, this finding does not imply that test scores overpredict performance for each individual black test taker. (See Wightman 1998a for graphs presenting data of the black and white law school students whose actual first-year performance in law school exceeded their predicted performance.)

In a comprehensive review of the literature on differential validity and differential prediction, Linn (1990, 310) provided the following references, summaries, and generalizations about research findings with regard to minority and majority groups:

1. Predictive validities (American College Testing Program 1973; Breland 1979; Duran 1983; Linn 1982a; Ramist 1984)
   a. Tests and previous grades have a useful degree of validity for black and Hispanic as well as white students.
   b. Predictive validities typically are lower for black than for white students at predominantly white colleges.
   c. At predominantly black colleges, validities are comparable to those [for freshmen in general] at predominantly white colleges.
   d. Typically validities are slightly lower for Hispanic than for white students.
2. Differential prediction (American College Testing Program 1973; Breland 1979; Duran 1983; Linn 1982a; Ramist 1984)
   a. Freshman GPA typically overpredicted for black students.
   b. Overprediction is usually greatest for black students with above-average scores on predictors and negligible for students with below-average scores on predictors.
   c. Overprediction is found for Hispanic students, but less consistently and by a smaller amount.
3. Statistical artifacts may contribute to overprediction (Linn 1983).
4. Differential course-taking patterns may mask the amount of over-prediction to some extent and partially account for the lower validities found for minority students (Elliott and Strenta 1988).
5. Inferences about bias on the basis of differential validity or prediction findings require assumptions that grades are themselves unbiased measures.
6. Results for graduate and professional schools, while more limited, are generally consistent with those at the undergraduate level, except that there is less indication that predictive validities are lower for minority group students (Braun and Jones 1981; Powers 1977; Linn 1982a).

Studies more recent than those reviewed by Linn, although limited in number, continue to confirm the earlier findings about differential predictive validity. For example, Young (1994) confirmed that the phenomenon still existed for a sample of 3,703 college students. He concluded that for women, but not for minorities, the difference in predictive validity appeared to be related to course selection. Similarly, Noble (1996) showed that both ACT scores and high school grade point averages slightly overpredicted success in standard freshmen courses for black students relative to white students and for men relative to women. Wightman and Muller's (1990) analysis of data from law school students found no differences in validity for black, Mexican American, or other Hispanic students. Their data also continued to demonstrate that on average, LSAT scores, used alone or in combination with UGPA, slightly overpredicted first-year averages in law school for black, Mexican American, or other Hispanic students.

Implicit in the analyses of differential validity and differential prediction described in this section is the assumption that the criterion (typically first-year grades) is unbiased. Currently, research to test the accuracy and the impact of that assumption is lacking. A key factor that is not explained by any of the studies of differential prediction is the cause for the overprediction. Linn (1990) ascertains that it seems likely the result is due to many factors, including both statistical artifacts and educationally relevant factors. Testing organizations and testing professionals have focused much attention on uncovering and understanding the statistical artifacts, as evidenced in the research cited in this section. The greatest shortage of current research seems to be in the areas of how to remedy the educationally relevant factors and how to integrate information about remedies with the test development efforts in order to provide new and more meaningful assessment options.

Another important consideration in dealing with questions of bias in standardized testing is the bias in selection that results from overreliance on test scores in the admission process even if there is no bias in the test scores themselves. Linn (1990, 320) emphasizes that "because the predictive validity of test scores and previous academic records are modest and the group differences in average scores are large, selection based solely on the basis of these quantitative predictors would have substantial adverse impact for Black and Hispanic applicants and exclude many minority students who would succeed if given an opportunity." Research that examined Linn's hypothesis is reviewed in the section on the consequential basis of test validity.

Coaching

The general topic of test validity is also related to the topic of test preparation or coaching. Coaching is used as a generic term here to refer to any of a broad number of activities ranging from relatively short-term review of test familiarization materials to extensive long-term instruction in the subject matter covered on the admission test. Research suggests important distinctions between the two extremes with respect not only to their effect on subsequent test performance but also their relationship to later academic achievement.

Virtually all of the higher education admissions testing programs provide some test familiarization materials free of charge to prospective test takers. They also market a wide array of test preparation materials, ranging from previously used intact test forms to computer-based instructional material. Printed and computer-based test preparation materials are also offered by commercial organizations that are independent from the organizations that produce the tests. In addition, a number of not-for-profit as well as commercial test preparation courses are offered. The cost of the available test preparation materials and services ranges from only a few dollars for the purchase of a previously used test form to nearly a thousand dollars for enrollment in some commercial test preparation courses. One consequence of the differential costs associated with test preparation options is that various options are not equally available to students with different financial resources. As important, some evidence suggests that students from different ethnic/racial groups do not equally understand the value of test preparation. For example, Mc-Kinley (1993) found that white LSAT takers tended to use the free and low-cost test preparation materials offered by the test publisher more often than black, Mexican American, or Puerto Rican test takers used them. He also found that white test takers tended to use a larger number of different methods of test preparation than did test takers from other subgroups.

The import of differential access to and use of test preparation opportunities is primarily related to the possible positive effect of test preparation on subsequent test performance. Two meta-analyses of the large number of studies dealing with the effect of test preparation on subsequent test performance (Messick and Jungeblut 1981; Powers 1993) both agree that test scores have been improved as a consequence of engaging in focused test preparation but that the average gains are generally modest. Messick and Jungeblut estimated that the first twenty hours of coaching were associated with an increase of approximately one-fifth of a standard deviation (19.2 points) on the SAT mathematics score. The same amount of coaching time was associated with an increase of less than one-tenth of a standard deviation (8.9 points) on the SAT verbal score. A study of the effects of professional coaching for African American students on the ACT showed similarly modest gains (Moss 1995). That is, after a six-week coaching course, the average increase among the study participants was 1.34 points. Whether gains of these magnitudes are worth the cost and the amount of preparation time required in order to achieve them is an individual decision.

A related question of interest is whether test takers from different ethnic groups benefit differently from exposure to short-term or moderate-term coaching. The limited available research that specifically compared test score gain across different ethnic groups revealed little difference among ethnic groups in the benefits, as measured by test performance, realized from engaging in test preparation activities (Messick 1980; Leary and Wightman 1983; Powers 1987). In a study that looked exclusively at black students, Johnson (1984) evaluated results from a test preparation program sponsored by the National Association for the Advancement of Colored People. The program's purpose was to increase the number of eligible black college applicants by raising their SAT scores. The evaluation report's conclusions—that overall the program was effective but the gains were modest—are consistent with other coaching research. In addition, the results reported by Johnson were mixed across clinics. Students from San Francisco and Atlanta showed statistically significant increases in test scores, whereas increases of approximately the same magnitude among students from New York were not statistically significant.

Several researchers have raised concerns that even the modest score increases associated with short-term test preparation are a potential threat to the validity of the use of these tests for admission decisions (see, e.g., Messick and Jungeblut 1981; Linn 1982b; Bond 1989). An early study that addressed this issue (Marron 1965) found that coaching led to an overprediction of academic performance. However, Marron's results have been questioned, primarily because of the lack of statistical rigor in his design and analysis. Several subsequent studies (Powers 1985; Jones 1986; Baydar 1990; Allalouf and Ben-Shakhar 1998) suggest either that test preparation may enhance rather than undermine predictive validity or that coaching had no negative impact on the predictive validity of the admission test.

Test preparation questions that focus on long-term academic preparation are distinct from questions about short-term or moderate-term coaching. The admission tests are designed to measure academic skills acquired over an extended period of time. If the tests are valid for that purpose, examinees who did not enroll in or do well in rigorous academic courses that provide the fundamental preparation for a college education should be expected to earn lower test scores than do examinees who engaged in adequate academic preparation. Addressing problems of inadequate long-term academic preparation may be more difficult and elusive than is providing short-term coaching solutions, but defining the relationships between academic preparation and subsequent test performance, and developing appropriate intervention may also provide more lasting positive outcomes. In cases in which shorter-term coaching—particularly coaching that focuses on test-taking strategies rather than underlying skills—results in score increases, Johnson's questions (1984) about whether improved SAT performance results in stronger college performance are central to concerns about coaching, test validity, and equity and fairness in the admission process.

There is research evidence to support the intuitive relationship between inadequate academic preparation and poor test performance (e.g., Chenoweth 1996; Pennock-Roman 1988). There also is research demonstrating increased test performance among minority students who are appropriately guided into academic programs or courses that provide the necessary long-term academic preparation. For example, in her study of Hispanic students in postsecondary education, Pennock-Roman (1988) not only found large differences in SAT scores between Hispanic and non-Hispanic white students but also found that those differences were associated with the type of academic courses taken. She concluded that the adequacy of Hispanic students' test preparation was one of the important factors in their relatively poor test performance. More directly relevant to improving test performance are the results from evaluations of the Equity 2000 program. A primary goal of that program is to encourage school systems to direct their minority students into college preparatory mathematics courses. A demonstration project supported by Prince George's County, Maryland, showed that successful completion of high school algebra and geometry was an important predictor of achieving SAT scores that qualified students for college admission (Fields 1997). The study indicated that programs like the one in Prince George's County are difficult to implement but also that they promise results that justify the extra effort.

Consequential Basis of Test Validity

In his seminal work on test score validity, Messick (1989) explained the need to incorporate the value implications and social consequences of interpreting and using test scores into the overall concept of test validity. Messick (1994, 3) later suggested that this could be accomplished by "scrutinizing not only the intended outcomes but also unintended side effects—in particular, evaluate the extent to which (or, preferably, discount the possibility that) any adverse consequences of the testing derive from sources of score invalidity such as construct-irrelevant test variance." Construct-irrelevant test variance refers to score variability that results from differences in factors that the test does not intend to measure. Cultural differences, language differences, and differential opportunity to learn (particularly in higher education admission tests that aim to assess skills that are independent of specific curriculum) have the potential to contribute to producing construct-irrelevant variance. A simple example of this concept would be a test intended to measure mathematical computation skills that is administered to examinees for whom English is a second language. If the task is presented through "word problems" or if the instructions are presented in language that is complex, low scores may reflect language limitations rather than low proficiency in the computational skills of interest.

The consequential basis of test validity is an issue for standardized higher education admission tests partly because the major tests used for admission purposes are "indeed culture dependent" (Linn 1982b, 285). Messick's depiction of social consequences as a validity issue has been a topic of controversy and debate within the measurement community (see, e.g., Linn 1997; Mehrens 1997; Popham 1997; Shepard 1997). The basis of the disagreement is whether the social consequences of test use fit appropriately under the validity umbrella; there is no disagreement that social consequences are an area that should be of concern to both test developers and test score users. Regardless of an individual's position about its place within the validity construct, Messick's representation has resulted in heightened attention to the issue of social consequences associated with test score use.

The consequences of overreliance on test scores from the perspectives of achieving diversity in higher education and affording educational opportunity for economically disadvantaged applicants have been well documented. For example, Willingham and Breland (1977) maintained that strict reliance on standard numerical indicators would have an adverse impact on several minority groups. Evans (1977) provided empirical evidence to demonstrate that below the very top of the LSAT score range, the proportion of black law school applicants who were accepted exceeded the proportion of white applicants with the same scores. More recently, Wightman (1997) used law school application and admission decision data to demonstrate that basing admission decisions exclusively on numerical indicators (i.e., test scores and previous grade point averages) would substantially reduce the proportion of admitted applicants from selected minority groups. More importantly, the law school data showed that the majority of minority students who would have been excluded from law school succeeded when they were given an opportunity. That is, on the basis of data from the fall 1991 entering class, no significant differences in graduation rate were found, within any of the racial/ethnic groups studied, between those who would have been admitted under the numerical model and those who would have been denied. The data on bar passage outcomes showed small differences between those who would have been admitted and those who would not within some, but not all, ethnic groups. The most compelling aspect of the bar admission data is that between 88 and 72 percent of minority law school students who would have been denied opportunity to enter law school under a numbers-only admission model were able to successfully pass the bar and enter the profession. Similar studies in other educational settings should be undertaken to help put in perspective the impact of selection based disproportionately on test score results.

Other social consequences resulting from heavy reliance on test scores in the admission process are less well researched. For example, little is known about the effect of lower test scores on decisions among tests takers with respect to whether to continue with the college application process as well as which schools to apply to. More research is required in several areas related to the social consequences resulting from test score use in higher education admissions. Such research should distinguish between issues of distributive justice and true sources of invalidity in order to guide potential remedies that might be proposed in response to research results. Messick (1994, 8) pointed out that "it is not that adverse social consequences of test use render the use invalid but, rather, that adverse social consequences should not be attributable to any source of test invalidity such as construct under-representation or construct-irrelevant variance." For example, to the extent that differences in test scores among members of different ethnic groups represent true differences in educational opportunity, heavy reliance on test scores would have adverse social consequences that are questions of distributive justice but are not sources of invalidity within the test. Alternatively, to the extent that score differences are attributable to factors such as different tendencies to guess on multiple-choice questions or speediness factors on tests designed to be power tests, there exist sources of construct-irrelevant variance that impact the validity of the test.

Use and Misuse of Admission Test Scores in Higher Education

The majority of testing programs provide advice and warning to both test takers and score users about appropriate score use, emphasizing the limitations of those scores. Even so, there is concern about overreliance on test scores in the admission process. The potential for misuse of test scores has been exacerbated by recent moves to pit concepts of merit and academic standards against the benefits of diversity and educational opportunity offered through affirmative action programs. Despite extensive evidence to the contrary, test scores are being portrayed as an accurate, objective indicator of merit. This section reviews relevant research on appropriate and inappropriate use of test scores and other indicators of academic achievement in the admission process and examines the changing public attitudes about test score use.

Reliance and Overreliance on Test Scores in Making Selection Decisions

The amount to which admission decisions rely or overly rely on test scores varies from institution to institution and also varies across undergraduate, graduate, and professional schools. University of Virginia's dean of admissions in 1997, John Blackburn, claims that "we see the SAT, and I think most colleges and universities see the SAT, as one factor among many that would be important in making decisions about students" (U.S. News Online 1997). Consistent with his assessment, in a national survey of admission practices, data confirmed that admission test scores were not the only or even the primary factor that schools claimed influenced their admission decisions. The major factors identified by schools and the importance attached to them are identified in Table 3.5. Grades in college preparatory courses received the highest ratings in the category "considerable importance." These findings are consistent with the previously reported data showing that for most under-

TABLE 3.5

Admission Trends, 1995: Factors Influencing
Admission Decisions, by Percentage

	Considerable Importance	Moderate Importance	Limited Importance	No Importance
Grades in college preparatory courses	80	10	7	3
Admission test scores	47	38	9	6
Grades in all subjects	41	40	14	5
Class rank	39	33	19	9
Essay/writing sample	21	34	24	21
Counselor recommendations	19	48	23	10
Teacher recommendations	18	46	23	13
Interview	15	30	34	22
Work/extracurricular experiences	7	35	40	17
Ability to pay	3	7	16	73
Personal recognition programs	1	12	41	45

SOURCE: National Association for College Admission Counseling, 1995.

graduate schools, high school grades are slightly better predictors of college performance than are test scores. Only 47 percent of the respondents rated the importance of admission test scores as "considerable," although another 38 percent rated their importance as "moderate."

Despite statements by schools describing the way in which test scores are used in the selection process, at least some empirical data imply that the relationship between test scores and admission decisions might be stronger than is suggested here. A now well-known example is the way the University of Texas law school used LSAT scores and grades as reported in *Hopwood*. Correlational data also suggest a strong relationship between test scores and admission decisions. Willingham (1988) reported a correlation of 0.37 between SAT score and undergraduate admission decisions and 0.36 between high school grade point average score and undergraduate admission decisions. Wightman (1997) reported a correlation of 0.33 between LSAT score and law school admission decisions and 0.28 between undergraduate grade point average score and law school decisions. When the two variables were considered simultaneously, in a logistic regression prediction model, Wightman (1997) reported a correlation of 0.78 between predicted and actual admission decisions for white law school applicants. In other words, LSAT score and

UGPA together accounted for approximately half of the variance in law school admission decisions. The correlations between predicted and actual admission decisions were substantially lower for other racial ethnic groups, suggesting that test scores and grades were less important to admission decisions for minority applicants than they were for white applicants. Even when the correlation data confirm a very strong relationship, correlations alone are not sufficient to determine whether scores are much more important factors than they are acknowledged to be or whether they are simply very highly correlated with the several other factors that were also taken into consideration. Another consideration that is related to the importance of test scores and grades is the number of applicants relative to the number of available places. Test scores most likely play a larger role in decisions within those schools that are the most competitive. More systematic research across a variety of schools and applicant populations would be required to empirically address those kinds of issues of use and overuse of test scores in admission decisions.

Previous Grades as an Alternative to Test Scores

Some available research suggests that test scores could be eliminated from the admission process. Predictive validity data presented earlier show that high school grades tend to be better predictors of subsequent college academic performance than are SAT or ACT scores. Further, data showed that although adding test scores to the prediction model improved prediction over grades alone, doing so had little effect with respect to changing the admission decision for individual applicants. But to evaluate the consequences of abandoning the use of test scores in the admission process, we need to consider some of the problems inherent in the use of grades alone.

Course grades are not always reflective of the skills, abilities, or knowledge of individual students. They can depend, at least partly, on the expectations of the instructors, the abilities of other students in the class, and the style and personality fit between student and teacher. Grades are frequently inflated, especially at schools in which a large proportion of students aspire to achieve admission to competitive institutions. Also, grades frequently are interpreted with respect to the academic reputation of the school at which they were earned. In a discussion of this topic, Linn (1982a, 284) correctly points out that "the lack of comparability of grades from one school to another, from one curriculum to another, or from one college to another is a potentially important source of un-fairness. The student who attends a school with less demanding standards for grades is given an advantage relative to his or her counterpart attending a school with more demanding standards." One way schools have dealt with grades from differentially demanding schools is to use a school-based adjust-ment to an individual's grades. The problem with that approach is that the stu-dent from a disadvantaged background who attended a high school or under-graduate school at which students typically do not excel is penalized, thus reducing the value of his or her demonstrated achievements. Some research has sought to analyze the disadvantage to middle-class and lower-middle-class students that would arise from eliminating test scores from the admission pro-cess. Stanley (1977–78, 31–32) remarked that the SAT had "a decidedly de-mocratizing effect on certain kinds of selective colleges that, before the advent of the SAT, tended to rely heavily for their students on high status private schools and the most academically prestigious public schools."

Finally, data suggest that test scores are not so much the barriers to admis-sion that many believe them to be. Analysis of law school data investigated the decision outcomes of a "numbers-only" admission process. The data showed that, regardless of whether the process was modeled by UGPA and LSAT score combined or by UGPA only, the consequence would have been a sub-stantial reduction in the overall number of minority applicants who were of-fered admission to ABA-approved law schools (Wightman 1997). Those re-sults are consistent with the Crouse and Trusheim (1988) findings that an admission policy that rejected applicants with predicted grades below some predetermined level would lead to the same admission decision for most ap-plicants, regardless of whether high school grades were used alone or in com-bination with SAT scores.

Using Test Scores to Define Merit

It was not that long ago that public sentiment about testing focused on its limitations and its overuse—particularly for purposes for which tests were not intended and were not validated. One example is the Nairn/Nader re-port (Nairn and Associates 1980), which represented a major public relations attack not only on the standardized tests used in higher education admissions but also on the Educational Testing Service as the maker and administrator of the majority of those tests. Measurement professionals then prepared a variety of position papers defending the tests as well as their appropriate use from both Nairn/Nader's and other earlier attacks against them (see, e.g., Cronbach 1975; Astin 1979; Linn 1982b).

The public mood about the role of standardized testing shifted during the mid-1990s. Performance on standardized tests is now often portrayed as an impartial demonstration of academic merit (or lack thereof). This shift in perception about standardized testing was fueled at least in part by the ongoing debate about affirmative action and the ruling by the Fifth Circuit in *Hopwood*. The tension in American ideology between the concepts of merit and distributive justice (or equality of outcomes) predates the *Hopwood* ruling. To most Americans, the concept of merit implies that people should succeed as a consequence of ability and hard work, not as a consequence of whom they are or whom they know (Kluegel and Smith 1986). In the abstract, this definition frames merit as a neutral concept that is independent of the emotional or political debate of affirmative action. During much of the affirmative action debate, little attention was paid to developing a definition of merit that could be embraced by the general public. The *Hopwood* ruling and the media reporting of it have had a role in formulating such a definition for the public. That is, the form of the complaint, the court's response to it, and the media's representation of the court's decision imply that test scores and grades are the overriding determinants of who is "entitled" to the limited resources in higher education. Opponents of affirmative action have seized this definition with zeal. Columnist John Leo (1997, 22) laments examples of admission procedures based on practices other than that of ranking applicants by test scores and grades as signs of "the gathering assault on good grades, test scores, and nearly all known indicators of merit and academic achievement." He goes on to attribute efforts to reduce the emphasis on test scores in the admission process as "drummed up to protect the excess of an affirmative action movement in deep trouble with the courts and the American people." In an opposing view, Harvard law professor Christopher Edley, Jr. (1997) chides critics of affirmative action for treating "paper and pencil tests as if they were complete and accurate measures of merit" as well as for "speak[ing] of preferences with robotic regularity because polling shows that the public generally supports affirmative action while opposing preferences."

The measurement community has never suggested that test scores could or should serve as a surrogate for merit. As noted previously, that community has been both clear and forthcoming about the limitations of test scores and the necessity of looking at a variety of factors in making admission decisions. Proponents of using test scores as indicators of merit ignore important contributions that diversity among the student body makes to the educational experience of all students. Consequently, they fail to identify the potential to bring diverse perspectives and experiences to the educational setting as a characteristic "meriting" admission. In responding to Initiative 200—an anti–affirmative action initiative in the state of Washington—the regents there unanimously approved a statement that included the following: "Among the educational resources the university has to offer, is a diverse student body" (Carson 1998). Although many educators agree that a diverse student body enhances educational experiences by sharing broader perspectives and challenging assumptions, there is limited formal research to support these conclusions. More systematic objective work is needed to define and document the concept of merit beyond the narrow confines of test scores and grades. Chapter 5 reviews the literature and discusses the existing research on this topic.

The Future of Admission Testing in Higher Education

The current use of standardized test scores in the admission process needs to be examined against a variety of alternatives, particularly in the wake of *Hopwood* and California's Proposition 209. These alternatives range from eliminating the use of scores altogether to a major reconstitution of the content and format of admission tests and to the way that scores from those tests are developed and reported. This section identifies various options to relying routinely on scores from traditional multiple-choice paper-and-pencil admission tests; it also summarizes and synthesizes current and ongoing research that evaluates these alternatives.

Eliminating the Use of Test Scores in the Admission Process

Possible overreliance by colleges and universities on standardized tests, as well as the potential that test scores would have negative consequences for applicants' decisions about if and where to apply to college or graduate school, became a concern in higher education long before the current political anti–affirmative action climate emerged. In the mid-1980s, Bates College, Union College, and Middlebury College retracted their requirement that applicants submit SAT scores as part of the application process, allowing them to substitute alternate achievement test scores including the ACT. After that decision, Bates undertook a five-year study comparing Bates GPAs of students who submitted SAT scores with the GPAs of students who did not. They found no difference in GPA at Bates as well as slightly lower attrition rates for nonsubmitters compared with submitters (Bates College 1998). Thus, in 1990, Bates further revised its policy to make the submission of any admission test scores optional for their applicants. Bates faculty cite the following reasons for the decision: inconsistent prediction of academic performance by test scores; inflated perceptions about the importance of test scores in the selection process; and two ethical issues related to the use of test scores—the possibility that test scores place students from multicultural, rural, or financially depressed backgrounds at a disadvantage, and the likelihood that teachers and students misdirect their energies to the activities of test preparation (Bates College 1998). Research related to each of their concerns was reviewed in earlier sections of this chapter.

The decision by Bates College did not result in widespread adoption of optional test score policies among other colleges. Only about two hundred colleges and universities no longer rely on standardized testing for their admission criteria (Rodriguez 1996). The sheer volume of applications to be processed, particularly at large state universities, is one reason for the continued use of standardized test scores. For example, Dr. Ricardo Romo, vice provost at the University of Texas at Austin, in a discussion about schools that have abandoned use of standardized tests as an admission criterion, noted that most of them are smaller colleges and universities. At the University of Texas, which receives twenty thousand applications per year, test scores have served as "another benchmark" (Rodriguez 1996). Another reason for continued use is the utility of the scores when they are used appropriately. John Blackburn, dean of admissions at the University of Virginia, reported that the SAT is "a measure that shows us how students can solve problems in quantitative or mathematical areas on one section, and then how well they use the language in English." He acknowledged that "we at the University of Virginia have never discussed eliminating the requirement or making it optional" (U.S. News Online 1997).

Recent developments in California as well as in the Fifth Circuit may bring some change in the number of schools requiring applicants to submit test scores as well as in the way test scores are used in many selection processes. For example, a recommendation to eliminate the use of the SAT as an entrance requirement was included in the recent report of the University of California's Latino Eligibility Task Force, which has been publicly endorsed by Richard C. Atkinson, the president of the University of California system. In Texas, some schools already have reconsidered their use of standardized test scores, often substituting the practice of basing admission on test scores with the policy of automatically admitting the top 10 percent from each high school. In fall 1997, the University of Texas completely abandoned its policy of automatically admitting students based only on their test scores. Previously, a score of 1,250 or higher on the SAT resulted in automatic admission (Rodriguez 1996).

Alternatives to Multiple-Choice Standardized Paper-and-Pencil Assessment

The key factors that influenced the growth of the college admission testing program at the beginning of the twentieth century remain factors in their use today. Specifically, curriculums vary substantially among different secondary schools, and grading standards are inconsistent and can be unreliable. Among the most rigorous and competitive colleges and universities, selection committees seek indicators to help ensure that applicants are properly prepared to undertake the required work. They also seek measures of relative academic potential as one factor to help them choose among a pool of qualified applicants whose number exceeds the available places in the class. Although one possibility might be to eliminate the use of standardized tests altogether, others would be to force schools to explore other options to fairly and reliably indicate the student characteristics they seek, and to develop assessment alternatives to replace or supplement the traditional multiple-choice standardized paper-and-pencil test.

Alternatives that take the form of changes in test format, content, and mode of presentation have been proposed as possible revisions or extensions to reliance on standardized multiple-choice higher education admission tests that began more than a half century ago. Considering alternatives is especially appealing in response both to the expansion of educational opportunity nationwide that has occurred over the past fifty years and to the increasingly multicultural society that is currently served by higher education. Sedlacek and Kim (1995, 1) noted that "if different people have different cultural and racial experiences and present their abilities differently, it is unlikely that a single measure could be developed that would work equally well for all."

An alternative to the multiple-choice format that has received substantial attention from both the testing community and the educational community in recent years is performance-based assessment. The National Center for Fair and Open Testing (a.k.a. FairTest) has long been an advocate of replacing the SAT, ACT, and similarly structured graduate and professional admission tests with "performance based assessments, such as teacher observations, essays, portfolios, and open ended questions that encourage real thought" (Natale 1990). In performance assessment, judgments are made about test takers' knowledge and skills from direct observation of their performing the tasks to be assessed or from inspection by trained evaluators of their work products. Proponents of performance assessment expected that this assessment alternative would be devoid of the bias believed to be manifest in the traditional multiple-choice test format. Unfortunately, the research results do not suggest that between-group performance differences disappear when performance assessment tools are used to evaluate academic skills and accomplishments (Linn, Baker, and Dunbar 1991). Adding a performance-based component to traditional assessments also failed to reduce group differences in observed scores. For example, an Analytical Writing Assessment component was recently added to the GMAT. Simulations to determine which applicants would be offered admission suggested that the addition of the Analytical Writing Assessment score would noticeably increase the number of women who would be offered admission but would have no impact on the number of minority applicants (Bridgeman and Mc-Hale 1996). Adopting performance assessments also introduces a series of practical and psychometric issues that have not been resolved. These include the time and resources needed to evaluate a tremendous volume of potential test takers (the College Board alone currently administers more than two million SATs per year). They also include issues of test score generalizability, because in most situations, performance is assessed on the basis of a very small sample of test takers (Linn 1994).

Another alternative to current admission testing practice is to incorporate noncognitive measures into the assessment package. Much promising work in this area has been reported in the literature. Tracey and Sedlacek (1984) measured eight noncognitive variables using the Noncognitive Questionnaire (NCQ). The NCQ includes the following variables: positive self-concept or confidence; realistic self-appraisal, especially academic; an understanding of racism and an ability to deal with it; preference for long-term over short-term goals; availability of a strong support person to whom to turn in crisis; successful leadership experience; demonstrated community service; and knowledge acquired in a nontraditional field. Tracey and Sedlacek (1984) have demonstrated the reliability, construct validity, and predictive validity of this instrument. Specifically, they showed that the correlation between scores on the NCQ and college grades was approximately the same as the correlation between SAT scores and college grades for both black and white students. In addition, the multiple correlation of both the SAT and NCQ with college grades exceeded the correlation of either predictor alone. Their data also showed that the NCQ significantly predicted persistence for blacks but not for whites. The significant relationships between the NCQ and academic performance have been replicated with other samples of black students (see, e.g., Rogers 1984; Tracey and Sedlacek 1985, 1987a, 1987b) as well as with a sample of specially admitted students (White and Sedlacek 1986). The significant role of noncognitive factors has also been shown using instruments other than the NCQ (see, e.g., Pickering, Calliotte, and McAuliffe 1992). However, the results have not always been consistent. Some researchers failed to replicate the findings of Sedlacek and colleagues with different samples of black undergraduates (Arbona and Novy 1990; Hood 1992). Fuertes and Sedlacek (1995) found that only one of the noncognitive measures—an understanding of racism and an ability to deal with it—was a significant predictor of academic performance for Hispanic undergraduates and that none was predictive of Hispanic student retention over a nine-semester period. And Williams and Leonard (1988) found cognitive measures to be more important than noncognitive indicators for black undergraduates in technical programs (e.g., computer science and engineering). The importance of the potential role of noncognitive factors in identifying academic success of students independent of traditional cognitive assessments, coupled with the unresolved inconsistencies in previous research, makes this an area in need of continued investigation and refinement.

Recent advances in technology may hold the most promise for spawning assessment alternatives that will better serve the admission goals of colleges and universities both to ensure academic standards and to provide equal access and opportunity. Several major testing programs, including the GRE, the GMAT, and teacher testing programs, already have successfully implemented national computer-administered testing programs. The benefit from computerized testing is not in the change from paper and pencil to computer administration per se but rather in the potential for new definitions of what is tested and how test scores and ancillary information about applicants are reported. For example, the power of computer-administered tests have the potential to help move assessment instruments away from multiple-choice formats without the loss of processing speed and reliability in scoring that were problematic in the early days of essay-type admission tests. Testing programs already have made some progress in designing computer-scored open-ended items to replace traditional multiple-choice item types. There are several documented examples. Plumer (1997) illustrated non-multiple-choice item types that are under development for the LSAT. Bennett (1994) described an electronic infrastructure under development at ETS that would allow future tests to measure constructs not currently measured and not redundant with those that are currently measured. One example would be a measure of how effectively potential students might profit from instruction. According to Bennett (1994, 11), "the general method for measuring this construct, known as 'dynamic assessment,' involves presenting the student with a task just above that individual's level, providing hints or other instruction and retesting performance." Another example provided by Bennett was a measure of the ability to generate explanations. Powers and Enright (1987) demonstrated the value of this skill for graduate students, but routine assessment of the skill was prohibitively expensive at that time. Bennett suggested that technology under development could make the scoring cost-effective.

Much work remains to be done in this area, particularly with respect to evaluating differential performance on the revised item formats among members of different ethnic groups. The related research on performance assessment, referenced earlier, raises a caution that test development efforts focused simply on changing the question format in a computer-administered testing mode may do little or nothing to change the performance gap between white and nonwhite test takers.

One of the benefits of computer-adaptive test methodology is the opportunity to reduce somewhat the number of items administered to a test taker without loss of accuracy of measurement. One potential gain to be realized from this reduction is to retain the base testing time but use that time to offer multiple formats to assess the same constructs, allowing test takers multiple opportunities to demonstrate their abilities. A second is to assess an increased number of factors for each test taker within the same amount of testing time. The latter could allow the assessment process to move away from the single admission test score and toward a comprehensive assessment system. Such a system could assess a variety of cognitive and noncognitive constructs, could be formative as well as summative, and could present a profile of each applicant across a variety of dimensions that were important to an admitting institution. Such a system could provide a viable alternative to the impossible task of attempting to develop a single test that could fairly assess the academic potential of students from a broad range of cultures, backgrounds, and talents. It also could help meet the concerns of public institutions, which are required to treat all applicants similarly, as well as help meet the needs of all institutions to clearly define in advance the criteria that they would consider in the selection process.

Summary and Highlights

This chapter has identified the issues that must be evaluated when the utility and consequences of using test scores in the admission process are considered from the perspectives of academic standards, equity, and access. It has also gathered into one place the research evidence that supports or refutes beliefs about standardized testing and equal access, and has identified gaps in the existing research.

A history of the development of standardized testing and its use in a higher education system with changing demographics and changing societal expectations provided the backdrop against which to examine technical questions about standardized testing. A review of past and ongoing litigation stemming from issues related to equal access and use of test scores provided insight into how tests can be used in making admission decisions and how litigation has helped frame public perception of the issues.

The majority of the questions asked about the use of standardized tests in the admission process fall under the general category of validity. The core question is:

- Do test scores add any useful information to the admission process?

But the question takes on many forms, such as

- Do test scores predict future academic performance?
- Do they predict academic performance beyond the first year?
- Do they predict any outcomes other than GPAs?
- Are they biased?
- Do they predict differently for nonmajority than for majority test takers?
- Does differential prediction deny opportunity to some groups of test takers?
- Can students "in the know" beat the test by learning a set of tricks?
- Does expensive short-term coaching raise test scores, thus undermining the validity of the test and increasing the score gap between rich and poor?
- What are the social consequences of heavy reliance on test scores in making admission decisions? Do those consequences derive from sources of test score invalidity?

A substantial body of research has been conducted by social scientists to address these questions. That research was cited and summarized in this chapter. Overall, the research provided strong evidence in support of the validity of standardized admission tests as one factor in the admission process. The research also found that the commonly used standardized admission tests are valid for members of different racial/ethnic groups, refuting the often expressed concern that test scores are valid only for middle-class white applicants. Despite the impressive amount of research designed to address questions like those posed above, additional work is required. Some of the existing research is dated and needs to be repeated using current test forms and current test-taking populations; some needs to be extended to other testing programs and/or test-taker populations; and some new or still unanswered questions need to be addressed. A variety of research issues needing additional work are presented in discussions throughout the chapter and are extracted here. They include the following observations and recommendations.

- Much of the differential validity research is dated and needs to be replicated or updated.
- Test bias research that examines the predictive accuracy of the test for different groups typically is based on the assumption that the outcome variable (e.g., FYA) is not biased. Research to test the accuracy of that assumption is lacking.
- Many studies found that test scores overpredicted academic performance for some ethnic groups. There is a dearth of research focused on explaining that finding.
- Many questions about the social consequences of heavy reliance on test scores in the admission process are not well researched. New work needs to distinguish between issues of distributive justice and sources of invalidity in order to guide potential remedies.

The discussion of appropriate test use distinguishes between statistical evidence of predictive validity and practical evidence of utility. Research highlighting the small differences in outcomes such as class rank or GPA that are associated with differences in test scores, as well as research demonstrating academic and professional success among applicants with the lowest test scores, is presented within the context of the discussion of test utility.

A review of the available evidence about test score use leads to the conclusion that test scores can make important contributions to fair and equitable admission practice when used as one of several factors in making decisions. This is especially true when they are used as a tool to help interpret other academic indexes such as previous grades. However, the summary of the debate on using test scores to define merit shows how misuse or overuse of test scores can be a disservice both to standardized testing and to higher education. Empirical research that would help define merit beyond the confines of test scores and grades is lacking and greatly needed.

Finally, possible alternatives for the future of admission testing were explored along a continuum ranging from eliminating the use of tests altogether to expanding the role of testing by expanding both the constructs measured and the form and format through which the measurement is accomplished. Technological advances are paving the way for the latter. Significant research is in progress, but much work needs to be done before the potential benefits might be realized.

Chapter Four

SOCIAL PSYCHOLOGICAL EVIDENCE
ON RACE AND RACISM

Shana Levin

Racial dynamics on college campuses are influenced by the same racial stereotypes and group-based power differentials that operate in the real world. A variety of theoretical perspectives has been developed to understand the complexity of race relations in the United States. Research on racial dynamics spans
many social science disciplines, including education, sociology, anthropology,
and organizational and social psychology. Each of these fields offers a unique
perspective on the dynamics of race relations. This chapter uses the social psychological research literature as a prime example of how the issue of diversity
in higher education can be understood through the lens of social science.

Two critical questions in the policy debate about diversity in higher education are whether race matters in everyday life and whether race should
matter in institutional policies. The first is an empirical question; the second,
a prescriptive judgment. One cannot decide whether race should matter in
policy decisions without first recognizing the many ways in which race does
matter in society. Social psychological research is rich with examples of how
race adversely affects social perceptions, attitudes, and behaviors. Most of this
research is focused on individual and intergroup processes rather than on institutional structures, which are discussed more extensively in Chapters 2 and
5 of the book. This chapter provides an overview of social psychological research on race and racism, and demonstrates its relevance to the issue of diversity in higher education.

Racial Attitudes

As we look back over the years of the post–Civil Rights era, we see a positive trend in the self-reported racial attitudes of white Americans, especially in their attitudes toward African Americans. The demise of legalized racial segregation and discrimination was followed by a sharp decline in blatant, "old-fashioned" racism, which centered on the notion of biologically based black racial inferiority (McConahay 1986). Today, national surveys show that white Americans overwhelmingly endorse the principles of racial equality and integration (Schuman et al. 1997). The National Opinion Research Center at the University of Chicago has collected survey data from cross-sectional samples of the white American population since 1942. The trends that occur for most of the items measuring support for principles of equal treatment are quite similar and can be shown using attitudes toward school integration as an example. In response to the question "Do you think white students and black students should go to the same schools or separate schools?" asked in 1942, 32 percent of the white respondents answered "same" and 68 percent answered "separate." In response to the same question asked in 1995, 96 percent of the white respondents answered "same" and only 4 percent answered "separate" (Schuman et al. 1997). This positive trend is also reflected in surveys of white college students, which show a steady decline in negative characterizations of blacks over the last sixty years. For example, whereas 75 percent of a sample of white college students surveyed in 1933 selected the trait "lazy" to describe blacks, only 2 percent surveyed in 1996 did so (Dovidio and Gaertner 1996).

Although these positive trends in self-reported racial attitudes indicate that the fundamental norms with regard to race have changed, many researchers argue that underlying negative attitudes toward African Americans and other minority groups persist, albeit in a new guise. Although most whites no longer blatantly oppose the ideals of racial equality and integration, many show subtle and often unconscious biases toward members of minority ethnic groups. These newer forms of unintentional racial biases are exhibited by many whites who, on a conscious level, endorse egalitarian values and believe themselves to be unprejudiced. These biases persist inconspicuously but can have grave effects on social perceptions, attitudes, and behaviors. Two contemporary approaches to racial attitudes highlight different forms of racial bias: aversive and symbolic.

Aversive Racial Attitudes

Gaertner and Dovidio (1986) propose that many people harbor negative feelings about blacks (or members of other minority groups) on an unconscious level. These biased judgments against blacks are assumed to result from the socialization of nonminority children into the dominant racial biases in society and from the typical way in which individuals categorize people into social groups rather than expend limited cognitive resources to judge each person individually. Aversive racism refers to the unintentional expression of these antiblack feelings by people who sincerely endorse, on a conscious level, egalitarian values and principles. Unlike more blatant prejudice, which is expressed directly against people because of their race, aversive racism is more likely to be expressed when it can be justified on the basis of some factor other than race; in this way, aversive racists can maintain their self-image of themselves as unprejudiced. Rather than reflecting bigotry or hatred, the antiblack feelings held by aversive racists reflect fear and discomfort; their discriminatory behavior toward blacks is characterized more by avoidance than by intentional hostility.

Dovidio and Gaertner (1996, 1998) have found consistent support for the aversive racism framework across a broad range of situations. For example, in a study on personnel selection (Dovidio 1995, reported in Dovidio and Gaertner 1996), black and white job applicants were treated the same when the information provided about them was either uniformly positive or uniformly negative. However, white applicants were favored over black applicants when a combination of positive and negative information was provided about the candidates. That is, aversive racism was exhibited when the white evaluators were given more ambiguous information about the applicants; in this case, the evaluators were able to attribute their unfavorable evaluation of black applicants to the ambiguous information they received about the candidates rather than to their race. Aversive racism has also been shown to influence ostensibly "color-blind" college admissions decisions. In a related study, white participants evaluated white and black applicants for university admission (Kline and Dovidio 1982, reported in Dovidio and Gaertner 1996). The credentials of the applicants were systematically manipulated to produce poorly, moderately, or highly qualified applicants. Discrimination against the black applicant was greatest when the qualifications were high: although applicants of both races were evaluated very positively under these conditions, the white applicant was judged even more favorably than the black applicant. Bias was even more pronounced when evaluations were made on items less directly related to the information provided in the application. That is, when evaluators took less relevant information into account in their admissions decisions, they were even more biased against blacks. Therefore, even when equal access to employment or educational opportunities is provided in principle, unintentional racial biases may undermine equal outcomes in practice.

In addition to influencing employment and educational admissions decisions, aversive racism has also been found to impact whites' opposition to affirmative action. A study by Murrell et al. (1994) used a factorial survey design to assess the attitudes of white college students toward affirmative action as a function of the targeted group (blacks, physically handicapped persons, or elderly persons) and the framing of the policy (with or without social justification). The policies framed in terms of "no justification" emphasized the use of nonmerit factors in the selection process, such as preferential treatment and reverse discrimination, whereas the policies framed in terms of "having justification" emphasized achieving diversity or remedying historical injustices. Consistent with the aversive racism framework, whites were more opposed to affirmative action for blacks than for elderly and handicapped persons (there was no significant difference between the response to elderly and handicapped persons), particularly when their opposition could be justified on the basis of unfair procedures (a factor other than race). That is, the level of resistance to the policies presented without justification for blacks as the targeted group was higher than for all other targeted groups with or without justification. If affirmative action opposition was truly motivated by nonracial principles of fairness rather than by aversive racial attitudes, then these white students would have equally opposed affirmative action policies designed to help all groups, and policies presented without justification would not have generated any more opposition when blacks were the targeted group than when the elderly and handicapped were the targeted groups. These results therefore suggest that resistance to affirmative action, although in part the result of policy-based reactions, may also reflect subtle prejudice toward blacks among some individuals. At the same time, however, it is important to point out that these findings do not imply that *all* opposition to affirmative action is motivated by aversive racial attitudes as well. Other nonracial and racial factors need to be considered. An alternate form of contemporary racial attitudes is described by the symbolic racism perspective.

Symbolic Racial Attitudes

Symbolic racism was defined by Sears (1988, 56) as "a blend of anti-black affect and the kind of traditional American moral values embodied in the Protestant Ethic." Symbolic racism is measured by respondents' agreement with survey items indicating that blacks are pushing too hard for equality, that they are making unfair and illegitimate demands, that they get too much attention and sympathy from elites, that their gains are therefore often undeserved, and that racial discrimination is a thing of the past. This sort of racism is called symbolic because it is phrased in terms that are abstract and ideological, reflecting a person's moral code and sense of how society should be organized rather than having any direct bearing on the person's own private life, and because it is focused on blacks as a group rather than on any specific individual (Sears 1998). According to the symbolic racism perspective, many whites acquire both traditional American values and negative feelings about blacks through early childhood socialization. Symbolic racists express antiblack feelings in adulthood through beliefs that blacks are violating the traditional values they hold dear. For example, symbolic racists are believed to oppose redistributive social policies such as affirmative action because they perceive that blacks fail to uphold traditional American values such as individualism, hard work, and self-reliance. Using data from four representative surveys (the 1986 and 1992 National Election Studies, 1994 General Social Survey, and 1995 Los Angeles County Social Survey), Sears et al. (1997) found that among whites, higher levels of symbolic racism were associated with greater opposition to equal opportunity for blacks, greater opposition to federal assistance for blacks, and greater opposition to affirmative action for blacks. Moreover, the researchers found that symbolic racism was even more predictive of whites' opposition to policies that give special treatment to blacks than were political partisanship and nonracial values such as individualism and morality. Other studies have shown that racism strongly affects racial policy preferences even when race-neutral ideology is held constant. Using whites' responses to a nationally representative survey (the 1992 National Election Studies), Sears (1998) found that political conservatives were more likely than liberals (72 percent vs. 59 percent) to strongly oppose giving preferences to blacks in hiring and promotion, but those high in symbolic racism were much more strongly opposed to the policy than those low in symbolic racism (81 percent vs. 41 percent). Moreover, symbolic racism increased opposition to affirmative action among both conservatives and liberals alike. When policy decisions are based more on racial attitudes than on nonracial principles, they directly contradict national ideals of equality and fairness. Because opposition to redistributive social policies such as affirmative action is couched by symbolic racists in terms of blacks' violation of traditional American values rather than blatant prejudice against blacks, this contemporary form of racism is more subtle and insidious, but its impact can be as severe as that of the old-fashioned kind.

Both the aversive and symbolic racism perspectives describe the prevalence of racism at the level of the individual. Although they argue that racism has changed in form from its traditional expression in direct and overt ways to its contemporary expression in indirect and subtle ways, they support the notion that racism still exists in the minds of some individuals. There is substantial evidence that racism exists not only at the level of the individual but at the level of the institution as well.

Institutional Racism

Institutional racism refers to "those established laws, customs, and practices which systematically reflect and produce racial inequities in American society" (Jones 1997, 438). As Jones points out, when institutional practices or policies systematically create disadvantage for racial minority groups and their members, it doesn't really matter what any specific person's *intentions* were. From this perspective, remedying institutional racism does not involve changing individuals' racist intentions as much as it involves restructuring institutional practices in order to increase equality of opportunity.

Sidanius and Pratto (1999) cite evidence of institutional racism in several different domains, including housing, retail and labor markets, the criminal justice system, and the educational system. Evidence for institutional racism in the housing market is indicated by dramatic differences in mortgage loan refusal rates as a function of race (reported in Sidanius and Pratto 1999). Specifically, national data released in 1990 indicated that blacks' mortgage applications for conventional loans were refused at more than twice the rate as those of whites. In an even more comprehensive study of mortgage lending in the Boston area during 1990, researchers from the Boston Federal Reserve Board found that after controlling for all the relevant variables hypothesized to affect loan decisions (including characteristics of the applicant and the loan itself, and factors associated with the risk and cost of default), the probability of loan denial was still 8.2 percentage points higher for blacks and Latinos than for whites (Sidanius and Pratto 1999). Evidence for institutional racism in the retail market is indicated by an audit study conducted by Ian Ayres (1995, reported in Sidanius and Pratto 1999). In this study, a team of thirty-eight white and black male and female auditors were sent into the same car dealerships to negotiate the best deals they could for more than four hundred new cars (the auditors were equivalent in all respects except for their race and sex). Controlling for all other differences between the auditors, including bargaining strategy, the results showed that compared with the final offers made to white men, car dealers made significantly higher final offers (after negotiation) to black men ($1,133.60 higher than for white men), black women ($446.30 higher than for white men), and white women ($215.70 higher than for white men). Evidence for institutional racism in the labor market is indicated by employment audit studies in which equally qualified and matched pairs of white and minority job applicants (equivalent in all essential ways including education, age, job experience, etc.) are sent out for the same job vacancies (reported in Sidanius and Pratto 1999). In summarizing the cumulative discrimination against blacks in employment audits in the United States, Bendick (1996, reported in Sidanius and Pratto 1999) found that (a) whites obtain interviews at a 22 percent higher rate than do blacks; (b) whites receive job offers at the interview stage at a 415 percent higher rate than do blacks; (c) once whites are made a job offer, there is a 17 percent chance that they will be offered a higher salary than will blacks for the same position; (d) once an employer expresses interest in a job candidate, the likelihood that a white applicant will be steered to a less-qualified job is 37 percent lower than it is for a black applicant; and (e) access to additional job vacancies is 48 percent greater for white than for black job applicants.

In the criminal justice system, members of minority groups have been found to face more severe legal sanctions than whites (e.g., more arrests, more convictions, and harsher prison sentences), even after taking into account all other legally relevant factors such as type and severity of crime and prior criminal record (Sidanius, Levin, and Pratto 1998). An interaction between race and gender has also been found, indicating that black men experience more unfair treatment by institutions (e.g., police) than do black women

(Gallup Organization 1997; for a review, see Sidanius and Pratto 1999). Despite the difficulty of disentangling race from class (given that racial minorities have a disproportionately low socioeconomic standing), racial inequalities are not reducible to class inequalities: disparities in racial outcomes persist even when differences in socioeconomic standing are taken into account (Sidanius and Pratto 1999).

These examples of institutional racism demonstrate the powerful ways in which race structures the society in which we live. Institutional racism perpetuates racism in the minds of individuals by feeding negative stereotypes about members of disadvantaged groups. For example, institutional racism in the criminal justice system creates a disproportionate population of African Americans in prison, which perpetuates negative stereotypes of African Americans as violent and hostile. These stereotypes are then unconsciously applied when individual African Americans are judged by others, creating prejudice of an implicit, unconscious, unintentional nature (Banaji and Greenwald 1994). In a study of the automatic and controlled components of stereotyping and prejudice, Devine (1989) activated the racial stereotype of African Americans held in the minds of white college students by presenting culturally stereotypic words (e.g., lazy) below conscious awareness. To vary the degree of activation, Devine presented one hundred words to two groups of white participants: for one group, eighty of these words were relevant to black racial stereotypes (high prime condition); for the other group, only twenty of these words were race-relevant (low prime condition). Participants in the high prime condition were more likely to judge the ambiguous behavior of a fictional character as more aggressive and hostile than were participants in the low prime condition, which is consistent with the negative stereotype of African Americans that had been activated in the high prime condition. Moreover, the effect was the same for participants who scored high and low on an explicit measure of modern racism (McConahay 1986). Stereotypes thus exist in the minds of individuals and, once activated, can influence the social perceptions and judgments that people make about individual members of stereotyped groups. Banaji and Greenwald (1994) argue that each act of implicit stereotyping can be seen as an implicit individual reproduction of beliefs about the collective. In other words, social structure (e.g., stratification of the criminal justice system by race) causes cognitive structure (e.g., greater attributes of violence and hostility in judgments of individual African Americans). In this way, institutional racism becomes translated into individual racism.

Another domain in which negative stereotypes exist about African Americans is the educational system. If we look at the relative outcomes of whites and blacks in this system, we see that whites receive more education than blacks, and this difference is greater for college graduates than for high school graduates (reported in Jones 1997). In 1993, 82 percent of whites versus 76 percent of blacks had graduated from high school by the age of twenty-five (a 6 percent difference), and 23 percent of whites versus 12 percent of blacks had earned a college degree by that age (almost double the high school difference). Another indication of educational attainment is reflected in achievement, as measured by performance on the Scholastic Aptitude Test (SAT). A comparison of blacks' and whites' 1992 SAT scores indicates that blacks scored approximately a hundred points lower than did whites on both the verbal and mathematical sections of the SAT (reported in Jones 1997). Furthermore, evidence shows that even when blacks have the *same* SAT scores as whites, their college GPAs are about one-third of a point lower than those of their white counterparts (Jones 1997). Assuming that blacks and whites who have the same SAT scores have comparable initial skills, the lower academic performance of African Americans must result from something other than skill deficits.

Stereotype Threat

One factor that may play a role in the differential academic performance of blacks and whites is what Steele and Aronson (1995; Steele 1997) have called stereotype threat. Stereotype threat is the fear of confirming or being judged by negative stereotypes often held by other people about one's own group. For example, when a group is negatively stereotyped in the academic domain, group members who are identified with the domain may be afraid that they will confirm or be judged by the negative stereotypes held by others about their group. This type of stereotype threat is experienced in situations in which one is at risk of confirming the stereotype to oneself and to others. For example, African Americans face negative stereotypes about their intellectual abilities. They therefore face the threat of confirming these negative stereotypes when taking a test that is diagnostic of intellectual ability. This threat arouses two basic reactions: (1) anxiety based on the fear that one will verify or be judged by the stereotype, and (2) disidentification with the academic domain, or rejection of academic performance altogether as an indication of self-worth. Anxiety and disidentification with the academic domain may interfere with performance and undermine the motivation to achieve. It is important to point out that the threat is posed by *group* ability stereotypes, not beliefs about one's own ability. The threat of negative group stereotypes can actually impair academic performance so that individuals perform at a level below their true ability. This line of research therefore offers a new interpretation of group differences in standardized test performance: they are due at least in part to differences between blacks and whites in the threat posed by negative stereotypes about their group's academic ability.

Steele and Aronson (1995) tested the model of stereotype threat by having black and white Stanford University students take a test composed of the most difficult items from the verbal Graduate Record Exam (GRE). Because the participants were students from a highly selective university, the researchers assumed that the students cared about their test performance and were identified in this academic domain. In one study, the participants were told either that the test was *diagnostic* of their intellectual ability—a situation high in threat because the stereotype about blacks' intellectual ability was made relevant to their performance on the test—or that the test was *nondiagnostic* of their intellectual ability—a situation low in threat because the negative stereotype was not related in any way to their performance on the test. Controlling for differences in their initial skill levels, the results showed strong evidence of stereotype threat: blacks performed equal to whites in the nondiagnostic condition but performed more poorly than whites did in the diagnostic condition. This finding supports the claim that it is the threat inherent in the situation that interfered with performance. A second experiment produced the same pattern of results with an even more subtle manipulation of stereotype threat. All the participants were given the nondiagnostic instructions, and then just before taking the test, half of them were asked to record their race on a demographic questionnaire (race prime), and the other half were not asked to record their race on the questionnaire (no race prime). Steele and Aronson (1995) reasoned that if the stereotype threat was linked to the group, then linking the participant to his or her group would make the stereotype more salient and would affect performance, in a manner similar to the diagnostic condition of the first study. As expected, there was no racial difference in performance when the racial stereotype was not primed. This finding supports the previous study in which the test showed no racial difference in performance when the test was not diagnostic of ability. However, when race was primed, black participants underperformed relative to their white counterparts. Taken together, the results of both studies indicate that stereotype threat increases when one's racial group affiliation is made salient and when the diagnostic properties of the test are made salient. This stereotype threat may be a possible source of bias in standardized tests, a bias that comes not from the actual content of the items but from differences between blacks and whites in the threat posed by societal stereotypes to undermine their test performance.

The implications of this line of research are that tests, as measures of performance, are not only indicative of individual ability but also of institutional climate. If merit is tied to performance in a domain in which minority groups suffer from the threat of negative stereotypes, then ignoring race in merit-based selection procedures unfairly disadvantages members of these minority groups. Given the racism that exists at an institutional level, and the reproduction of social structures in the cognitive structures (i.e., stereotypes) of individuals, "color-blindness" may perpetuate racial inequities as a result of the operation of unintentional racial biases among whites and stereotype threat among blacks. The use of "race-neutral" or "color-blind" admissions policies in higher education is not independent of race; indeed, the negative effects of race are always part of the equation because of the racialized society in which we live. Race-conscious admissions policies can help counteract the negative effects of institutional and individual racism, and thereby level the playing field for members of all racial groups.

Social Psychological Theories of Racial Conflict

Although there is overwhelming evidence that racial disparities exist in many different domains in American society and that institutional racism perpetuates individual racism, the social psychological research literature offers different explanations for why these phenomena occur and, more specifically, why there is opposition to redistributive social policies designed to reduce racial inequities. Three main social psychological theories examine the individual and intergroup processes that drive racial conflict: realistic group con-

TABLE 4.1

*Comparison of the Processes Driving Racial Conflict
as Proposed by Three Social Psychological Theories*

Theory	Primary Force Driving Racial Conflict
Realistic group conflict theory	Competition between groups over scarce resources and perceived threats to group position.
Social identity theory	Individuals' motivation to achieve a positive identity by favoring their own group over other groups.
Social dominance theory	Individuals' desires for group inequality and the domination of "inferior" groups by "superior" groups.

flict theory, social identity theory, and social dominance theory. (See Table 4.1 for a comparison of the processes driving racial conflict proposed by these theories.)

Realistic Group Conflict Theory

According to realistic group conflict theory (Bobo 1983, 1988) and the group position and perceived threat hypothesis (Bobo 2000), group conflict and ethnocentric attitudes and behaviors are primarily functions of realistic competition between groups over scarce resources and perceived threats to group position. Whites, as members of the dominant group in the United States, develop attitudes and beliefs that defend their privileged, hegemonic social position. The dominant group seeks to legitimize the current inequalities through these group-interested ideologies and to perpetuate them by engaging in discriminatory behavior. In this light, whites' opposition to redistributive social policies such as affirmative action is viewed not as a reflection of negative feelings or beliefs about minority groups per se but rather as a reflection of defense of group privilege in a conflict over valued social resources, status, and power. From this perspective, the affirmative action debate is one about the place racial groups should occupy in American society. Using data from the 1992 Los Angeles County Social Survey—a random-digit-dialed, computer-assisted telephone survey of adults living in Los Angeles County—Bobo (2000) found support for realistic group conflict predictions: the more whites perceive that the advancement of blacks (in terms of employment and housing opportunities, political influence, and economics) comes at the expense of the advance-

ment of members of other groups, the more they perceive that affirmative action for blacks has negative effects. Significantly, Bobo (2000) also found support for symbolic racism predictions: the higher whites' levels of symbolic racism, the more they perceive negative effects of affirmative action. Moreover,
in a regression model that includes social background variables (age, education, sex, income), ideology and values (conservatism, inegalitarianism, individualism), and racial attitudes (affect, stereotypes, perceived threat, symbolic
racism), perceived threat and symbolic racism contribute the lion's share to the
overall 33.2 percent of the variance explained in perceptions of the negative
effects of affirmative action. These results reveal the powerful effects of racial
attitudes in explaining some whites' perceptions of the negative impact of affirmative action.

Social Identity Theory

According to social identity theory (Tajfel and Turner 1986), individuals hold
conceptualizations of the self at both an individual and a group level. Personal
identity refers to those aspects of the self that differentiate one individual from
others within a given social context. Social identity refers to those aspects of
the self that relate to group membership or that are defined in terms of the
groups to which one belongs. When group boundaries are made salient, individuals categorize people as members of their own group (in-group) or as
members of another group (out-group), and start to compare their group with
other groups on the basis of some evaluative criteria. Individuals are motivated
to achieve and maintain a positive image of their in-group. One way they
may do so is by comparing their in-group with out-groups perceived to be inferior on some evaluative dimension. This preference or favoritism places their
in-group at an advantage relative to the out-groups. When there is a power
differential, in-group favoritism can have dramatic implications for the unequal distribution of economic and social resources. For example, social identities based on race will trigger evaluative comparisons with other racial
groups. Individuals are motivated to achieve a positive social identity by fa-
voring their own racial group over other racial groups. This in-group favoritism may translate into resistance to affirmative action policies when these
policies are perceived to benefit members of other racial groups at the expense
of one's own racial group. Some members of groups with greater access to resources may thus oppose redistributive social policies such as affirmative ac-

tion because these policies threaten to reverse the favorable evaluation of their group relative to other groups.

Social Dominance Theory

According to social dominance theory (Sidanius 1993; Sidanius and Pratto 1999), individuals differ in the degree to which they desire unequal status relations between groups in society. In surveys of college students and adult random samples, individuals who want groups at the bottom of the social hierarchy to be kept down and dominated by groups at the top of the hierarchy have been found to endorse a variety of ideologies that justify greater levels of social inequality, such as racism, individualism, and the Protestant work ethic (Sidanius and Pratto 1999). Racist beliefs reinforce the social hierarchy because they portray racial-status differences as being legitimately based on inherent differences in group members' ability and potential. Other ideologies such as individualism and the Protestant work ethic lack specific racial content but still function to reinforce racial inequality because they attribute the lower status of blacks to lack of ability and motivation. Survey data of college students and adult random samples indicate that support for these "system-justifying" ideologies translates into greater opposition to redistributive social policies such as affirmative action (Sidanius and Pratto 1999). From this perspective, then, the primary driving force behind some opposition to affirmative action is individuals' desires for group inequality and the domination of "inferior" groups by "superior" groups. This approach directly contradicts claims that all opposition to affirmative action is rooted in "principled" adherence to ideologies such as individualism and the Protestant work ethic. Rather, endorsement of these ideologies is viewed as a way for individuals who want to maintain the social hierarchy to justify their racially motivated opposition to affirmative action. In a study using a random sample of white adults from Los Angeles County surveyed in 1996, Sidanius et al. (1999) found three results consistent with social dominance theory: (1) desires for social dominance were positively associated with the three system-justifying ideologies of political conservatism, symbolic racism, and classical racism; (2) both symbolic racism and social dominance orientation were found to have direct positive effects on opposition to affirmative action; and (3) consistent with the expectation that desires for social dominance will also have an indirect effect on racial policy preferences, mediated by a series of system-justifying ideologies, social dominance orientation was found to have an indirect positive effect on opposition to affirmative action, with political conservatism, classical racism, and symbolic racism as the mediators. These results indicate that we must take into account the powerful effects of group dominance motives on opposition to redistributive social policies such as affirmative action. In a second study using a random sample of nonblack (white, Asian, and Hispanic) adults from Los Angeles County, surveyed in 1996, Sidanius et al. (2000) drew similar conclusions from a comparison of the social dominance and principled politics approaches to affirmative action opposition. Proponents of the principled politics model argue that political conservatives are ideologically opposed to affirmative action policies, regardless of the beneficiaries of the policies, because the policy violates ideals of fairness and individual responsibility. Contrary to the claims made by those holding the principled politics position, Sidanius et al. (2000) found three main results consistent with the social dominance approach: (1) nonblack conservative respondents were most opposed to affirmative action when blacks were the beneficiaries (as opposed to women or the poor), and were especially so when they themselves were well educated; (2) the greater the social dominance orientation of the highly educated white respondents, the more they perceived affirmative action to be "unfair"; and (3) consistent with the notion that "unfairness" perceptions serve as system-justifying ideologies, most of the correlation between social dominance orientation and general affirmative action opposition among highly educated white respondents was mediated by the perception of affirmative action as "unfair." If beliefs about fairness are driven by desires for social dominance, then some persons who claim to oppose affirmative action policies because they are unfair may be using the fairness argument to justify group-dominance-motivated opposition to affirmative action policies.

In sum, given the current racial-status hierarchy, "color-blindness" will reinforce the racial status quo as a result of the operation of unintentional racial biases, group identity processes, group competition, and group dominance motives. These processes contribute to the unequal treatment of minority groups and generate opposition to redistributive social policies designed to ameliorate their condition. Social psychological research therefore suggests that a race-neutral or color-blind approach is unfair because it ignores the many ways in which race matters in society. A mound of social science evidence thus supports Justice Harry Blackmun's opinion in the *Bakke* case that "in order to get beyond racism, we must first take account of race. There is no other way. And in order to treat some persons equally, we must treat them differently" (438 U.S. 407, 1978).

Fairness Beliefs

As Justice Blackmun's opinion indicates, responses to affirmative action reflect underlying notions of fairness. For some, fairness requires treating people as individuals, and for others, fairness requires taking into account the collective representations that matter in society. Ferdman (1997) frames this fairness debate in terms of a distinction between the "individualistic perspective" and the "group perspective." Proponents of the individualistic perspective argue that it is unfair to pay attention to ethnicity because ethnic group memberships should not influence the opportunities and outcomes of individuals in society. Proponents of the group perspective, on the other hand, argue that it is unfair *not* to take ethnicity into account because of the power differentials that exist between ethnic groups in society. According to this latter perspective, ignoring ethnic group membership obscures the significant ways in which these power differentials influence the opportunities and outcomes of members of different ethnic groups. Despite differences between the individualistic and group perspectives in their prescriptions for how fairness can best be achieved, the two perspectives share the same underlying notion that fairness involves two basic principles: equal access to opportunities and equitable assignment of rewards. If, consistent with the individualistic perspective, affirmative action policies violate principles of equality of opportunity and equity of rewards, they should be judged as fundamentally unfair and opposed. If, on the other hand, they operate to ensure equality of opportunity and equity of rewards as the group perspective argues, then they should be judged as fair and supported.

Individualistic Perspective

The individualistic view is deeply rooted in American values of meritocracy. A meritocratic reward structure is one in which advancement is determined by individual ability and talent. From the individualistic perspective, selection procedures and outcomes are fair when all individuals, regardless of ethnicity, are judged by the same established criteria of competence. Individual skills and achievements are viewed as legitimate criteria by which to judge individual competence because they are thought to be objective and orthogonal to ascribed characteristics such as race. Because race is considered to be irrelevant to judgments of individual competence, proponents of the individualistic perspective argue that race should not be taken into account in merit-based selection procedures.

Contrary to these arguments in favor of the individualistic perspective, there is ample social psychological evidence that race is not irrelevant to judgments of individual competence. For example, the study on personnel selection by Dovidio (1995, reported in Dovidio and Gaertner 1996) mentioned earlier found that white job applicants were favored over black applicants when a combination of positive and negative information was provided about the candidates. In the related study in which white participants evaluated white and black applicants for university admission (Kline and Dovidio 1982, reported in Dovidio and Gaertner 1996), the researchers found that discrimination against the black applicant was greatest when the qualifications were high. According to the equity principle of distributive justice, a relationship is equitable when all individuals receive the same relative outcomes in proportion to their inputs. For members of all ethnic groups to receive equitable outcomes in terms of college admissions decisions, the "inputs" of members of all groups must be judged by the same standard. Contrary to the equity principle, these studies show that race impacts judgments of individual competence in ways that disadvantage minority applicants for college admissions.

Eberhardt and Fiske (1994) assert that existing power differentials not only disadvantage minority groups but also privilege majority groups because they create the illusion that the qualifications of majority group members are more merit-based than are those of minority group members. That is, the authors argue that contrary to popular belief, merit-based selection is not independent of group membership. Rather, absent an explicit affirmative action policy targeting minority groups, members of majority groups are conferred a competitive advantage by the implicit assumption that their achievements are more merit-based than are those of minority group members. Research conducted by Major, Feinstein, and Crocker (1994) supports this argument. In an experimental paradigm, men and women were randomly selected or rejected for a leadership role under one of three procedures: selection based solely on sex (group-based selection), solely on merit (individual merit-based selection), or on both sex and merit. The researchers found that, unlike women, men evaluated their skills more favorably after being preferentially selected on the basis of sex than after being selected on the basis of merit. One possible explanation for this finding is that men may feel that their group membership entitles them to more positive outcomes in the leadership domain because they assume that their group membership is related to performance in that domain. In support of this explanation, Major, Feinstein, and Crocker (1994) found that men, but not women, believed that the leadership role would be performed better by men than by women. In addition, they found that men were more confident than women that they would be selected to be a leader. When these initial differences in self-confidence and perceptions of leadership ability were held constant in subsequent analyses, differences between men and women in their responses to the sex-based selection procedures disappeared. These results indicate that members of majority groups are advantaged by the implicit positive association between their group membership and performance in a domain in which their group enjoys positive stereotypes (e.g., the leadership domain). Furthermore, results of the stereotype threat research conducted by Steele and Aronson (1995) indicate that members of minority groups are disadvantaged by the implicit negative association between their group membership and performance in a domain in which their group suffers negative stereotypes (e.g., the academic domain). According to Clayton and Tangri (1989, 181), "including such a factor [as race] does not unbalance an equitable state, but rather restores balance by adjusting for the positive weighting of majority group membership that is ingrained within the system."

Group Perspective

An alternate system of allocating opportunities and rewards is advocated by the group perspective (Ferdman 1997). In this view, a fair system is one in which all groups are afforded equal opportunity. To ensure equal opportunity at the group level, we must take group membership into account in comparisons between individuals because group-based power differentials and the long history of discrimination against minority groups have restricted minority access to the vital resources necessary to compete as individuals. According to the group perspective, using the same standards to judge individuals from majority and minority groups is unfair because differences in power prevent the two groups from having equal opportunity.

Although there is overwhelming evidence that racial disparities exist in many different domains in American society, including the educational system, and that these racial disparities are the result, at least in part, of institutional racism, individual racism, and stereotype threat, the question remains as to how best to remedy them. Research on aversive racism (Dovidio, Kawakami, and Gaertner 2000) and implicit stereotyping and prejudice (Banaji and Greenwald 1994) suggests that methods focusing exclusively on individual change in conscious awareness of racial attitudes will be ineffective. As Banaji and Greenwald (1994) argue, sociocultural realities influence how individuals interpret the social world and make judgments. Through redistributive social policies such as affirmative action, we can effectively transform social structure and ultimately change cognitive structure. Given the evidence that aversive racism is expressed by many individuals who consciously endorse egalitarian principles, legislated social change has the benefit of effecting cognitive change without relying on individuals to consciously adopt nondiscriminatory behaviors.

Similarly, research on stereotype threat (Marx, Brown, and Steele 1999) suggests that effecting change within individuals by consciously raising expectancies about their performance in a domain in which their group suffers from negative stereotypes will not reduce stereotype threat effects. Rather, the solution is to create performance environments in which stereotype-threatened individuals can trust that interpretations of their performance will be free of the taint of negative stereotypes. In their research investigating the viability of such a solution, Brown and Steele (1999, reported in Marx, Brown, and Steele 1999) varied two conditions of the typical stereotype threat paradigm. First, before taking the difficult verbal GRE–type exam, participants completed a shorter verbal task on which they either performed well or poorly, thereby implicitly setting their performance expectations for the second task. Then just before beginning the second test, students received one of two instructions that manipulated stereotype threat: the diagnostic instructions used in earlier experiments (stereotype threat condition) or diagnostic instructions combined with a statement that this particular test was *racially fair* (no stereotype threat condition). In the latter condition, presenting the test as one that could be trusted by black students was presumed to make negative racial stereotypes irrelevant to performance on the diagnostic test, thereby eliminating stereotype threat. The results showed that under the stereotype threat condition, raising expectancies by giving students a previous success did not eliminate the underperformance of black students relative to their white counterparts. However, the "race fair" condition did eliminate black students' underperformance, even when their expectancies had been lowered by a previous failure. The authors conclude that perceptions of the test's racial fairness may have raised blacks' test performance by creating an environment free of racial mistrust. Taken together, the results of social psychological research on race and racism suggest that until the institutional climate is taken into account, individual abilities will not be judged fairly by merit-based selection procedures.

Social Categorization

Objections to affirmative action stem not only from beliefs that the policy is unfair but also from beliefs that treating people differently on the basis of their group membership is antithetical to the goal of achieving a society in which opportunities and outcomes are independent of group membership. From this perspective, categorizing people by ethnic group highlights group differences and thereby engages people's natural tendency to identify with their group, favor their own group over other groups, and defend their group's interests in conflicts over resources such as university admissions. Much social psychological research has demonstrated the profound effects of social categorization. Creating group boundaries or highlighting existing ones can strongly influence the perceptions, evaluations, and judgments of members of one's own ingroup as well as members of out-groups. For example, sorting individuals into in-groups and out-groups causes people to view members of out-groups as more similar to one another (Wilder 1981) and generates more negative evaluations (Tajfel 1981) and stereotypic perceptions of (Rothbart 1981), and negative attributions for (Pettigrew 1979), the behavior of out-group members than in-group members.

However, other research has shown that there may be advantages to recognizing the social category membership of individuals. For example, Ferdman (1989) found that in an organizational setting, making people in the dominant group pay attention to categorical information about those in the subordinate group (i.e., information related to their group membership) did *not* lower evaluations of subordinate group members. Rather, white managers evaluated Hispanic managers most positively when they were presented with both individuating features (e.g., hobbies) *and* categorical information (e.g., membership in ethnic organizations), and least positively when they were presented with individuating information alone. In another study, Clayton (1996) examined attitudes toward social categorization among two samples of college students and found that although students were generally opposed to categorizing individuals on the basis of their group membership, opposition to affirmative action (1) varied depending on whether the beneficiaries were grouped according to race, gender, religion, sexual orientation, or college major, and (2) was not based solely on objections to social categorization. Affirmative action for ethnic minority group members received more negative ratings than did affirmative action for women, which is consistent with the findings of Sidanius et al. (2000) reported previously.

These results disconfirm the view that objections to affirmative action policies are solely based on a reluctance to identify people according to their social group. They also indicate that some resistance to affirmative action, although apparently based on objective standards of justice, is actually influenced by subjective reactions to the group that will benefit from the policy. Consistent with these findings are those indicating that among the most important predictors of opposition to affirmative action are negative racial attitudes, in the form of symbolic racism (Sears 1998; Sears et al. 1997), aversive racism (Dovidio, Mann, and Gaertner 1989; Murrell et al. 1994), social dominance orientation (Sidanius et al. 1999, 2000), and perceived threat to the privileged position of whites (Bobo 2000). The preponderance of empirical research therefore suggests that fairness requires taking race into account in affirmative action policies, because race influences social perceptions, attitudes, and behaviors in ways that disadvantage members of minority groups.

In sum, the social psychological research literature presents two main predictors of affirmative action opposition: racial attitudes and fairness beliefs. Dovidio and Gaertner's aversive racism framework further contends that racial attitudes and fairness beliefs are intimately related: their research demonstrates that "although concerns about the fairness of affirmative action programs may be articulated as reasons to oppose these programs, subtle [racial] biases may be operating by influencing these perceptions of fairness, which in turn affect the intensity of the negative reactions" (Dovidio and Gaertner 1996, 68). As mentioned previously, Sidanius et al. (2000) also found a positive relationship between group dominance motives and perceptions that affirmative action is "unfair"; in fact, they found that one way in which people with strong desires for social dominance justify their opposition to affirmative action is by claiming that it is an unfair policy. If beliefs about fairness are tainted by negative racial attitudes and group dominance motives, then some opposition to race-conscious policies based on these notions of fairness must be motivated by desires for *inequality* of opportunity rather than by desires for *equality* of opportunity.

Dimensions of Diversity in Higher Education

Given the evidence of racism in American society and the observations derived from theories of race relations and fairness, the challenge we face today is how to use these observations to facilitate the goals of diversity in higher education. Smith (1995b) has developed a framework outlining four important dimensions of diversity in higher education: representation, campus climate and intergroup relations, education and scholarship, and institutional transformation. The dimension of representation focuses on the inclusion and academic success of previously underrepresented groups, particularly African Americans, Latinos, and American Indians. Efforts to increase the access and success of members of these groups have been motivated by social justice and equity concerns. The second dimension, campus climate and intergroup relations, addresses the campus setting within which diverse groups of students interact. The focus of this dimension is on creating a positive learning environment and intergroup atmosphere for the benefit of all groups of students. The dimension of education and scholarship focuses on ways to incorporate diverse perspectives and knowledge bases into teaching methods, curricula, and areas of scholarly inquiry so as to better educate all students to live in a multicultural society. Lastly, institutional transformation focuses on the ways in which institutions must be restructured to fulfill the educational mission of diversity in all of its dimensions.

Theories of race and race relations have tended to focus narrowly on issues of representation and climate. The contact hypothesis, perhaps the most influential model to emerge from social psychological research on race, was developed primarily to address the dimension of campus climate and inter-group relations. The contact hypothesis was refined by Gordon Allport (1954) during the era of legalized school segregation, when a primary concern was how to reduce prejudice and hostility between members of segregated groups when they came into contact with one another in desegregated environments. The model specifies a number of critical conditions that must be present for intergroup contact to reduce prejudice and lead to positive intergroup rela-tions: members of different groups must have equal status within the contact situation; they must work together cooperatively in the pursuit of common goals; contact must be close enough to lead to perceptions of common inter-ests and common humanity among the group members; and the contact must be sanctioned by institutional supports (e.g., by university administrators and policies).

The issue of diversity that we face today raises different questions than those addressed by the contact hypothesis. In the post–Civil Rights era, there is a widespread belief in the equality of opportunity, despite the reality of persisting racial inequalities. The challenge we face today is how educational institutions can treat people as individuals in order to ensure equality of op-portunity, while at the same time acknowledging the persisting inequalities that demonstrate how race continues to matter in society. This issue involves all four dimensions of diversity: (1) how to incorporate both individual char-acteristics and group membership into selection and evaluation procedures to promote access and success for underrepresented groups on college campuses; (2) how to facilitate positive intergroup relations by recognizing that individ-uals assimilate into larger groups to meet needs for identity and belonging, but that individuals within groups vary widely from one another and should therefore not be subject to group stereotypes; (3) how to educate students to live in a society in which individual differences and collective representations contribute to a diversity of perspectives; and (4) how to restructure institu-tions of higher education so that they fulfill their mission of diversity.

An Integrated View

The fundamental question, then, is whether people should be categorized and treated as group members, or whether they should be decategorized and treated as individuals within institutions of higher education. According to the group perspective, group membership must be taken into account in decisions of access because of power differentials between groups, and it must be taken into account in terms of climate because membership meets basic human needs for group identity and belonging. According to the individualistic perspective, group membership must *not* be taken into account in decisions of access because it is irrelevant to more objective merit criteria, and it must *not* be taken into account in terms of climate because it exaggerates group differences and thereby exacerbates intergroup conflict. The problem with traditional research paradigms is that they have couched these two perspectives as a false dichotomy, and they have focused on one perspective to the exclusion of the other. Ferdman (1997) proposes that one way to reconcile these seemingly contradictory individualistic and group perspectives is to integrate them into a new view of fairness that promotes both the protection of group rights and the acknowledgment of individual differences. This integrated view offers a new framework for understanding the complexity of contemporary race relations. Rather than focusing on either the individualistic or the group perspective, or on one dimension of diversity rather than another, this new paradigm attempts to incorporate both the individualistic and group perspectives into an integrated framework that can be applied to all four dimensions of diversity.

Previous research on the first dimension, representation, demonstrates the utility of factoring both group membership and individual characteristics into selection and evaluation procedures in order to increase minority access and success on college campuses. For example, Nacoste (1990, 1994, 1996) has examined how psychological responses to affirmative action vary as a function of the weight given to group membership and individual characteristics in selection procedures. Affirmative action procedures that give weight to group membership, but give *more* weight and consideration to individual achievement-related characteristics, are evaluated as procedurally fairer than those that give the most weight to group membership. Therefore, this research suggests that individual characteristics and group membership be combined, although differentially weighted, in the selection process so that the procedures used to enhance minority access to higher education are considered fair. Furthermore, universities should reveal the nature of their weighted selection procedures so that these procedures will be perceived to be fair by both beneficiaries and nonbeneficiaries of affirmative action. As the research literature consistently demonstrates, perceptions of fairness are important determinants of support for affirmative action policies (Clayton and Tangri 1989; Nacoste 1989).

The criteria used to guide selection procedures have also been found to influence self-evaluations and performance expectancies among beneficiaries of affirmative action (Major, Feinstein, and Crocker 1994). Cognitive theories of emotion posit that when people achieve positive outcomes such as college admission and successful academic performance, they are likely to experience more positive affect and evaluate themselves and their attributes more favorably when they can attribute these outcomes to internal factors such as ability or merit (Weiner 1985). When positive outcomes are attributed to benefits based on group membership, beneficiaries are less certain they could have achieved these outcomes solely on the basis of their personal merit or deserving. This "attributional ambiguity" about personal deserving is expected to reduce self-evaluations and performance expectancies. However, Major, Feinstein, and Crocker (1994) found that affirmative action procedures perceived to be based on *both* individual merit and group membership reduced ambiguity about the extent to which selection was deserved and enhanced the self-evaluations of the competence of beneficiaries. These increased feelings of competence may then lead to enhanced academic success among minority beneficiaries of affirmative action. Once again, for affirmative action selection procedures to be successful in enhancing minority access and success, it must be made clear that selection is based on individual merit as well as group membership. Incorporating both selection criteria increases perceptions of fairness and reduces attributional ambiguity about the personal competence of those selected, thereby reducing negative responses to affirmative action procedures.

Two additional dimensions of diversity, institutional viability and institutional goals to educate students to live in a diverse society, will also be promoted to the degree that unique perspectives derived from the intersection between individual and group identities are represented on college campuses. For an institution to be viable, it must promote both the individual and group interests of members of the university community (i.e., students, faculty, staff, board of trustees) and society at large. And for an institution to fulfill its mission of educating all students to live in a multicultural society, it must expose students to the breadth of perspectives offered not only by members of different ethnic groups but also by different individuals within the same ethnic group whose life experiences vary dramatically. The contact hypothesis suggests that exposure to the tremendous variation between individual members of the same ethnic group will reduce the use of racial stereotypes and increase perceptions of similarity among members of different ethnic groups on the basis of common individual interests (Allport 1954). Students will be better prepared to live in a diverse society if they learn to appreciate similarities with and differences from others based on both individual and group characteristics.

A fourth dimension of diversity, intergroup climate, will also be enhanced to the degree that individuals are able to recognize similarities with and differences from members of other ethnic groups. Previous research has shown that one way to improve relations between different groups is to create a superordinate or common in-group identity that emphasizes what everyone has in common and meets needs for assimilation, while at the same time respecting individuals' needs for differentiation into smaller ethnic subgroups. In their research on the common in-group identity model, Gaertner et al. (1994) found that intergroup bias among students attending a multicultural high school was lower when students perceived the student body as one superordinate group than when they perceived the student body as composed of separate subgroups. Importantly, the researchers also emphasize that the development of a common in-group identity does not necessarily require each group to completely give up its subgroup identity, just so long as diverse group members conceive of themselves as members of different groups that are all playing on the same team. For example, Gaertner et al. (1994) found that intergroup bias was lower when students thought of themselves simultaneously as "Americans" (superordinate group) and as members of their particular ethnic/racial subgroup than when they thought of themselves only as members of their particular ethnic/racial subgroup. The final conclusion to be drawn from this research is that sharing a superordinate in-group identity with members of other ethnic groups decreases intergroup bias, even when the superordinate identity (e.g., American) and ethnic subgroup identity (e.g., white, black, Asian, Hispanic) are both important to individuals.

Huo et al. (1996) drew similar conclusions in their research on the group-value model of justice. According to this model, people will accept decisions made by authorities when they feel they are being treated fairly, even if they do not obtain desired outcomes. When evaluations of an authority figure are based more on relational issues (treatment with respect and honesty) than on instrumental issues (outcomes), then conflicts are less likely to arise when people receive unfavorable outcomes. Consistent with the model's predictions, Huo et al. (1996) found that when employees described conflicts with supervisors from different ethnic backgrounds than their own, they were more satisfied with the interaction when they felt they were treated with respect and benevolence, regardless of whether or not the conflict situation was resolved in their favor. Important to our discussion of intergroup climate are findings that even people who identified strongly with their ethnic subgroup focused more on relational issues than on instrumental issues in their evaluations of authorities, as long as they also identified strongly with the superordinate group (i.e., the work organization). These findings suggest that intergroup conflict on multicultural college campuses will be minimized, even when there are disparities in outcomes, when the diverse groups of students identify with a superordinate in-group (regardless of whether or not they also identify with their particular ethnic subgroup).

Both of these identity and justice models suggest that identification with a common in-group or superordinate group will result in a more positive intergroup climate. They also emphasize that the development of a common in-group identity will still have positive effects, even when people identify strongly with their ethnic or racial subgroup. Gaertner et al. (1994) suggest that in practice, a common in-group identity may be activated by increasing the salience of an existing common group membership (e.g., as Americans) or by introducing factors perceived as shared by group members (e.g., a common enemy of the state). This recategorization of different groups into one group is viewed as a particularly powerful and pragmatic strategy not only for reducing subtle forms of intergroup bias but also for improving reactions to affirmative action (Dovidio and Gaertner 1996). For example, in a survey study of middle-class white adults, Smith and Tyler (1996) found that respondents who identified strongly as Americans had more positive attitudes toward affirmative action than did those who had a weak American identity, even when the strength of the subordinate white identity was equivalently high. In terms of process, the salience of a common in-group identity may reduce the degree to which opposition to affirmative action is driven by ethnic group identity, competition, and dominance motives. That is, if people derive a sense of belonging and identification from a common in-group, then their social identity will not be bolstered by feelings of superiority to fellow in-group members (rather, their identity needs will be fulfilled through favorable comparisons with people outside the common in-group), they will not view their interests as competing with those of fellow in-group members, and they will not view their position of dominance as threatened by the demands of fellow in-group members. Rather, recategorizing different racial groups into a common in-group would focus on the need for affirmative action policies in terms of the beneficial consequences for the society as a whole in meeting the demands of all four dimensions of diversity: increasing the inclusion and academic success of minority groups; improving the campus climate within which diverse groups of students interact; better educating all students to live in a pluralistic society; and restructuring institutions to fulfill their commitments to diversity.

Conclusion

The dominant ideology in the United States is one that encompasses a belief in widespread opportunity, individual responsibility for achievement, and equity principles of justice (Kluegel and Smith 1986). According to this dominant ideology, fairness requires treating people as individuals. However, social psychological research suggests that fairness requires taking race into account, because race influences social perceptions, attitudes, and behaviors in ways that disadvantage members of minority groups. Research on unintentional racial biases, group identity processes, group competition, and group dominance motives demonstrates the need for affirmative action. The challenge of future research on diversity in higher education will be to establish how educational institutions can treat people as individuals while at the same time acknowledging the collective representations that matter in society. Promising research directions are offered by empirical studies on successful selection and evaluation procedures that take into account both individual characteristics and group memberships (e.g., Major, Feinstein, and Crocker 1994), and successful ways to improve campus climate by creating a superordinate or common in-group identity that emphasizes what everyone has in common, while at the same time respecting individuals' needs for differentiation into smaller ethnic subgroups (e.g., Gaertner et al. 1994). These studies suggest that an integrated framework incorporating both the individualistic and group perspectives will enable us to understand the complexity of contemporary race relations in a way that traditional research paradigms focusing on a single perspective have failed to do.

In this chapter, the social psychological research literature is used as a prime example of how social scientists have advanced our understanding of racial dynamics. One limitation of this research literature is its primary emphasis on individual and intergroup processes rather than institutional structures, which are discussed at greater length in Chapters 2 and 5 of the book. Although limited in focus, this knowledge base is highly relevant to the public debate about diversity in higher education. Social psychological research on race and racism reveals inequities in American society that contradict principles of racial equality and fairness. The use of race-conscious admissions policies in higher education can help mitigate the individual and intergroup processes that perpetuate these inequities. A more level playing field in admissions policies will ensure members of all ethnic groups equal access to the opportunities and equitable assignment of the rewards that higher education affords.

Chapter Five

THE EDUCATIONAL BENEFITS
OF DIVERSITY: EVIDENCE
FROM MULTIPLE SECTORS

Jeffrey F. Milem

The attack on affirmative action, coming as it does out of
tremendous anxiety in a changing world, is an opening
for a more progressive vision.

C. R. LAWRENCE III *and* M. J. MATSUDA,
We Won't Go Back: Making the Case for Affirmative Action

This chapter presents the broad range of social science evidence on the benefits of diversity in higher education in order to illuminate a central issue that is often missed in the debate over affirmative action—that supporting diversity in colleges and universities is not only a matter of social justice but also a matter of promoting educational excellence. I start by examining the mission of an institution of higher education.

The mission of an institution of higher education tells us what a college or university is about, what it values, what it holds to be true. Educational policies, programs, and practices emerge from the mission of the institution (Kuh et al. 1991). Few would disagree with the assertion that institutions of higher education have a unique responsibility to develop in students the knowledge, skills, and competencies they need to be active members of society.[1] As inhabitants of an increasingly diverse country that is inextricably connected to a larger "global" community, we must reconsider what it now means to be an active and productive member of society. As colleges and universities have recognized and responded to these trends, their mission statements have undergone a process of dramatic transformation. Increasingly, institutional mission statements at colleges and universities across the country affirm the role of diversity in enhancing teaching and learning in higher education (Alger 1997). Administrators (e.g., see Bollinger 1997; Rudenstine 1997; Shapiro 1995), academics (e.g., see Astone and Nuñes-Womack 1990; Duster 1993; Hurtado et al. 1998, 1999; Smith et al. 1997; Tierney 1993), and national educational associations (see note 1) offer compelling arguments about the ways diversity expands and enriches the educational enterprise through the benefits it provides to individual students, to colleges and universities, and to our society and our world. In a statement endorsed by the presidents of sixty-two research universities (including eight Ivy League institutions and more than thirty public research universities), the American Association of Universities argued:

> We speak first and foremost as educators. We believe that our students benefit significantly from education that takes place within a diverse setting. In the course of their university education, our students encounter and learn from others who have backgrounds and characteristics very different from their own. As we seek to prepare students for life in the twenty-first century, the educational value of such encounters will become more important, not less, than in the past.
>
> A very substantial portion of our curriculum is enhanced by the discourse made possible by the heterogeneous backgrounds of our students. Equally, a significant part of education in our institutions takes place outside the classroom, in extracurricular activities where students learn how to work together, as well as to compete; how to exercise leadership, as well as to build consensus. If our institutional capacity to bring together a genuinely diverse group of students is removed— or severely reduced—then the quality and texture of the education we provide will be significantly diminished. (Association of American Universities 1997)

Yet as the momentum for diversity reaches unprecedented levels on campuses across the country, institutional leaders find they must respond to attacks levied against something they have identified as a central part of the educational missions of their campuses. Moreover, it is becoming apparent that for many campuses, decisions about campus diversity will be made in courtrooms rather than in classrooms or boardrooms. This is not to say that the higher education community can or should have no role in influencing these decisions. Legal challenges to the use of race in college admissions require that attorneys, policy makers, scholars, and institutional leaders across the country search for empirical evidence that documents the benefits of diversity and provides evidence of persistent discrimination and inequality in higher education. This is not an easy task. When members of these diverse communities come together to discuss strategies for addressing these issues, they quickly learn that they usually do not speak the same language when it comes to diversity. What is compelling evidence for diversity in the eyes of a social scientist, or a college president, or a dean of students, may not meet the standards of evidence that are applied by an attorney or a Supreme Court justice.

Liu (1998) offers a persuasive argument for "why, as a *legal doctrine*, educational diversity should qualify as a 'compelling interest.'" His law review article thoughtfully and convincingly argues for "placing the diversity rationale squarely within the existing norm of equal protection doctrine. In other words, it is an effort to legitimize an educational policy in the language of constitutional law" (383). Liu does this by illustrating how the remedial and diversity rationales for affirmative action do not differ substantively in any ways that would make either argument more constitutionally "compelling." The diversity rationale essentially asserts that diversity adds to the educational experience of students who attend institutions that are racially and ethnically diverse. A key provision in defending the diversity rationale in court cases that challenge it involves the ability of an institution to provide a "strong basis in evidence" to support the assertions made regarding an institution's interest in educational diversity. Liu asserts that "as a starting point, it seems reasonable to require a university invoking the diversity rationale to define and substantiate the educational needs that its admissions policies purport to meet" (431). In arguing the diversity rationale in court, institutional leaders must be able to describe clearly the ways in which a diverse student body adds to their educational programs (Liu 1998).

As indicated elsewhere in this book, the value of diversity in higher education is also being questioned in the court of public opinion. Although the public generally lends its support to democratic ideals of fairness, equity, and equality of opportunity, the debate over affirmative action is constructed in such a way that vocal portions of the public argue that affirmative action violates the very principles that led to its creation. Chapter 4 of this book provides us with valuable insights into why this may occur. The approval of ballot initiatives in California and Washington, and efforts to bring similar initiatives to the ballot in other states, indicates that many in our population do not understand the value of diversity in colleges and universities, nor do they understand the ways in which diversity enriches our individual and collective experiences.

Through a multidisciplinary analysis of the research literature, this chapter examines studies that help to increase our understanding of the benefits of diversity in colleges and universities. Perhaps unlike no other time in our history, scholars from a variety of disciplinary backgrounds have the opportunity to demonstrate the ways in which their research findings provide evidence of the educational outcomes of diverse institutional environments. As this body of research evidence continues to build, it will help to ensure that the benefits of diversity are located at the center of the educational enterprise. This chapter illustrates how scholarship that documents the value of diversity in institutions of higher education, from a variety of disciplines and perspectives, can be used to inform and enhance the argument for diversity on campus. Classic and contemporary research are used to inform the debates surrounding affirmative action and other policies designed to create and maintain diverse learning environments.

Conceptual Framework for Understanding the Educational Benefits of Diversity

This chapter uses a four-dimensional framework to better understand and describe the benefits of diverse college campuses. Research indicates that racial and ethnic diversity in higher education benefits (1) individual students, (2) higher education institutions, (3) the economy and private enterprise, and (4) society. *Individual benefits* refers to the ways in which the educational experiences and outcomes of individual students are enhanced by diversity on campus. *Institutional benefits* refers to the ways in which diversity enhances the ability of colleges and universities to achieve their missions— particularly as diversity relates to the missions of teaching, research, and service. *Economic and private-sector benefits* refers to the ways in which diversity enhances the economy and the functioning of organizations and businesses in the private sector. *Societal benefits* are defined as the ways in which diversity at colleges and universities affects lives, policies, and issues beyond the walls of the university, including the achievement of democratic ideals, the development of an educated and involved citizenry, and the delivery of necessary

TABLE 5.1

Educational Benefits of Diverse College and University Campuses

Type of Benefit	
Individual Benefits	Institutional Benefits
• Enhanced critical and complex thinking ability • Higher levels of social/historical thinking • Enhanced ability to understand diverse perspectives • Improved openness to diversity and challenge • Enhanced classroom discussions • Greater satisfaction with the college experience • Higher levels of student persistence • Improved racial and cultural awareness • Greater commitment to increasing racial understanding • Perceptions of a more supportive campus racial climate • Increased wages for men who graduate from higher institutions of "quality"	• More student-centered approaches to teaching and learning • More diverse curricular offerings • More research focused on issues of race/ethnicity and gender • More women and faculty of color involved in community and volunteer service

services to underserved groups (e.g., those with low income, the elderly, those who lack adequate health care).

This chapter has drawn from research and writing in the areas of critical race theory, economics, education, feminist studies, health policy, law, medicine, organizational behavior, organizational effectiveness, psychology, social psychology, and sociology. Table 5.1 provides a summary of the findings of this analysis within the framework of the four dimensions of the previous paragraph. The following discussion describes in more detail the evidence about the many ways in which diverse college environments benefit us all. In general, this information shows that diversity serves a compelling interest both for institutions of higher education specifically and for all members of our increasingly heterogeneous society generally.

TABLE 5.1 (continued)

Educational Benefits of Diverse College and University Campuses

Type of Benefit	
Economic/Private Sector Benefits	Societal Benefits
• Cultivation of workforce with greater levels of cross-cultural competence	• Decreased occupational and residential segregation in society
• Attraction of best available talent pool	• Greater engagement with social and political issues
• Enhanced marketing efforts	
• Higher levels of creativity and innovation	• Decreased stereotyping and lower levels of ethnocentrism
• Better problem-solving abilities	• Higher levels of service to community/civic organizations
• Greater organization flexibility	
• Affirmative action in employment leads to:	• Increased service by physicians of color to the most medically underserved communities
—decreased job discrimination	
—decreased wage disparities	• Greater equity in society
—decreased occupational segregation	• A more educated citizenry
—increased occupational aspirations for women and people of color	
—greater organizational productivity	

Individual Benefits

Much of the research about higher education traditionally has examined the ways in which individual students grow and change while in college (see, e.g., Astin 1977, 1993; Feldman and Newcomb 1969; Pascarella and Terenzini 1991). In recent years, more of this research has focused on the ways in which racial dynamics on campus influence student outcomes. The most abundant research evidence supporting arguments for the continued use of affirmative action in college admissions exists in the area of how individuals benefit from diversity. Research evidence regarding the individual benefits of diversity suggests that diversity enhances student growth and development in the cognitive, affective, and interpersonal domains.

This educational benefit is universal in that all students learn from it, not just minority students who might have received a "bump" in the admissions process. Indeed, majority students who have previously lacked significant direct exposure to minorities frequently have the most to gain from interaction with individuals of other races. The universality of this benefit distinguishes the diversity rationale from the rationale of remedying discrimination, under which minority students receive special consideration to make up for past injustices to their racial group (Alger 1997, 21–22).

Conceptualizing Diversity

Before discussing the ways in which racial and ethnic diversity benefits individual students, it is important to define *diversity*. Building upon the work of Gurin (1999) and Chang (1999c), I argue that there are three types or dimensions of diversity that have an impact on student outcomes. The first, *structural diversity*, refers to the numerical and proportional representation of students from different racial/ethnic groups in the student body (Hurtado et al. 1998, 1999). A second type of diversity involves *diversity-related initiatives* (i.e., cultural awareness workshops, ethnic studies courses, and so forth) that occur on college and university campuses. Although demographic shifts or changes in the structural diversity of campuses frequently provide the stimulus for diversity-related initiatives (Chang 1999b), some colleges and universities incorporate these types of initiatives even though their campuses are racially and ethnically homogeneous. The final dimension of diversity, *diverse interactions*, is characterized by students' exchanges with racially and ethnically diverse people as well as diverse ideas, information, and experiences. People are influenced by their interactions with diverse ideas and information as well as diverse people.

These three dimensions of diversity are not mutually exclusive. In fact, we are most frequently exposed to diverse information and ideas through our interactions with diverse people. Moreover, although diversity-related initiatives benefit students who are exposed to them—even on campuses that are almost exclusively white—their impact on students is much more powerful on campuses that have greater structural diversity (Chang 1999a). In sum, although each dimension of diversity can confer significant positive effects on educational outcomes, the impact of each is believed to be enhanced by the presence of the other dimensions of diversity (Chang 1999b; Gurin 1999; Hurtado et al. 1998, 1999). Conversely, the impact of each type of diversity is believed to be diminished in environments in which the other dimensions are absent.

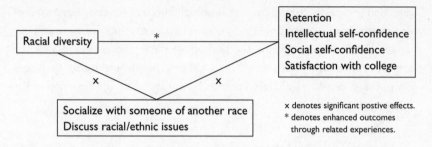

FIGURE 5.1   Model for understanding the educational efficacy of racial diversity (derived from Chang 1999a).

The empirical work of Mitchell Chang is very helpful in illustrating these three types of diversity and the impact they have on students. Chang (1996) found that maximizing cross-racial interaction and encouraging ongoing discussions about race are educational practices that are beneficial to students. The findings of this study revealed that socializing across race and discussing racial/ethnic issues have a positive effect on students' likelihood of staying enrolled in college, their overall satisfaction with college, their intellectual self-concept, and their social self-concept (Chang 1996). However, when the effects of increased structural diversity are considered without involvement in activities that provide students with opportunities to interact in meaningful ways cross-racially, students of color were likely to report less overall satisfaction with their college experience (Chang 1996). Thus, increasing *only* the structural diversity of an institution without considering the influence that these changes will have on other dimensions of the campus racial climate is likely to produce negative effects for students at these institutions. Moreover, Chang's work shows that the larger the representation of racially diverse students at an institution, the greater the likelihood that students will report that they have engaged in interactions with other students who are different than they are. In an extension of this earlier research, Chang (1999a) found that structural diversity (represented by the enrollment of students of color at an institution) was an essential ingredient in providing opportunities for this interaction to occur. (Chang's model summarizing the educational efficacy of diversity is presented in Figure 5.1.) In short, as an institution becomes more structurally diverse, the greater the likelihood that students will have opportunities to socialize across racial groups and to discuss racial issues. As this interaction increases, the campus environment becomes more supportive of diversity-related practices, which in turn enhances students' learning and educational experiences. Hence, the findings of these studies suggest that the impact of each type of diversity (structural diversity, diverse interactions, and institutional diversity-related initiatives) is enhanced by the presence of the other types of diversity.

Theoretical Considerations Regarding the Impact of Diversity on Individuals

Gurin (1999) makes a persuasive argument about higher education's unique opportunity to enhance the cognitive and psychosocial development of college students. She argues that undergraduates are at a critical stage in their human growth and development at which diversity, broadly defined, can facilitate greater awareness of the learning process, better critical thinking skills, and better preparation for the many challenges they will face as involved citizens in a democratic, multiracial society. Gurin asserts that "universities are ideal institutions to foster such development" (103).

Erikson's (1946, 1956, cited in Gurin 1999) work on psychosocial development indicates that individuals' social and personal identity is formed during late adolescence and early adulthood—the time when many attend college. Environments such as higher education facilitate the development of identity. For example, among the conditions in college that facilitate the development of identity is the opportunity to be exposed to people, experiences, and ideas that differ from one's past environment (Gurin 1999). Moreover, the college environment can accentuate the normative influence of peer groups. Diversity and complexity in the college environment "encourage intellectual experimentation and recognition of varied future possibilities" (Gurin 1999, 103). These conditions are critical to the successful development of identity.

Gurin (1999) uses the work of Piaget (1971, 1985) as a conceptual and theoretical rationale for how diversity facilitates students' cognitive development. According to Gurin, Piaget argues that cognitive growth is facilitated by disequilibrium, or periods of incongruity and dissonance. He also argues that for adolescents to develop the ability to understand and appreciate the perspectives and feelings of others, they must interact with diverse individuals in equal status situations. This facilitates the process of "perspective taking" and allows students to progress in intellectual and moral development. For "perspective taking" to occur, both diversity and equality must be present (Gurin 1999).

Piaget worked primarily with children and adolescents, but the applicability of his research to the development processes of college students has been well established by Perry (1970), who used an explicitly Piagetian model in his study of the cognitive development of college students at Harvard. Perry's theory outlines the intellectual and ethical development of college students, by use of a nine-stage model that traces the development of students' thinking about the nature of knowledge, truth, and values and the meaning of life and responsibilities (King 1978). Specifically, Perry's theory examines students' intellect (how they understand the world and the nature of knowledge) and their identity (how they find meaning for their place in the world) (King 1978). Key to the successful progression of students through the developmental stages in this theory is the ability to recognize the existence of multiple viewpoints and "the indeterminacies" of "Truth" (Pascarella and Terenzini 1991, 29). As students progress to the higher stages of development in the Perry schema, they develop commitments to beliefs, values, behaviors, and people. The process of developing these commitments is dynamic and changeable, and it is triggered by the students' exposure to new experiences, new ideas, and new people. Perry (1981) suggests that this process of development is likely to extend throughout our lives.

A growing body of research in social psychology indicates that it is inappropriate to assume that active engagement in learning occurs as a matter of course during the college years (Gurin 1999). In fact, what previously had been assumed to be active engagement in learning is actually a more automatic response, or "mindlessness" (Langer 1978, cited in Gurin 1999). This "mindlessness" is the result of learning that already has occurred and that has become so customary that thinking proves unnecessary. In the absence of what Coser (1975, cited in Gurin 1999) describes as complex social structures, people work off of scripts or schemas that do not require active thinking processes.[2] Coser asserts that people who interact with more complex social structures exhibit a heightened sense of individuality while simultaneously showing a more complex attentiveness to the social world. This body of theoretical work strongly suggests that racially and ethnically diverse learning environments can effectively provide the types of complex social structures that stimulate the development of active thinking processes (Gurin 1999).

Types of Individual Outcomes

In considering the outcomes of diversity for individuals, it is helpful to understand what is meant by *outcomes*. Gurin (1999) describes two major types of outcomes that are influenced by campus diversity. *Learning outcomes* refers to the active learning processes in which students become involved while in college, the engagement and motivation that students exhibit, the learning and refinement of intellectual and academic skills, and the value students place on these skills after they leave college. *Democracy outcomes* refers to the ways in which higher education prepares students to become involved as active participants in a society that is becoming increasingly diverse and complex. The democracy outcomes of diverse learning environments are discussed in detail in the section of this chapter that considers the societal benefits of diversity.

To the categories of outcomes described by Gurin (1999), Milem and Hakuta (2000) propose two other types. The first, *process outcomes*, reflects the ways in which students perceive that diversity has enriched their college experiences. Measures of student satisfaction and perceptions of campus climate are examples of outcomes included in this category. These measures can also be thought of as *intermediate outcomes* (Astin 1991) because of the unique role they play in students' development. They can be viewed as meaningful educational outcomes, but they also can be viewed as a source of influence on other types of outcomes. For example, student satisfaction is frequently studied as an important outcome of the college experience. However, satisfaction can also be examined for the possible influence that it has on other important outcomes (such as persistence, achievement, and so forth). Similarly, students' perceptions of the campus racial climate can be viewed as outcome measures. However, they are also important (as intermediate outcomes) when they are examined for the influence they have on other important student outcomes. A final type of outcome reflects the *material benefits* that students accrue when they attend diverse colleges. Examples of material benefits include an increase in potential salary/wages, the attainment of advanced graduate or professional degrees, and/or better job placements for students educated at more diverse institutions and/or who benefit from affirmative action in college admissions.

Discussion of Research Findings of Diversity and Individual Outcomes

Students' learning outcomes are enhanced in a number of ways by their experience of diversity in college. Students who interact with others from diverse backgrounds show greater relative gains in critical thinking and active thinking. Pascarella, Whitt, et al. (1996) report that students who participated in racial and cultural awareness workshops showed measurable gains at the end of their first year of college in what the researchers argue are critical thinking skills. In another study using these data, Pascarella, Edison, et al. (1996) studied changes in students' openness to diversity and challenge after their first year of college.[3] After controlling for precollege characteristics (including levels of openness to diversity and challenge at the time the students first entered college), the authors found that students who perceived their college as nondiscriminatory, had participated in racial and cultural awareness workshops, and had interacted with diverse peers were likely to report greater openness to diversity and challenge after their first year in college.

In an extension of this study, Whitt et al. (1998) examined factors that predicted openness to diversity and challenge after the second and third years of college. They found that after controlling for the effect of individual student characteristics, the same predictors that explained openness at the end of the first year were still operative after the second and third years. In addition, openness was greater among those who had engaged in conversations with other students in which diverse ways of thinking and understanding were emphasized.

Research on the impact of a curriculum enhancement project in a sequence of human development courses adds to our understanding of the impact that exposure to diverse ideas and information can have on college students. A study by MacPhee, Kreutzer, and Fritz (1994) found that certain types of curricular and pedagogical interventions enhance students' openness to diversity as well as their critical thinking skills. Mixed research methods (quantitative and qualitative) were employed to examine the impact of the curriculum transformation that occurred in these courses. The findings from the quantitative analyses suggested that student attitudes toward out-groups (particularly the poor) were broadly influenced by the transformation of the curriculum. They also showed small but statistically significant changes in students' racial attitudes. The qualitative analyses revealed three primary findings: (1) students demonstrated that they had developed a number of critical-thinking skills; (2) levels of ethnocentrism among students declined; and (3) students who had enrolled in these classes were able to make an appropriate distinction between poverty and ethnicity as developmental risk factors (Mac-Phee, Kreutzer, and Fritz 1994).

Gurin (1999) provides additional evidence about the ways diversity enhances these learning outcomes. Analyses were conducted on behalf of the University of Michigan for use as evidence in the two lawsuits that challenge the university's use of race as one factor in undergraduate and graduate/professional admissions decisions. The analyses use data gathered by the university as well as longitudinal data from a national sample of undergraduates gathered by the Higher Education Research Institute at the University of California, Los Angeles (UCLA). These analyses were conducted to document the educational outcomes of diversity for students at the University of Michigan as well as for students across the nation.

Students who reported higher levels of contact with diverse ideas, information, and people were more likely to show growth in their "active thinking processes," which were represented by increases in measures of complex thinking and social/historical thinking (Gurin 1999).[4] In addition, students who had greater exposure to diversity were more likely to show higher levels of intellectual engagement and motivation. Further, students who had greater exposure to diversity were likely to report that they had higher postgraduate degree aspirations. The analyses also showed that exposure to various types of diversity had different relative impact, depending on the students' racial/ethnic background. Although white students were more likely to benefit from exposure to diverse ideas and information and exposure to diverse peers, African American students were more likely to benefit from interactions with diverse peers. Moreover, African American students experienced positive learning outcomes when they were exposed to close friends of their *own race*. In other words, for African American students to fully benefit from diversity, they must have contact with diverse peers as well as interaction with same-race peers (Gurin 1999).

Springer et al. (1996) found that greater interaction with diverse people and ideas decreased the gap in views of campus climate frequently found between students of color and white students. In studies of the impact of college climate on the racial attitudes and views of white men and women, Milem (1992, 1994) found that students who participated in more frequent discussions of social and political issues talked more frequently about racial/ethnic issues, socialized with someone from another racial/ethnic group, attended a racial awareness workshop, or enrolled in ethnic studies courses were more likely to report increased levels of racial and cultural awareness and greater commitment to the goal of promoting racial understanding four years after entering college. This suggests that greater interaction with diversity in college helps students develop greater understanding and appreciation of the perspective of groups other than their own. These outcomes are similar to the outcomes of active thinking and perspective taking discussed in the analyses performed by Gurin (1999).

With regard to the process outcomes of diversity, Astin (1993) found that faculty members' emphasis on diversity in their courses had positive effects on students' overall satisfaction with college. Villalpando (1994) reported similar findings regarding the relationship between satisfaction and the extent to which faculty included racially/ethnically diverse materials in their courses. This finding was as true for white students as for students of color. Tanaka (1996, cited in Smith et al. 1997) found that a more supportive campus climate as evidenced by campus efforts to create a multicultural environment and to include racial/ethnic material in the curriculum had positive effects on students' sense of community and their overall satisfaction with college.

A recent study of students attending Harvard University and University of Michigan law schools provides additional information about the process outcomes of diversity, especially as they pertain to legal education (Orfield and Whitla 1999). A survey conducted by the Gallup Organization was administered by telephone to 1,800 law students attending these two schools. Survey results indicate that these law students believed their interactions with diverse people and ideas while in law school enhanced their learning and thinking in fundamental ways.

Specifically, the overwhelming majority of students (90 percent) indicated that their exposure to racial and ethnic diversity while in law school had a positive impact on their educational experience. Moreover, the students reported that being in a racially diverse environment enabled them to engage in discussions with others that enhanced their learning. Nearly two-thirds of the students indicated that diversity improved in-class discussions. More than six in ten (62 percent) indicated that diversity improved their ability to work and to get along with others. Approximately eight in ten students (78 percent for Harvard students and 84 percent for Michigan students) reported that discussions with students from different racial and ethnic backgrounds significantly affected their views of the U.S. criminal justice system. The majority of students also reported that their discussions with students from different racial and ethnic backgrounds significantly influenced their views about civil rights and conditions in various social and economic institutions. In sum, students who attended two of the most highly selective law schools in the country indicated that diversity was an essential aspect of their legal education.

An emerging body of evidence also documents the material benefits that accrue to students of color who attend selective colleges and universities as well as to white students who attend the same institutions. In their study of the outcomes of racial diversity in selective colleges and universities, Bowen and Bok (1998) reported that black students who attended selective institutions were five times as likely as all black students nationwide to earn advanced degrees (professional degrees or Ph.D.'s). Black men in the entering cohort of 1976 reported average postgraduate annual incomes of $82,000—twice the average earnings of black college graduates nationally. Black women graduates of selective institutions earned an average of $58,500 annually—80 percent more than black women graduates nationwide (Bowen and Bok 1998).[5] Daniel, Black, and Smith (1997) examined the relationship between college quality and the wages of young men. Not surprisingly, the authors found that young men who attended a higher-quality college earned higher wages. These "returns" were significantly higher for black than white men. The study also found that both black and white men who attended selective colleges with more diverse student bodies had higher earnings (although the returns were somewhat higher for white than for black men).

Faculty Views on the Importance of Racial and Ethnic Diversity in Higher Education

Apart from students, faculty members may be the campus constituency best positioned to assess the ways in which diversity affects the opportunities that students have to learn and develop while in college. Data from a recent national survey of college and university faculty conducted by the Higher Education Research Institute (HERI) at UCLA offer a vivid and informative picture of how faculty view racial/ethnic diversity in higher education. Approximately 55,000 faculty nationwide, drawn from all institutional types in the higher education system, completed the survey (see Sax et al. 1999 for more information about this survey). Three of the survey items are particularly helpful in determining how faculty value racial and ethnic diversity in higher education.

Faculty overwhelmingly believe that a diverse student body enhances all students' educational experience. More than 90 percent of the faculty surveyed agreed with the statement that "A racially/ethnically diverse student body enhances the educational experience of all students." Women were more likely than men to endorse this statement (95.4 percent of women agreed compared with 87.7 percent of men). Faculty support was evident across institutional type ranging from a low of 86.1 percent at private, two-year institutions to a high of 93.3 percent at private four-year colleges.

One misperception forwarded by many who oppose the use of race as one factor in college admissions is that this process leads to the enrollment of unqualified or underprepared students. Because faculty members are the institutional representatives primarily responsible for facilitating teaching and learning, they are uniquely positioned to address this misperception. Findings from the HERI faculty survey indicate that faculty convincingly refute this assertion. Only 28 percent of the faculty surveyed agreed that "Promoting diversity leads to the admission of too many underprepared students." Although one-third of male faculty agreed with this statement (33.6 percent), fewer than one in five female faculty did so (18.4 percent). Faculty at private, two-year colleges were most likely to agree with the statement (37.9 percent), whereas faculty at private, four-year colleges were least likely to agree (24.9 percent).

One cluster of items from the survey assessed the importance faculty place on items that represent different goals of undergraduate education. One item asked faculty to indicate how important they felt it was for undergraduate education to "Enhance students knowledge of and appreciation for other racial/ethnic groups." Nearly 60 percent of faculty nationwide responded that this goal was either very important or essential. Faculty at private, two-year institutions were most likely to indicate that this goal was very important or essential (69.7 percent), whereas more than half of the faculty at public universities (50.9 percent) reported that it was very important or essential.

When viewed together, these findings suggest that faculty members—those primarily responsible for the teaching and learning that occurs in the classroom—believe that racial and ethnic diversity is a central part of the teaching and learning missions of our higher education institutions.

Summary

Students' learning outcomes are enhanced in a number of ways by their experiences with diversity in college. Students with more experience of diversity show greater relative gains in critical and active thinking. They also are more likely to show evidence of greater intellectual engagement and academic motivation. Students who have more experience with diversity show greater relative gains in intellectual and social self-concept. Finally, higher levels of experience with diversity predict higher levels of retention and increases in degree aspirations. Black students who attend selective institutions are more likely than those who attend less selective institutions to pursue a graduate or professional degree after completing their bachelor's degree.

Research findings also suggest that process outcomes are enhanced by campus diversity. Students who interact with diverse people and ideas report higher levels of satisfaction with their collegiate experience. Moreover, students who experience higher levels of diversity are likely to report a greater sense of community while in college. More extensive interaction with diverse people and ideas decreases the gap between students of color and white students' views of campus climate. This suggests that greater experience of diversity in college helps students develop the ability to understand and appreciate the perspective of groups other than their own.

The findings from an emerging body of research suggest that students who are educated in more racially diverse selective institutions are likely to accrue greater material benefits than are students who attend selective institutions that are more homogeneous. In addition, black students who were educated at selective institutions earn much higher salaries than do their peers who attended other colleges and universities.

Finally, data from a recent national survey of college and university faculty offer important information about faculty views of the relationship between campus diversity, teaching, and learning. The data suggest that faculty believe that racial and ethnic diversity enhances the teaching and learning that occur on their campuses. The many findings summarized in this section provide compelling evidence that diversity benefits individuals in a variety of important ways.

The Impact of Diversity on Higher Education Institutions and Their Missions

Racial and ethnic diversity influences not only student outcomes but also the campuses where it exists. Emerging literature on the institutional benefits of diversity indicates that increased diversity has a transformative effect on colleges and universities (Chang 1999b; Hurtado et al. 1998, 1999; Smith 1995a; Smith et al. 1997) and enriches the overall educational environment on campus. Empirical evidence illustrates the ways in which faculty diversity transforms and enriches the educational missions of colleges and universities.

How Faculty Diversity Enhances Teaching and Learning

In a recent study of the impact of diverse faculty on the research, teaching, and service missions of the university, Milem (1999) found that women faculty and faculty of color contributed to the diverse missions of the university in ways not typical of white male faculty members. This study analyzed the relationship between the race/ethnicity and gender of faculty members and a variety of outcomes related to the three central missions (teaching, research, and service) of higher education institutions.[6]

Even after Milem controlled for other factors known to influence faculty job performance, he found that including women and people of color as faculty members enriches the three primary missions of the university. Race and gender are significant predictors of use in the classroom of active learning methods—methods that have been shown to positively influence the learning process. The use of active pedagogy provides students with opportunities to interact with peers from different backgrounds through class discussions, collaborative learning methods, and group projects. Research suggests that these activities both contribute to a campus climate that is more supportive of diversity and lead to positive outcomes for the students involved (see, e.g.,

Astin 1993; Chang 1999a; Gurin 1999; Hurtado et al., 1998, 1999; Smith et al. 1997).

A diverse faculty provides students with a greater opportunity to encounter readings and research that address the experiences of women and members of different racial/ethnic groups (Milem 1999). This is another form of "interaction"—interaction with diverse ideas—that can lead to positive student outcomes. Interacting with diverse course content provides all students with opportunities to understand the experiences of individuals and groups who differ from them in various ways. Moreover, the engagement of diversity through readings and class materials provides students of color with opportunities to see themselves and their experiences represented in the curriculum.

As for the research mission of the university, faculty of color and women faculty expand the boundaries of current knowledge through the research they produce. They are much more likely than are white male faculty to engage in research that extends knowledge of issues pertaining to race/ethnicity and women/gender in society (Milem 1999). Study findings suggest that faculty of color and women engage in service-related activities with greater frequency than do their white male colleagues (Milem 1999). Thus, students who attend institutions with higher proportions of women faculty and faculty of color are more likely to be exposed to faculty who are student-centered in their orientation to teaching and learning. They also are more likely to experience a curriculum that is more inclusive in its representation of the experiences and contributions of women and racial/ethnic minorities in society. Finally, they are more likely to interact with faculty who are engaged in research on issues of race and gender. On the basis of these analyses, Milem (1999) argues that through their unique contributions to the three primary missions of higher education (research, teaching, and service), women and faculty of color play a specialized and fundamental role in the teaching and learning process.

In a related study that explored the relationship between the climate for racial/ethnic diversity and aspects of the role performance of college and university faculty, Milem (2001) found that measures representing different components of the institutional climate for diversity at colleges and universities were significant predictors of teaching outcomes. Specifically, if faculty perceived other faculty at their institution to be more student-centered in their pedagogical approaches and/or to place greater value on diversity, these faculty were more likely to report that they had employed active teaching methods in the classroom, modified their curriculum to ensure that the perspectives of women and racial/ethnic minorities were represented, attended faculty development sessions designed to assist them in incorporating these issues into the content of their courses, and engaged in research on issues of race/ ethnicity. These findings indicate that the organizational climate matters and that the climate is shaped directly and indirectly by greater representation of women and people of color on the faculty (Milem 1999, 2001).

Summary

When college and university leaders engage diversity as part of their institutional mission, they find that diversity helps transform their campuses in fundamental and positive ways that support student learning. This transformation involves changes in who is taught, what is taught, and who teaches. These studies indicate that paying attention to the institutional context in which diversity is promoted is paramount if institutional leaders are to successfully use campus diversity to enhance the teaching and learning missions of their institutions. Moreover, the evidence suggests that campus climate has a significant role in shaping how faculty approach their work.

Benefits of Diversity to the Economy and Private Sector

Diversity in higher education not only confers benefits on individuals, colleges, and universities but also provides meaningful benefits to businesses and the private sector. In fact, much of the research on the institutional benefits of diverse organizations has been completed by private businesses. Business leaders indicate that increasingly dynamic and highly competitive domestic global markets have created a demand for workers who have cross-cultural competencies that allow them to function effectively in these increasingly diverse marketplaces. Finally, research suggests that diversity in the workplace is good for business in that it increases the flexibility and economic viability of businesses in ways that enable diverse businesses to maximize their earnings.

Essential Skills for Workers in a Global Economy

A report by the RAND Corporation (Bikson and Law 1994) provides important information about the human resource needs that result from the rapidly developing global economy. Officials from sixteen multinational corporations and sixteen institutions of higher education in four cities (Los Angeles, New York, Chicago, and Houston/Dallas) were interviewed. The cities were chosen on the basis of evidence that they were "aware of and actively responding to an increasingly global economic environment and are thus likely to be on the cutting edge regarding issues of globalism" (vii).

The study addressed four primary areas: the ways in which globalism was understood by corporations and colleges; the human resource needs presented by these views of globalism; the steps that colleges and corporations take (or can take) to prepare workers who meet these human resource needs; and the measures that still must be taken to produce a workforce that will be competitive in a global economy.

Bikson and Law (1994) reported that the academic and corporate communities were in consensus about how the movement toward globalism affects the human resource needs of corporations that want to remain economically competitive. Their research suggests four types of human resource needs that workers must possess: (1) domain knowledge; (2) cognitive, social, and personal skills; (3) previous experience and on-the-job training; and (4) cross-cultural competence. Domain knowledge includes knowledge in specific subject matter areas. Bikson and Law's study suggests that colleges currently produce graduates with strong domain knowledge. However, citing concerns about the preparation of students in K-12 education, some respondents questioned colleges and universities' abilities to continue to do this. Corporate leaders expressed concern that students' cognitive, social, and personal skills are not being developed. Cognitive skills include decision making, problem solving, and learning how to learn. Social skills include the ability to function effectively in work groups with others of diverse backgrounds. Personal skills include flexibility and adaptability, openness to new ideas and approaches, empathy for the perspective of others, commitment to high-quality work, and innovation. These skills are directly related to many of the individual outcomes of diversity discussed elsewhere in this chapter. Previous work experience and on-the-job-training pertain to opportunities for students to apply their domain knowledge and social and personal skills in work settings while in college. Cross-cultural competence was identified as the most critical human resource need, in part because it "crosses over" the other categories:

> It involves some domain knowledge (in relation to other cultures) as well as social skills and personal traits that enhance crosscultural communication and cooperation. . . .
>
>   Crosscultural competence, then, chiefly entails a widened knowledge base plus openness and adaptability to different cultural perspectives—and the willingness to learn whatever else is needed to deploy domain skills effectively in new contexts (including, perhaps, functionality in another language). Although these sound like the sorts of prerequisites universities are well-suited to fulfill, they are what corporations find in shortest supply among entry-level candidates. (Bikson and Law 1994, x, 26)

Cross-cultural competence is comprised of cognitive and affective dimensions. Unfortunately, many students have not been sufficiently exposed to other cultures to learn how to work effectively with individuals who are different than they are. Bikson and Law (1994) assert that colleges must find ways for students to communicate regularly across communities of difference, both globally and domestically, so that students can develop the cross-cultural competencies that are important for organizational competitiveness.

If colleges are to meet the challenges presented by increasingly diverse global and domestic economies, they must make changes in many areas, including curriculum, extracurricular activities, faculty development, and cooperative ventures (Bikson and Law 1994). The authors offer specific recommendations about ways institutions can meet these needs: "Colleges should make better use of the cultural diversity already available in their student bodies and localities to cultivate global awareness and crosscultural competence" (xiv). Finally, students "should use the cultural diversity of their own campuses and localities to develop crosscultural competence" (xv). Clearly, diverse colleges and universities offer environments for learning that provide students with opportunities to develop the critical skills and competencies required in domestic and global economies calling for workers who are cross-culturally competent.

Ways in Which Diversity Enhances
Organizational Performance

In a review of the impact of cultural diversity in organizational settings, Cox (1993) suggests that three types of organizational goals are achieved by managing diversity effectively. These goals pertain to moral, ethical, and social responsibility; legal obligations; and economic performance. Cox cites research evidence indicating that a relationship exists between the affective and achievement outcomes of individuals and dimensions of diversity (gender, race, and age). The specific outcomes cited include job involvement levels, employee turnover, promotability ratings, and levels of value congruence.[7] Cox asserts that properly managing diversity leads to lower turnover rates, greater use of flextime work scheduling, and greater work team productivity. Organizations that capitalize on their diversity should enjoy a competitive cost advantage (Cox 1993; Reskin 1998).

Research evidence supports the idea that diverse work teams promote creativity and innovation (Cox 1993; Reskin 1998). Organizational diversity has been shown to enhance productivity by better utilizing workers' skills (Reskin 1998). Kanter's (1983) study of innovation in organizations found that the most innovative companies deliberately establish heterogeneous work teams. Kanter notes that innovative organizations are more likely to have effectively combated racism, sexism, and classism within their ranks. They also are likely to employ more women and nonwhite men.

Nemeth (1986, cited in Cox 1993) indicates that racial/ethnic minority viewpoints stimulate consideration of previously unconsidered alternatives in work groups. In a related study, after holding ability levels constant, heterogeneous work groups were judged to be more creative than homogeneous groups (Triandis, Hall, and Ewen 1965, cited in Cox 1993). Other research (McLeod, Lobel, and Cox 1993) indicates that in a brainstorming exercise, racially diverse groups of Asians, blacks, whites, and Latinos generated ideas of the same quantity, but of higher quality, than did racially homogeneous groups.

Citing evidence of the "group think" phenomenon,[8] Cox's synthesis of research indicates that diverse groups are more likely to do a better job of problem solving than more homogeneous groups. Because homogeneous groups tend to be inordinately concerned with maintaining cohesiveness, they are more likely to be victims of this problem. On the basis of the research of

Nemeth (1985) and Nemeth and Wachter (1983), Cox (1993, 35) argues that because groups with minority members were more likely than homogeneous groups to generate higher levels of critical analysis in problem solving, "culturally diverse workforces have the potential to solve problems better because diverse groups (1) bring a greater variety of perspectives to bear on the issue, (2) have a higher level of critical analysis of alternatives, and (3) have a lower probability of group think."

The final organizational benefit of diversity identified by Cox (1993, 35) pertains to the flexibility of organizations that have more racially diverse members. Research suggests that "members of racial/ethnic minority groups tend to have especially flexible cognitive structures." Cox contends that the process of managing diversity is likely to enhance organizational flexibility, whereas organizations that are not supportive of diversity tend to be rigid and inflexible, as evidenced by narrow thinking and narrowly defined evaluation criteria.

In addition to detailing the many benefits that accrue for more diverse organizations, Cox identifies a set of problems that may result as organizations attempt to diversify themselves. For example, diversity can lead to lower levels of cohesiveness. Although cohesiveness has been shown to enhance morale and communication, there is no evidence that it enhances work performance. Diverse organizations also tend to communicate less effectively. As a result, members' anxieties may rise, conflict may increase, and members may feel less comfortable in the group (Cox 1993). Similarly, theory and research in race relations suggest that conflict increases as the presence of minorities increases in a given organizational context (Blalock 1967). Despite these "growing pains," Cox (1993, 39) asserts that the advantages of more diverse organizations far outweigh the disadvantages: "In certain respects, then, culturally diverse work groups are more difficult to manage effectively than culturally homogeneous work groups. In view of this, the challenge for organizations . . . is to manage in such a way as to maximize the potential benefits of diversity while minimizing the potential disadvantages."

The imperative of addressing diversity in the work place is underscored by the fact that the proportional representation of women and men of color continues to increase in the United States as well as the global workforce (Judy and D'Amico 1997; Cox 1993). In the United States, the representation of whites in the workforce is expected to decrease from 76 percent in 1995 to approximately 68 percent by 2020. Although Asian Americans show the greatest proportional growth in the population, Latinos show the greatest growth in terms of absolute numbers and will account for 36 percent of the total population increase between 1990 and 2020 (Judy and D'Amico 1997). These changes will be felt more dramatically in particular regions of the country. For example, in California, 42 percent of the population in 2020 will be Latino, 18 percent Asian, and 33 percent white (Judy and D'Amico 1997). If organizations are to successfully meet their human resource needs, they must hire and retain workers from diverse groups.

Consumer markets are likewise becoming more diverse. People of color currently represent more than $500 billion in consumer spending in the United States (Cox 1993). Because research indicates that sociocultural identity affects buying behavior, having a diverse organization can potentially help organizations sell their goods or services in an increasingly diverse marketplace. This occurs through the increased public relations value for businesses and organizations identified as managing diversity well. Moreover, a diverse workforce helps organizations identify the ways in which culture affects consumers' buying decisions. Finally, market research indicates that people of color are more likely to do business with individuals from their own cultural group (Cox 1993).

Research on the Impact of Affirmative Action in the Workplace

The views that individuals hold regarding the appropriateness of the use of affirmative action programs in higher education are clearly associated with their views about affirmative action in other domains, as suggested by Levin in Chapter 4. Another area in which the use of affirmative action has been widely contested is in the area of employment. Reskin (1998), in a recently completed review of the research literature about the impact of affirmative action programs in employment, indicates that affirmative action programs have increased the representation of minority men and women in the workforce. According to Reskin (1998, 93), "Although many Americans would prefer a labor market that never takes race or gender into account, as long as employers and employment practices routinely discriminate against minorities and women, the choice is not between meritocracy and affirmative action, it is between discrimination and affirmative action." Affirmative action in employment has led to greater access to professional, managerial, and craft occupations for minority men and women and has lessened wage discrimination (Reskin 1998). Carnoy (1994, cited in Reskin 1998) estimates that at least one-third of the earnings gains for African American and Latino workers during the 1960s can be attributed to declines in wage discrimination resulting from antidiscrimination legislation and affirmative action programs.

Reskin (1998) summarizes findings from a number of studies that compared outcomes for firms with and without affirmative action programs. These studies suggest that opportunities for white women and African American men were much greater at firms that practiced affirmative action than at firms that did not. Other studies indicate that employment discrimination is less likely to occur in firms and industries that actively promote affirmative action in employment. Research suggests that occupational segregation has steadily decreased over the past three decades: "By preventing discrimination, affirmative action has opened thousands of jobs to women and minorities that discrimination had formerly closed to them" (Reskin 1998, 54). Although the decline in occupational segregation has been accompanied by a decline in wage disparities, significant wage disparities between blacks and whites remain.

Affirmative action programs in employment help raise the career aspirations of minorities and women. In the same way that some people lower their aspirations if they perceive limited opportunities in a given field, research indicates they will pursue opportunities in fields they perceive as being open to them (Kanter 1977; Reskin and Hartmann 1986; Markham, Harlan, and Hackett 1987; Jacobs 1989; Cassirer and Reskin 1998, all cited in Reskin 1998). By reducing the perception that discriminatory barriers block access to certain lines of work, affirmative action curtails women and minorities from self-selecting for certain jobs and/or promotions (Reskin and Roos 1990, cited in Reskin 1998).

Opponents of affirmative action allege that beneficiaries of these programs engage in a process of self-doubt about their abilities and qualifications for the jobs they receive (Steele 1990, cited in Reskin 1998). However, research suggests that stigmatization by others poses much greater risk than self-stigmatization. Employers can greatly reduce the risk of stigmatization by providing accurate information about their affirmative action programs (Reskin 1998).

Much of the resistance to affirmative action programs comes from those who perceive that they are at risk of being penalized. One of the most frequent criticisms of affirmative action is that it involves "reverse discrimination." Research suggests that "reverse discrimination is rare both in absolute terms and relative to conventional wisdom" (Reskin 1998, 72). For example, Steeh and Krysan (1996, cited in Reskin 1998) found that only 5 to 12 percent of whites indicated that they felt their race had cost them a job or promotion, compared with more than one-third of African Americans. However, such findings seem to conflict with popular views about the prevalence of "reverse discrimination." Between 66 and 80 percent of whites (compared with about 25 percent of African Americans) surveyed during the 1990s reported that they thought African Americans with lesser qualifications had been given jobs or promotions over "more qualified" whites (Taylor 1994; Davis and Smith 1994; Steeh and Krysan 1996, cited in Reskin 1998).

Data from the Equal Employment Opportunity Commission (EEOC) indicate exceptionally low proportions of reverse discrimination charges in employment. Only 4 percent of the discrimination claims filed with the EEOC between 1987 and 1994 charged reverse discrimination (Norton 1996, cited in Reskin 1998). Of the cases that actually made it to court between 1990 and 1994, only 2 percent charged reverse discrimination (U.S. Department of Labor, Employment Standards Administration, cited in Reskin 1998). "Finally," Reskin (1998, 73) reported, "allegations of reverse discrimination are less likely than conventional discrimination cases to be supported by evidence."

Summary

Leaders in the private sector indicate that colleges and universities are not providing graduates with skills that are essential to their ability to achieve success in increasingly diverse and competitive global and domestic economies. These business leaders are calling on leaders in higher education to better utilize the racial and ethnic diversity on their campuses to provide students with opportunities to develop cross-cultural competency, a critical human resource need that business leaders have identified as lacking in entering workers.

Research on the organizational impact of diversity suggests that when it is managed correctly, diversity benefits organizations by helping attract the best available talent, enhancing marketing efforts, increasing creativity and innovation, improving problem-solving abilities, and improving organizational flexibility. Research indicates that affirmative action in employment has led to decreased job discrimination, decreased wage disparities, decreased occupational segregation, increased occupational aspirations for women and people of color, and greater organizational productivity. There is little empirical evidence that supports the view that those who benefit from affirmative action suffer from self-stigmatization. Finally, evidence supporting charges of reverse discrimination is "rare both in absolute terms and relative to conventional wisdom" (Reskin 1998, 72).

Societal Benefits

The earlier sections of this chapter discuss evidence of the ways diversity benefits students, higher education institutions, and businesses and the economy. One final category of outcomes remains to be discussed. These outcomes focus on the ways in which higher education prepares students to function effectively as citizens of an increasingly diverse society. This section describes the ways in which participation by diverse students in higher education helps meet some of the basic needs of those in society who are most underserved.

Democracy Outcomes

Democracy outcomes refers to the ways in which higher education prepares students to become involved as active participants in an increasingly diverse and complex society. Gurin (1999) suggests that three major categories—citizenship engagement, racial/cultural engagement, and compatibility of differences—characterize democracy outcomes. *Citizenship engagement* refers to students' interest in and motivation to influence society and the political structure as well as to students' participation in community and volunteer service. *Racial/cultural engagement* refers to students' levels of cultural awareness and appreciation and their commitment to participating in activities that promote racial understanding. *Compatibility of differences* refers to an understanding by students that there are common values across racial/ethnic groups, that group conflict can be constructive when it is handled appropriately, and that differences do not have to be a divisive force in society. Another type of democracy outcome discussed by Gurin relates to students' ability to live and work effectively in a diverse society. Specifically, this refers to the extent to which college prepares students to succeed after college and the extent to which students' college experience breaks a pattern of continuing segregation in society.

The research supports the view that students' interaction with diverse people and ideas while in college has a positive impact on the student. The extent to which students interacted cross-racially is influential in determining the amount of acceptance students report for people from other cultures, the rate at which they participate in community service programs, and the amount of growth they exhibit in other areas of civic responsibility (Bowen and Bok 1998). Similarly, involvement in more racially diverse environments and activities leads to higher levels of cultural awareness and acceptance and increased commitment to the goal of improving racial understanding (Milem 1992, 1994; Sax and Astin 1997). Conversely, the absence of interracial contact adversely influences students' views toward others, students' support for campus initiatives, and educational outcomes. White students who had the least social interaction with individuals of a different background were less likely to express positive attitudes about multiculturalism on campus (Globetti et al. 1993).

Research on School Desegregation

Many studies of desegregation have found that the segregation of minorities that occurs in educational settings tends to be perpetuated over stages of the life cycle and across institutional settings (Braddock 1985). Most of the research pertaining to the effects of desegregation has been done in K-12 rather than in institutions of higher education. Hence, this section on the impact of school desegregation is included here.

Braddock, Crain, and McPartland (1984, 261) affirm that "school desegregation is leading to desegregation in several areas of adult life," including college, social situations, and jobs. Their analyses indicate that desegregation changes the attitudes and behaviors of whites and blacks. This is apparent in diminishing racial stereotypes and lessened fears of hostile reactions in interracial settings among white adults who were educated in desegregated settings as children.

Braddock (1985, 11) asserts that "one of the most important aspects of racial segregation is its tendency to perpetuate itself." This is true for both majority and minority individuals. For example, research suggests that segregation in elementary and secondary schools is perpetuated in college. Braddock (1980) and Braddock and McPartland (1982) found that black students who had attended desegregated elementary and secondary schools were more likely to attend desegregated colleges. Early school and community desegregation tends to promote adult desegregation in work environments (Braddock and McPartland 1989). This is especially true for blacks living in the northern United States, where the relationship between school and community desegregation has been less confounded. Braddock, McPartland, and Trent (1984) found that blacks and whites who had attended desegregated schools were more likely to work in desegregated firms than were their peers who had attended segregated schools. In an extension of this earlier work, Braddock, Dawkins, and Trent (1994) found that whites who attended desegregated schools were more likely to work with blacks or Latinos. Moreover, black and Latino students who attended desegregated schools were more likely to work in environments in which they had white co-workers.

In related findings, Braddock and Dawkins (1981) found that students, particularly blacks who attended desegregated high schools, were more likely than students who attended segregated high schools to receive better grades in college. Another study demonstrates a greater likelihood of persistence in college among those blacks who attended desegregated high schools (Green 1982). Despite these findings on the positive impact of desegregation, segregation at the high school level is actually increasing (Orfield and Eaton 1996). Thus, college may be the first (and only) place at which many students encounter and interact with someone of a different race or ethnicity (Hurtado et al. 1998, 1999). Opportunities to interact with diverse peers in college can help disrupt the perpetuation of segregation in our society, because research indicates that high levels of engagement with diversity in college lead to engagement with diversity after college (Gurin 1999). According to Gurin,

> Diversity experiences during college had impressive effects on the extent to which graduates in the national study were living racially and ethnically integrated lives in the post-college world. Students who had taken the most diversity courses and interacted the most with diverse peers during college had the most cross-racial interactions five years after leaving college. This confirms that the long-term pattern of segregation noted by many social scientists can be broken by diversity experiences during college. (Gurin 1999, 133)

Civic and Professional Involvement

Bowen and Bok (1998) argue that one of the central goals of institutions of higher education is to educate students to become good citizens. Many colleges and universities select students with the expectation that they will give something back to society through their involvement in professional, social, and civic organizations. In recent years, institutions have extended their belief in the value of this mission to the need to diversify their student bodies. These institutions understand the obligation they have to educate and to develop an expanded pool of "black and Hispanic men and women who could assume leadership roles in their communities and in every facet of national life" (Bowen and Bok 1998, 156). As our society becomes increasingly diverse, the need for leaders who represent the needs, interests, and perspectives of diverse communities is increasing dramatically.

Studies of student involvement in community and civic service suggest that students of color who are educated at selective institutions are much more likely than their white peers to "give back" to society once they graduate. In their study of black and white students who attended institutions with selective admissions policies, Bowen and Bok (1998) found that black students who attended these institutions were likely to be widely involved in civic and community activities. The study analyzed data representing the experiences of two cohorts of students. Data pertaining to the earlier cohort of students (1976) indicated that black students were more likely than their white peers to be involved in community and civic organizations. Moreover, black men were much more likely than white men to be involved in leadership positions in organizations with a civic focus. This was especially true in organizations focusing on social service, youth, and school-related activities. Black women were more likely than white women to report that they held leadership positions "in community, social service, alumni/ae, religious, and professional groups" (160). Finally, black students were more likely than white students to report that they held positions of leadership in multiple civic and community organizations.

Data from this study also indicate an indirect relationship between attending the most selective institutions and holding leadership positions in community and social service organizations. Black students who attended the most selective institutions were more likely to hold leadership positions. This is explained largely by the fact that these students were more likely to have obtained advanced degrees than peers who attended less selective institutions.

Moreover, black students who obtained advanced degrees were more likely than their white peers to be involved in community and social service organizations. This is true for lawyers (21 percent involvement by blacks compared with 15 percent by whites), physicians (18 percent for blacks compared with 9 percent for whites), and most dramatically for Ph.D.'s (33 percent for blacks compared with only 6 percent for whites). According to Bowen and Bok (1998, 192), "The black alumni/ae of these schools have already demonstrated a marked tendency to 'give something back' through participation and leadership outside the workplace as well as within it. This civic spirit, revealed through actions taken rather than good intentions expressed, and demonstrated over time through volunteering in schools, neighborhoods, museums, and civic associations of every kind, is surely one important indicator of 'merit.'"

Benefits Accruing from Diversification of the Medical Profession

According to Nickens, Ready, and Petersdorf (1994, 472), "Producing a physician work force that reflects this country's rich diversity is important not only for reasons of social equity, but also to ensure the delivery of health care that is competent both technically and culturally." The health care crisis faced by residents of low-income communities, and specifically low-income communities of color, is striking. This crisis is largely the result of insufficient access to health care providers by people in these communities. The national average for physician-to-population service ratio is one physician for every 387 people. However, more than 2,700 areas in our country have been identified as having a shortage of health professional coverage. In these areas, the average is one physician for every 3,500 people or more (Health Resources and Services Administration 1995). Approximately one person in five in our country lives in an area designated as having insufficient health care coverage. These areas are found in rural and urban settings across the United States. In low-income neighborhoods in Chicago, Los Angeles, Houston, and New York, the physician-to-population ratio can be as extreme as one physician for every 10,000 to 15,000 people. When the physician-to-population ratios in underserved communities are contrasted with those ratios in affluent communities, the differences are staggering. Although low-income people of color in Los Angeles face a physician-to-population ratio of between 1:10,000 to 1:15,000, residents of Beverly Hills, California, enjoy a physician-to-population ratio of 1:25 or 1:30, that is, one physician for every 25 or 30 people (Komaromy et al. 1997).

Living in poverty dramatically increases the likelihood a person will live in an area that has insufficient health care coverage. In 1995, 11.2 percent of whites in our society lived at or below the poverty level. The figures for blacks and Hispanics (U.S. Bureau of the Census 1998) were dramatically higher.[9] Census data indicate that nearly one in three blacks (29.3 percent) and Hispanics (30.3 percent) lived in poverty in 1995. We see even greater disparities when we examine the poverty rate for children who were born in 1995: 41.5 percent of black children and 39.3 percent of Hispanic children were born into families at or below poverty level, whereas 15.5 percent of white children were born into similar economic circumstances.

Statistics reported by the Census Bureau (1998) tell us something about the consequences of this crisis, particularly its effects on people of color in our country. These data reveal that the infant mortality rate for black children in our country remains significantly higher than that for white children. In 1995, for every 1,000 births that occurred, 16.22 black male babies and 13.74 black female babies died before they reached the age of one year. Conversely, only 6.98 white male babies and 5.55 white female babies faced a similar fate. Moreover, white children can expect to live significantly longer lives than do black children. The life expectancy for white men in 1995 was 73.4 years as compared with 65.2 years for black men. For white women, the life expectancy was 79.6 years as compared with 73.9 years for black women (U.S. Bureau of the Census 1998).

To address these and other concerns, the Association of American Medical Colleges (AAMC) launched its Project 3000 by 2000 program in the early 1990s. In an effort to meet the health care needs of the most underserved populations in our society, this program had a central goal of doubling the enrollment of underrepresented minority physicians by the year 2000 (Nickens, Ready, and Petersdorf 1994). The AAMC recognized that training more physicians of color is a critical first step in addressing the health care needs of low-income communities, particularly those of color. This belief is based on a number of studies that target the medical profession.

The medical community has conducted extensive research that establishes the societal value of racial and ethnic minority participation in the medical profession (the findings of these studies are summarized in Table 5.2). Key among these findings is the discovery that physicians of color are more likely than white physicians to provide care for underserved populations. Keith et al. (1985) have been cited widely as the first scholars to provide empirical evidence that minority physicians were significantly more likely than their white counterparts to provide health care to populations in our society that need it most. This was reflected in the type of medicine as well as in the geographic area in which minority doctors practiced. Nearly one-third more minority doctors than nonminority ones (55 percent and 41 percent, respectively) chose primary care specialties. Moreover, physicians of color were twice as likely as nonminority physicians (12 percent vs. 6 percent) to practice in areas that had been designated by the federal government as health-manpower shortage areas. This was true for all of the medical subspecialties included in the sample (not just primary care physicians). Finally, minority graduates were more likely than nonminority graduates to have Medicaid recipients as patients (31 percent for blacks, 24 percent for Latinos, and 14 percent for whites). Therefore, the authors argue, "by increasing the number of minority physicians, affirmative action programs have substantially improved access to care among minority populations" (Keith et al. 1985, 1523).

Recently, Komaromy et al. (1997) used data from the AMA master file to build on the findings of Keith et al. (1985) in their study of the practice patterns of physicians in California. Urban areas of poverty with high proportions of black and Latino residents had the worst physician-to-population ratios; poor urban areas with low proportions of black and Latino residents had nearly three times as many primary care physicians. The salience of race to health care availability is further evidenced by the fact that communities with high proportions of black or Latino residents were four times as likely as others to experience a shortage of physicians, regardless of level of community income (Komaromy et al. 1997).

Latino and black physicians were more likely to locate their practices in areas with the greatest need for primary care doctors; they also tended to locate their practices in poorer areas than white physicians did. Black physicians practiced medicine in areas in which the mean percentage of black residents was five times greater than in areas in which other physicians practiced. Black

TABLE 5.2

Findings from Studies of Practice Patterns of Minority Physicians

Study	Controls for Socioeconomic Status	Controls for Participation in Service-Related Financial Aid Programs	Primary Care Specialties	Service to Minority Populations	Service to Medicaid Patients	Service to Uninsured Patients	Service to Patients Reporting More Health Problems
Keith et al. (1985)			X	X	X		
Association of American Medical Colleges (1994)				X	X	X	
Moy and Bartman (1995)	X			X	X	X	X
Komaromy et al. (1997)			X	X	X	X	
Cantor et al. (1996)	X			X	X	X	
Xu et al. (1997)	X	X		X	X	X	

SOURCE: (X) indicates that these considerations/findings were evident in this study.

physicians cared for six times as many black patients as did other physicians. Similarly, Latino physicians practiced in areas with significantly more Latinos. Latino physicians cared for three times as many Latinos as did other physicians. These findings held in multivariate analyses even after controlling for the fact that greater proportions of people from these groups lived in the areas in which these physicians practiced. Black physicians were most likely to care for patients insured by Medicaid (45 percent of their patients, compared with 18 percent of white physicians' patients, 24 percent of Latino physicians' patients, and 30 percent of Asian physicians' patients). Latino physicians were more likely to provide care to patients without insurance (9 percent compared with 3 percent for black physicians, 4 percent for Asian physicians, and 6 percent for white physicians). These findings, according to Komaromy et al. (1997), suggest that black and Latino physicians play an essential role in providing health care for poor people and members of minority groups.

Other recent studies report similar findings. Cantor et al. (1996) found that minority and women physicians were much more likely than nonminority male physicians to serve minority, poor, and Medicaid recipients. Moreover, although the relationship between the physicians' socioeconomic background and tendency to serve these populations was weak, race and sex were the variables that most strongly and consistently predicted physicians' decisions to practice in these areas. Xu et al. (1997) report similar findings in a study that controlled for the effects of gender, family income, residence, and National Health Services financial aid obligations on practice patterns. Analyses of national data from the AAMC show that 40 percent of medical school graduates who were members of underrepresented minorities (blacks, Mexican Americans, mainland Puerto Ricans, and American Indians) indicated that they planned to practice medicine in underserved areas; less than one in ten (9 percent) of other medical school graduates expressed a similar desire. Nearly six in ten (60 percent) of medical generalists from underrepresented groups reported that they planned to practice in these areas, compared with just 24 percent of nonminority medical generalists. Moy and Bartman's (1995) study of physician practice patterns reported similar findings based on data gathered from a nationally representative sample of patients.

Each of these studies illustrates the important role that physicians of color play in addressing the health care needs of the most medically underserved communities in our nation. Physicians of color are significantly more likely to pursue medical specialties that address the needs of medically underserved people and to locate their practices in areas convenient to the medically underserved. Moreover, the salience of race in predicting service to these communities holds even after controlling for the effects of socioeconomic status, gender, and National Health Service financial obligations.

Changes to affirmative action policy in California and similar threats in other states present serious obstacles to increasing the representation of people of color in the medical profession. Despite efforts by members of the medical community to diversify the nation's medical schools, the number of applicants from underrepresented minority groups decreased 7 percent this year. The AAMC reported that the number of applicants from underrepresented racial/ethnic groups fell to its lowest point since 1992. The decrease was most evident among black male applicants, a steep drop of 15 percent. Through its Project 3000 by 2000, AAMC had hoped to have three thousand minority students enrolled in first-year medical classes by the year 2000. However, this goal was impossible for AAMC to reach; minority student enrollment in medical school in 1999—1,731 students—fell well below the goal (*Chronicle of Higher Education* 1999). One consequence of these attacks on affirmative action is that they further imperil the health and well-being of members of our society who live in medically underserved communities.

Summary

Research evidence clearly indicates that greater exposure to racial and ethnic diversity in college leads to growth in democracy outcomes. Students who have been exposed to greater diversity are more likely to demonstrate increases in racial understanding, cultural awareness and appreciation, engagement with social and political issues, and openness to diversity and challenge. They are more likely to exhibit decreases in racial stereotyping and ethnocentrism. Moreover, greater engagement with diversity while in college leads to growth in civic responsibility. This is evident in increased commitment to the goal of promoting racial understanding, greater involvement in community and volunteer service, and higher levels of involvement in community action programs. All of these outcomes are intimately related to what it means to be a productive citizen in an increasingly diverse, democratic society.

Research also indicates that interacting with diversity while in college disrupts the cycle of segregation that prevails in our society. Students who attend institutions with higher levels of diversity and report high levels of interaction with diverse people and information are more likely to live and work in desegregated environments after leaving college. Interacting with diverse ideas and people while in college encourages students to continue these behaviors throughout their lifetimes. Gurin's (1999) findings suggest that this is particularly true for whites. Interacting with diverse people is particularly significant here because college is likely to be the first time most students will have the opportunity to be educated and to live in a racially diverse setting.

Research suggests that students of color benefit our society through their high levels of service to community and civic groups as well as medically underserved populations. Bowen and Bok (1998) found that African American students were much more likely than white students to be involved in community and civic organizations as well as in the leadership of these organizations. Studies of physicians' practice patterns indicate that doctors of color are more likely to practice medicine in areas with populations that have the greatest need for health services. These areas include low-income urban and rural locations, locations with high populations of people of color, populations that rely on Medicare for their health insurance, and populations that do not have any health insurance.

Organizational Forces That May Make Diversity Difficult to Institutionalize

In her book summarizing the impact of affirmative action in employment, Reskin (1998) indicates that much of the race and sex discrimination that exists in the workplace is a function of the business practices of firms in which such discrimination takes place.[10] To illustrate this concept, Reskin offers two examples of factors that contribute to employment discrimination. The first occurs when employers rely heavily on informal networks to recruit their employees. The second occurs when firms require job credentials that are not necessary to perform a job effectively. Reskin (1998, 35) suggests that "structural discrimination persists because, once in place, discriminatory practices in bureaucratic organizations are hard to change." Reskin argues that bureaucratic organizations develop an inertia that tends to preserve these practices unless the organization is faced with genuine pressures to change itself.

Reskin's observations about the role of organizational inertia in the business sector suggest that similar forces may exist in colleges and universities. This is particularly true when we consider that colleges and universities, like many private businesses and firms, are highly bureaucratic organizations. Hence, we must critically examine the things that colleges and universities do as organizations that impede their efforts to successfully incorporate diversity as a central part of their institutional mission.

Although the American higher education system is large, diverse, complex, and decentralized, at the same time it is remarkably homogeneous (Astin 1985). This homogeneity can be seen in comparable approaches to undergraduate curriculum, remarkable conformity in the training and preparation of faculty, and similar administrative structures. Most educators view the higher education system from an institutional perspective as opposed to a systems perspective. This tendency toward an institutional perspective often leads to the implementation of policies and practices that weaken the system as a whole (Astin 1985).

Astin (1985 and 1991) argues that there is a tendency among institutions of higher education to place too heavy an emphasis on accumulating resources and enhancing their reputations. Astin asserts that excellence in American higher education has been traditionally equated with the academic reputation of an institution and/or with the resources it accumulates. In this traditional view of excellence, resources are measured by money, faculty, research productivity, and highly able students. Astin suggests that this traditional view of excellence results from the hierarchical nature of the higher education system.

A related perspective on these processes can be found in the concept of institutional isomorphism, first introduced by David Riesman (1956), also known as "institutional homogenization" or "institutional imitation" (Jencks and Riesman 1968; Pace 1974; DiMaggio and Powell 1983; Astin 1985; Levinson 1989; Hackett 1990; Scott 1995). In a discussion of the problem of institutional homogenization, Riesman (1956, 25) observed that "There is no doubt that colleges and universities in this country model themselves upon each other. . . . All one has to do is read catalogues to realize the extent of this isomorphism." He depicted the higher education system as being an "academic procession," which he described as a snake-like entity whose most prestigious institutions are at the head of the snake, followed by the middle group, with the least prestigious schools forming the tail. The most elite institutions carefully watch each other as they jockey for position in the hierarchy. In the meantime, schools in the middle are busy trying to catch up with the head of the snake by imitating the high-prestige institutions. As a result, schools in the middle of the procession begin to look more like the top institutions, while the institutions in the tail pursue the middle-range schools. Ultimately, institutional forms become less distinctive, relatively little real change occurs in the hierarchy, and the system of higher education struggles to move forward. Jencks and Riesman (1968) suggest that strong economic and professional pressures drive isomorphism in higher education, and they conclude that homogenization occurs faster than differentiation.

Astin (1985) contends that these forces have led to the development of a highly refined status hierarchy in higher education comprised of a few well-known institutions at the top, a bigger group of institutions with more modest reputations in the middle, and the biggest group consisting of institutions at the bottom of the hierarchy that remain virtually unknown outside of their geographic region. Conformity, Astin and others (Bowen 1977; Riesman 1956) argue, is the most pervasive consequence of this status hierarchy. Another consequence of the institutional hierarchy is that it tends to create a great deal of competition among institutions for resources "and for a higher place in the hierarchy as revealed in reputational surveys" (Astin 1985, 12). Research indicates that the single best predictor of an institution's place in the hierarchy of institutions is its selectivity (or average score of the entering freshman class on the SAT) (Astin and Henson 1977). When this thinking becomes pervasive, it is easy to see why there are strong incentives for institutions to view their students as a resource that can be used to enhance an institution's reputation.

When students are viewed as this sort of educational resource, and not as the focus of the educational enterprise, there is immense pressure to make institutional admissions policies more selective. Decisions to seek applicants with higher standardized test scores are not made for any compelling pedagogical or educational reasons. Rather, on the basis of this traditional view of excellence, institutional leaders believe that higher standardized test scores bolster the institution's reputation, which in turn, will cause more students to want to apply to the institution (Astin 1985). Faculty and administrators come to view selective admissions policies as essential to maintaining academic excellence or standards. Hence, institutions and institutional excellence come to be defined more by the "quality" of the people they admit and less by the educational experiences of students attending the institution (Astin 1985). This extremely limited definition of quality does not serve colleges and universities or any of their constituencies well.

This narrow view of educational excellence puts pressure on institutional leaders to place inordinate significance on standardized tests in the admissions process. When standardized test scores are used by institutional leaders as a way of enhancing their institution's reputation (i.e., "the average SAT score of our entering class is . . . "), test scores are clearly being used in a way that they were not intended. Using test scores in this manner reinforces in the minds of constituents that test scores are the primary, or even the only, indicator of merit or quality. This view of merit is clearly antithetical to the definition of merit that has been articulated by influential educational leaders and organizations across the country.

The Importance of Thoughtful Institutional Responses to Diversity

Although this chapter has cited research from a variety of sources that provide evidence of the many benefits resulting from diversity on college campuses, the focus of this discussion has not been on the importance of the institutional context(s) in which these benefits have been accrued. Having a diverse campus in and of itself does not guarantee that the educational benefits summarized in this chapter will accrue to students, to the institution, or to society. Liu (1998, 438) contends that "often neglected in the debate about diversity is the fact that achieving a racially diverse student body *by itself* is not sufficient to bring about desired educational outcomes. How that diversity is managed matters greatly." He further argues that "it is a mistake to understand the diversity rationale only as an issue concerning admissions rather than as an issue implicating broader institutional policy. . . . Thus, to establish a 'compelling interest' in educational diversity, a university must demonstrate clear, consistent internal policies and practices designed to facilitate interracial contact, dialogue, and understanding on campus" (439).

Work by Hurtado et al. (1998, 1999) documents the importance of the institutional context in shaping student outcomes and provides a framework for conceptualizing and understanding the impact of various dimensions of the campus racial climate. This framework was first introduced in a study of the climate for Latino students (Hurtado 1994b) and further developed in syntheses of research completed for policy makers and practitioners (Hurtado et al. 1998, 1999). According to Hurtado et al. (1998),

> Probably few areas of higher education and campus life in the recent past have had more attention paid to the policy dimension than has the issue of race on campus. Evidence of this can be found in policies and programs related to college admissions, financial aid, affirmative action, discrimination and harassment, and desegregation. Yet, at the same time, probably no area of campus life has been so devoid of policy initiatives than has the campus racial climate at individual institutions.

When considering the climate for diversity on campus, Hurtado et al. (1998, 1999) argue that most institutions usually focus on only one element of the climate, the goal of increasing the numbers of racial/ethnic students on campus. Although this is an essential goal that institutions must achieve, it cannot be the only goal. Other elements of the climate require attention and constitute key areas for focusing diversity efforts.

Hurtado et al. (1998, 1999) argue that central to the conceptualization of a campus climate for diversity is the notion that students are educated in distinct racial contexts. Both external and internal (institutional) forces shape these contexts in higher education. The external components of climate are comprised of two domains representing the impact of *governmental policy, programs, and initiatives* as well as the impact of *sociohistorical forces* on campus racial climate. The *institutional context* contains multiple dimensions that are a function of educational programs and practices. These include an institution's *historical legacy of inclusion or exclusion* of various racial/ethnic groups, its *structural diversity* in terms of the numerical and proportional representation of various racial/ethnic groups, the *psychological climate* that includes perceptions and attitudes between and among groups, as well as a *behavioral climate* dimension that is characterized by the nature of intergroup relations on campus.

Hurtado et al. (1998, 1999) conceptualize the institutional climate as a product of these dimensions. These dimensions are not discrete; rather, they are connected to each other. For example, a historical vestige of segregation has an impact on an institution's ability to improve its racial/ethnic student enrollments, and the underrepresentation of specific groups contributes to stereotypical attitudes among individuals within the learning and work environment that affect the psychological and behavioral climate. In short, although some institutions take a "multilayered" approach toward assessing diversity on their campuses and are developing programs to address the climate on campus, most institutions fail to recognize the importance of the dynamics of these interrelated elements of the climate.

Specifically, Hurtado et al. (1998, 1999) assert that many institutions pay attention only to increasing the structural diversity of their institution. When this happens, the outcomes of increased diversity are not necessarily positive. Race relations theory tells us that as the representation of minorities increases, the likelihood of conflict also increases. By paying attention to all aspects of the campus racial climate, colleges and universities are able to use this conflict in ways that are purposeful and to create positive educational experiences for students. The framework of Hurtado et al., and the many studies they cite to illustrate it, indicates that institutional leaders must make thoughtful and deliberate decisions about how diversity adds to the educational mission of their institution. Although Gurin (1999) argues correctly that structural diversity is necessary for other types of diversity to occur (diversity of ideas and information and diversity of interactions), increasing structural diversity alone is not sufficient for the benefits of diversity to transpire.

Actualizing the value-added educational benefits associated with diversity requires active engagement in institutional transformation (Chang 1999b; Smith 1995a; Smith et al. 1997).

When diversity is conceptualized and engaged as a transformative enterprise effecting change in multiple levels of the campus environment, colleges and universities maximize a broad spectrum of learning outcomes that, for the most part, cannot be achieved without racial diversity (Chang 1999b).

The transformation that occurs as institutions become more diverse goes to the heart of the educational enterprise in terms of what is to be taught, who is to teach it, and how it is to be taught (Garcia and Smith 1996). Those who view diversity as part of a transformative process hold the core belief that higher education should be held accountable to basic democratic ideals that require that it be more equitable and inclusive. Diversity initiatives are transformational in nature because they challenge "traditional assumptions about learning, but also other forms of privilege associated with learning" (Chang

1999b, 7). Chang argues that the transformative nature of diversity should be acknowledged when considering empirical evidence on diversity outcomes: "This is particularly important because widespread educational benefits associated with racial diversity emerge . . . out of institutional transformation and not out of pre-existing institutional functions and practices" (Chang 1999b, 8–9). In short, it is becoming increasingly apparent that only when the necessary conditions are in place can colleges and universities fulfill their mission to serve the "compelling interests" of the individual, the institution, the private sector, and the society.

Chapter Six

AFFIRMATIVE ACTION PRACTICES
IN A BROADER CONTEXT

Mitchell J. Chang, Daria Witt, and Kenji Hakuta

Although our nation has made significant strides in closing the racial gap in access to opportunity, we have not yet resolved what W. E. B. Du Bois in 1899 called the problem of the color line. It is becoming increasingly clear that there is no one solution. The issue of race and the struggle over equality invariably change over time. The changes coincide with our nation's economic, social, demographic, and political shifts. In the 1960s, for example, racism and inequality existed in blatant forms, and steps that could be taken to abolish them were clear. Although there was great disagreement over the pace at which reforms should take place and some disagreement over whether reforms should even take place, the goals of the civil rights activists were generally viewed as moral, justifiable, and unambiguous. Now that the most blatant forms of racism have been eradicated, civil rights activists target such issues as "aversive racism" and other forms of discrimination that are less tangible than legally enforced separate schools and separate bus seats. Perhaps because the more recent targets are less clear-cut, Americans have not been nearly as supportive of the civil rights agenda as they were in the sixties. Likewise, the education community has not been as successful in recent years in making the case for race-sensitive remedies, particularly the case for why such policies are good for white students. Accordingly, many have concluded that because the laws have been changed to be fair and to root out blatant forms of discrimination, equal access and equal participation are now commonplace. The evidence presented in this book, however, leads to a very different conclusion.

By addressing the many facets of racial dynamics in higher education, we have tried to reveal the complexity of the issues and their relevance to those court cases that challenge race-conscious college admissions policies. We want to expand the diversity debate beyond the benefits underrepresented students bring to a college campus or to the education of all students on that campus—a concern receiving much legal interest. We want to include in the debate, but not restrict it to, establishing distributive justice and compensating groups that have suffered discrimination in the past. Those issues are certainly very important and must be addressed adequately with or without affirmative action. We believe that the debate about diversity in higher education should also include a rich discussion about expanding the mission of higher education and transforming universities not only to provide the best education possible to *all* students but also to actively engage in fulfilling the broader democratic goals of our nation. These goals include, but are not limited to, expanding democratic participation in a way that truly embraces the spirit of *E Pluribus Unum*—out of many, one.

Failure to frame current higher education affirmative action practices in a broader context may well perpetuate and reinforce certain pernicious myths about the reality of racism in this country (that it has ended), about the campus climate (that universities are now inclusive), about the potential for underrepresented minorities to succeed (that they are inherently inferior), and about what constitutes merit (that it is best measured by test scores). The evidence presented in this book addresses these myths.

In Chapter 2, William Trent and associates show that a number of factors conspire to place African American and Latino/a students at risk of academic failure in the early stages of their educational experience. Thus Trent et al. stress the need to "level the playing field" by paying greater attention to schools that serve underprivileged students. In evaluating the "merit" of prospective applicants, they suggest that admissions committees look closely at the circumstances under which each student has been educated and the extent to which adequate opportunities have been provided. Moreover, admissions committees need to understand that race cuts across class and that a middle-class black student usually has not had the same opportunities as a middle-class white student, and a poor black student usually has not had the same opportunities as a poor white student. Trent et al. show that the likelihood of experiencing poverty, living in a single-female-headed household, residing in an urban area, and attending an urban school, for example, differs significantly by race. In addition, many minority parents with college degrees attended segregated, inferior schools, whereas most white parents with college degrees attended more challenging, academically superior schools (Miller 1999) that enhanced the cultural capital these parents can pass along to their children to assist in the children's academic success. Because tracking was even more common two decades ago than it is now, few minority parents have had the benefit of college preparatory programs, and few have attended selective colleges (Miller 1999). Indeed, the majority of African Americans enrolled in higher education are typically first-generation college students (Mickelson and Oliver 1991; Allen 1992). Because the playing field is not level, admissions committees ought to have the flexibility to broaden their definition of merit, enabling them to evaluate applicants on the basis of a sense of history and to consider the cumulative disadvantages that so many minority students have had to overcome.

Chapter 3 by Linda F. Wightman points to the need for a more precise but simultaneously broader definition of merit. When universities judge applicants solely on the basis of test scores and grade point average (GPA), they not only overlook many applicants (of all races and ethnicities) who would contribute greatly to the academic, intellectual, and social life of the university, but they also set themselves up for much greater scrutiny of their affirmative action policies. If admission were based exclusively on GPA and test scores (as it was at the University of Texas before the *Hopwood* decision), the only way a university could admit a substantial number of non-Asian students of color would be to have a two-tiered standard of admission, which heightens scrutiny over "merit." For Wightman, the larger issue is not whether institutions should abandon traditional indicators of merit; rather, for her the issue is that if admission practices are limited to considering only high school GPAs and test scores, then universities seemingly ignore the multifaceted nature of academic success. That earning a college degree requires more than just good test scores and previous academic achievement is well substantiated and well known to educators and admissions officers (Olivas 1992). Given current technological sophistication and the many widely recognized alternate measures of merit, colleges and universities should be able to establish a more comprehensive rubric that allows for greater precision of both objective and subjective indicators of merit for admissions purposes. Such a rubric that moves beyond the overemphasis on GPA and test scores would help to establish a more just admissions process and also facilitate public explanations of how admissions decisions are made.

Chapter 4 by Shana Levin documents the ways in which race is a major social psychological factor that structures American consciousness and social behaviors, often to the detriment of minority groups. Levin shows that the persistence of racism and discrimination in this country points to the need for universities to take race into account in their admissions decisions, not only because applicants of color have suffered racial injustices throughout their lives, but also because race pervades judgments of merit in subtle yet consistent ways that might work against minority students. Thus, she concludes, individual merit and group membership must both be considered when making admissions decisions. Chapter 4 also has implications for how best to embrace and foster diversity in institutions of higher education. One such implication is that ethnic identities need to be acknowledged and allowed to flourish, which, contrary to popular belief, enables underrepresented students to engage with, rather than disengage from, the broader campus community. Universities also need to work on establishing superordinate identities for students (e.g., sports teams, a feeling of membership in the university community) to facilitate interaction outside of racial and ethnic groups and to develop a greater sense of belonging for all students.

In Chapter 5, Jeffrey F. Milem's documentation of the rich variety of benefits that diversity brings to the individual, the institution, and society highlights the importance of maximizing the full spectrum of diversity on college campuses. Milem shows that the effective institutional strategies extend far beyond admitting a diverse student population. Indeed, the evidence Milem presents shows that structural diversity is not enough to bring about the many benefits of diversity. Universities must also foster environments in which students and faculty feel comfortable exploring and sharing different viewpoints and learning from one another. Ultimately, institutions should undergo a more fundamental transformation to reflect the changing population of their students and faculty, integrating all dimensions of diversity, including but not limited to student, faculty, and administrative composition, a more inclusive curriculum, and structured and continuing dialogue across racial and ethnic lines.

In addition to improving the intellectual life for all students and faculty, integrating the multiple dimensions of diversity, according to Milem, will help break down stereotypes, prevent the phenomenon of self-segregation or balkanization among different racial and ethnic groups, and produce a society beyond the university walls that is more integrated, understanding, and engaged in civic life.

Taken together, the chapters in this book make a concerted argument based on social science evidence that (1) racism in this country has yet to be eradicated; (2) campuses can still do much more to include underrepresented students and to maximize the educational benefits associated with having a diverse student body; (3) students' ability to compete academically for college admissions is highly influenced by multiple social forces that generally affect racial groups differently; and (4) merit cannot be measured by test scores alone. Given these conclusions, we believe that race-sensitive admissions practices still serve compelling interests for individual states and the nation as a whole. Regardless of what the future of such practices might be, which invariably will be decided by either the courts or the public, the issues identified here will not likely disappear even after hard decisions have been made.

At the level of college admissions, debates about merit and how best to measure who is meritorious, for example, will likely persist independent of affirmative action decisions. As we have emphasized throughout this book, diversifying our college and university campuses requires expanding current notions of merit. The issue is not whether the concept of merit and belief in meritocracy should or should not be commonly valued principles. After all, these concepts are an important part of American identity and culture. Rather, as civil rights lawyers Charles Lawrence and Mari Matsuda (1997) contend, the issue is that when merit is idealized and portrayed to operate in a system in which individuals are judged and rewarded only by their own talents and efforts, factors such as prejudice, privilege, inheritance, and accident of birth are not acknowledged as playing a part. Lawrence and Matsuda argue that although everyone knows that money and social networks lead to promising jobs, the belief that people can always pull themselves up by their bootstraps persists; as a consequence, the notion of privilege is obscured. Because of the prevalence of these beliefs, Lawrence and Matsuda contend that affirmative action policies, as well as other means of opening the doors to persons whose qualifications are different from those prescribed by traditional notions of merit, are easily framed in opposition to quality and worthiness. Framing merit in this way, however, is often at odds with reality.

According to Lawrence and Matsuda, common beliefs about meritocracy typically center on the notion that there is a "best" that is clearly definable and unambiguous, but real life actually requires a "world of multiple bests." For example, they point out that there is no "best" person to accompany a wilderness crew because a good crew requires diverse talents such as those of a naturalist, a paramedic, an experienced guide, and a good cook, all of whom work together to create a strong team of multiple valuable abilities. Yet because the "best" is widely believed to be quantifiable, many diverse, valuable talents are overlooked because they do not fit traditional notions of what the "best" is. Before affirmative action, women and racial and ethnic minorities were prohibited from even applying for jobs in fire departments, police departments, and other industries (including higher education) because they were judged categorically to be inferior to white males. Therefore, in most industries and in education, Lawrence and Matsuda conclude, privilege inevitably trumped merit. Conversely, affirmative action enables the consideration of the talents of those without privilege and helps to expand the notion of merit to include those who have been systematically excluded. Thus, Lawrence and Matsuda argue, affirmative action does not displace merit but actually reinforces it. Refuting allegations that affirmative action was in fact "reverse discrimination," the New York City Commission on Human Rights issued the following statement: "What is lost, therefore, to the majority is not a right, but an expectation of benefits flowing from illegal practices and systems, to which the majority class was never entitled in the first place" (quoted from Weiss 1997, 153).

In addition to logical flaws, other more insidious and deeply rooted obstacles for reconsidering and expanding the notion of merit stem from enduring assumptions about racial inferiority. Sociologist Jerome Karabel (1999) has analyzed the unique status of race in discussions of "preferences" granted to college and university applicants. As Karabel describes, no universities make admissions decisions on the basis of academic merit alone. Instead, universities give preferences to many characteristics in deciding whom to accept. Such characteristics might include where an applicant's parents went to school, whether an applicant's parents are donors or have political influence, where the applicant lives, how old the applicant is (older students are given preference), and whether the applicant has a disability; all are both commonly used and "institutionally sanctified" characteristics. Despite this, Karabel notes that of the many non-achievement-related characteristics (many of which are also immutable) that are awarded preferences by university admissions officers, race alone is considered "impermissible." Curiously, most people do not doubt that the child of an alumnus "deserves" the coveted admissions spot he/she is awarded, despite the fact that everyone acknowledges the preferences awarded to legacies. Moreover, concerns about the academic qualifications or inferiority of legacies are not regularly raised to challenge this common admissions practice. In contrast, the assumption that underlies arguments against affirmative action is that the racial minorities admitted through affirmative action are inherently unqualified and inferior to their fellow students.

Because of the "rumors of inferiority" and the narrow definitions of merit, affirmative action is often mistakenly viewed as compensating for deficiencies in people rather than deficiencies in the system, thus generating intense opposition against the policy (Crosby 1994). There is little recognition on the part of most white Americans of the current inequalities and racism within the system. The "rumors of inferiority" pervade much more than opposition to affirmative action. They translate into lower expectations by teachers for their students of color, often resulting in students receiving an inferior and "dumbed-down" curriculum. They translate into employers not hiring people of color or not promoting them because the employers assume these minorities do not have the capacity to perform at a high standard. They result in admissions officers evaluating black applicants as inferior to white applicants who have the same credentials. They result in the unequal treatment of people of color by police officers, bankers, shopkeepers, lawyers, and realtors.

Most white Americans want so much to believe that the end of legal discrimination and segregation has brought about universal equality for all racial groups. Despite this goodwill, there is a general lack of awareness on their part about the very separate lives lived by most blacks and Latinos. Few white Americans set foot in inner city neighborhoods and inner city schools that are predominantly black or Latino. Neighborhoods across America are almost as segregated as they were in the days before the civil rights movement. Sugrue (1999) charges that most children attend schools in which their classmates are of their own race and class. The societal and personal costs of this segregation are severe for people of all races. According to Sugrue, the stark separation that exists among people of different races in residential patterns, education, social functions, and everyday life affords little opportunity to combat the misconceptions, stereotypes, and hostility that lie at the root of the separation. Schoolchildren, he maintains, do not have the benefit of learning from people of different backgrounds who might have perspectives, experiences, customs, and ideas that are different from their own. Furthermore, persistent residential segregation, he adds, results in a great disparity in the quality of job opportunities and networks, education, social services, and wealth for members of different racial groups. Sugrue notes that such separation is reflected in the results of numerous public opinion surveys that reveal the large divide between blacks and whites on many social and political issues. For example, although whites generally believe that discrimination is rapidly disappearing and equal opportunity exists, blacks tend to believe that discrimination is intensifying and that they personally have been denied job opportunities because of their race (quoted in Sugrue 1999). It is obviously difficult for different racial groups to develop a strong sense of compassion and understanding if they exist, essentially, in parallel worlds.

Affirmative action has always been a complicated issue because in many ways it is a policy that serves as a surrogate for the larger responsibilities of the government to rectify the wrongs it has abetted for so many years (Taylor 1999). Affirmative action policies acknowledge the nonexistence of equal opportunity by revealing that a subtle but very real privilege has contributed to the success of those who have "made it" in the system (Crosby 1994). As Crosby and Clayton (1990) point out, affirmative action is threatening to those with power because it exposes the so-called meritocracy for what it is and belies the claims of those who present their own achievements as "determined by merit alone" (Crosby 1994). In the following statement, the Citizens' Commission on Civil Rights (1984, 116) captures the perception of affirmative action as part of the moral obligation of American society to compensate those who have suffered from white privilege: "A society that, in the name of the [color-blind] ideal, foreclosed racially-conscious remedies would not be truly color-blind but morally blind. The concept of affirmative action has arisen from this inescapable conclusion." Although the spirit driving affirmative action may prove to be timeless, the actual policies are designed to be a temporary means of ensuring equal opportunity by remedying the significant underrepresentation of members of certain minority groups (Brest and Oshige 1995).

The question "How much diversity is enough?" is commonly posed by both proponents and opponents of affirmative action. The subtext of this question is, of course, "When will affirmative action no longer be necessary?" The answer, albeit unsatisfying, is that we do not know. The reason we do not know is that there are so many factors and processes that still require existing policies. As suggested earlier, issues about race and racism change over time, coinciding with economic, social, demographic, and political shifts. Until discrimination or at least its effects have been eradicated; until the educational playing field is leveled; until all students, regardless of race, class, and gender, have an equal opportunity to succeed in education; until society operates under a definition of merit in which a broad range of applicable talents can be considered and qualified applicants are not overlooked because they do not fit into traditional notions of merit—until all these issues are explored and remedied, we will need affirmative action. William Trent responded to the question of how much diversity is enough by saying that there is enough diversity when the "specter of exceptionality" has been lifted (personal communication, July 24, 1998). In other words, when minority students (e.g., black students at selective schools, women in engineering, Latino/as in law school) are no longer given the additional burden of having to represent their race and their gender, their numbers are adequate. When minority students no longer feel isolated and are represented in universities, in office buildings, in leadership positions in numbers that are commensurate with their numbers in the general population, there will be enough diversity. At such a time, existing affirmative action policies might be rendered obsolete.

We believe, however, that levels of diversity cannot and should not be legislated. Institutions of higher education have always operated under a high degree of academic freedom that has enabled them to define their own mission, their own admissions process, hiring process, and curricula. Universities need to be able to decide and clearly articulate how diversity serves the mission of their institution. This should be defined in terms of the type of education the university wishes to provide its students and the university's perception of its role in the broader society.

Universities are by no means the only party responsible for improving racial circumstances in this country and realizing our nation's democratic ideals. Elementary and secondary schools arguably may play an even more critical role in those endeavors. Without receiving a quality education in the early grades, for example, many students find it difficult to go on to college and succeed. Given this, we are deeply concerned that all too often, public schools that serve low-income minority students are poorly funded, that practices such as tracking continue to have a disproportionately negative impact on students of color, and that attempts at educating all students to thrive in a multiracial society are overly politicized. In addition, there is much misinformation passed along to students about how to apply to college, the existence of financial aid, and the need to take gatekeeping courses. The lack of quality information or outright misinformation prevents students whose parents are not knowledgeable about college admission requirements (who are disproportionately poor and minority) from ever applying to college and joining the ranks of future leaders. Attention to these and other K-12 educational issues, however, is often artificially juxtaposed with affirmative action efforts in higher education. In practice, the two go hand in hand; more often than not, however, educational policies treat each as independent of the other. Often we fail to consider broader solutions to educational issues, which may account in part for why affirmative action policies are typically judged in very narrow terms.

When we look beyond higher education, for example, the evidence suggests that affirmative action has been tremendously successful in its three decades of existence. Its success is amply demonstrated in a 1996 Citizens' Commission on Civil Rights report, which shows that the employment sector has undergone tremendous changes as a result of affirmative action. For example, the number of blacks employed as firefighters and police officers tripled or quadrupled between 1970 and 1990. Industries such as manufacturing, construction, trucking, and service have also diversified and added many more people of color to their managerial ranks. The report also notes the tremendous advances women have made in traditionally male-dominated fields such as architecture, economics, and law—advances that can be largely attributed to affirmative action. There has also been a tremendous increase in the number of racial and ethnic minority students attending college. According to the Commission on Civil Rights report, in 1970 only 4.5 percent of blacks over the age of twenty-five had completed four years of college; by 1980, the figure had risen to 7 percent, and by 1990, to 11.9 percent.

Perhaps of more relevance to this book is that greater diversity in college and university campus demographics has brought about a number of changes outside the realm of higher education. For example, Grissmer et al. (1994)

explored possible explanations for the tremendous increase in the verbal and math proficiency scores of black thirteen- and seventeen-year-olds between 1970 and 1990 on the National Assessment of Educational Progress (NAEP). The researchers found that although the scores of white teenagers increased by only approximately 0.1 standard deviation units in the twenty-year time period, the scores of black students increased by more than 0.6 standard deviation units, reducing the gap between the two racial groups' scores by one-half. Latino/a students also made significant gains between 1975 and 1990.[1] The scores of Latino/a seventeen-year-olds increased 0.2 standard deviations in math and more than 0.5 standard deviation units in verbal. According to Grissmer et al., the single most important factor that has contributed to black students' tremendous gains in test scores over the past twenty years is the increase in the educational level attained by black parents during the same period. In fact, almost half of the points black students gained on the NAEP test during these two decades can be attributed to rising parental education levels. Indeed Grissmer et al. note that the percentage of black teenagers whose mothers had completed college rose 52 percent between 1970 and 1990; the percentage of fathers who were college graduates increased 268-fold in the same twenty-year period.

Of course affirmative action is not the only cause of the improvement in the socioeconomic status of many minorities. Certainly many political, social, economic, and demographic changes have played a major part in the dramatic increase in the number of black college graduates (e.g., the desegregation of K-12 schooling and the consequent improved education for many minority students, the gradual demise of *legal* discrimination, and global competitiveness). Nevertheless, affirmative action can be credited for rapidly expanding the number of minorities admitted to previously all-white selective institutions and to jobs that permitted them to enter the ranks of the middle class, providing a better education and greater social and economic stability (Bowen and Bok 1998). In turn, these changes improved the chances that the children of these graduates would succeed academically. As William Taylor (1998, 13) remarks in reference to the increase in NAEP scores: "Many took full advantage of the opportunity, worked hard, got their degrees, found better and more remunerative jobs than their predecessors, married and formed stable families. All of this created an environment in which their children could achieve, as reflected on the NAEP assessment."

The effectiveness of affirmative action policies to date does not contradict our conclusion that they are needed as much today as ever. Judging from the accumulated body of evidence that points to the benefits of diversity for everyone, the continuing disparities in access and opportunities available to students of different races, the fallibility of test scores and grades as indicators of merit, and the persistence of racism and discrimination in American society, affirmative action has much left to accomplish. For these and other reasons noted throughout this book, sensible policies that seek to overcome the negative effects associated with race cannot avoid taking race into account. As such, class-based affirmative action, for example, will not adequately address the disparities that were originally created by practices designed to systematically exclude individuals of certain racial groups. It appears that substituting class for race in making college admissions decisions will do little to increase the numbers of underrepresented students of color, mainly because in absolute numbers, most poor people in the country are white. Such a substitution would also fail to account for racial disparities in academic performance, which are independent of class, as discussed by Trent et al. in Chapter 2.

Even more significant are the tremendous disparities that continue to exist across racial and ethnic groups in the employment sector. For example, the Citizens' Commission on Civil Rights (1996) report on the state of affirmative action showed that almost 97 percent of managers in Fortune 1000 and Fortune 500 service companies are white males. Less than 2.5 percent of senior-level management jobs in the private sector are held by black men and women. According to the commission, the wages of black men with professional degrees are only 79 percent of those of their white counterparts; the wages of black women with professional degrees are only 60 percent of those of white men. As Trent et al. point out in Chapter 2, despite the tremendous increases in the numbers of minorities attending college, there has been little progress toward parity because the eligibility pool of minority high school graduates has increased at a rate greater than their college attendance rates. In the realm of faculty employment, the American Council on Education (1995) reports the "gross underrepresentation" of people of color on university faculties and the fact that the faculty of color who are present tend to be "clustered on the lower rungs of the professoriate" in non-tenure-track positions (quoted in Citizens' Commission on Civil Rights 1996, 31). As the report concludes: "The sad truth is that despite thirty years of civil rights laws, some people grow up untouched by them—cut off from access to services and opportunities which would make them full participants in society. While neither a panacea nor a substitute for economic growth, education and job training, affirmative action will continue to be needed as long as discrimination persists."

The multidisciplinary evidence presented in this book underscores the need for continued support of diversity through policies such as affirmative action. Although a *legal* rationale for affirmative action in higher education is somewhat limited to discussions about how diversity might serve a "compelling interest," we should not lose sight of the fact that the political, philosophical, and moral justifications of the policy stem from concerns about achieving justice, · fairness, and a reckoning with the consequences of past actions that persist into the present. Despite the solid, cumulative body of scholarship that provides clear support for affirmative action policies, public sentiment has been moving, in our view, in the wrong direction. Such detachment from the evidence is not difficult to explain. Many laws and policies that have come into existence during the past few years have reinforced ideas of "personal responsibility" and a "blaming" of the victim, relieving the onus on the government to address and fix deeply rooted social ills. Such policies are flawed because they assume a fair system in which persons of all racial, ethnic, class, and gender backgrounds are competing on a level playing field. The evidence in this book amply demonstrates the unevenness that exists on many parts of the playing field—an unevenness that those in power seem reluctant to acknowledge.

The pressing issues of diversity and affirmative action are more immediate and personal to the academy than almost any other social issue that we as researchers are called on to address. These issues affect the very composition of the classes we teach, the constitution of the faculties we are part of, and the atmosphere in which we work. These issues are also central to the very mission of higher education and the purpose that the academy serves in the broader society. According to Tierney (1997, 192), "public higher education is a public good" and has traditionally been defined as a vehicle for upward mobility for all people. As such, those institutions have a responsibility that extends beyond admitting only those applicants who score highest on a standardized test. They have, Tierney contends, an obligation to serve the public good by developing policies that "seek to advance, affirm, and expand participation in the democratic public sphere" (193). We also believe that the academy, with its ability to foster dialogues that engage different viewpoints and to bring together people from all walks of life for a common purpose, should play a greater leadership role in dismantling the segregation that has persisted during the forty-five years since the *Brown* decision. Our position is not only based on educational and moral grounds; it is supported by the cumulative research record.

The extent to which colleges and universities can play a more proactive role in dismantling segregation and in better serving the public good may well be decided in the nation's highest court. The widely divergent rulings in circuit-level courts regarding the constitutionality of race-conscious college admissions practices in recent years have led legal analysts to predict that the Supreme Court may soon weigh in on the issue. It appears that at least one of the two cases filed against the University of Michigan will likely go before the Supreme Court. At the time this book went to press, both sides in these two cases seemed determined to petition the Supreme Court for review if a favorable judgment was not received from the U.S. Court of Appeals for the Sixth Circuit. Similar cases that previously received widespread national attention had only recently been abandoned before reaching the highest court. Officials from both the University of Texas and the University of Georgia announced in November and August 2001, respectively, that they would not ask the Supreme Court to overturn separate lower court rulings that had struck down each university's race-conscious admissions policies. Unlike the cases involving those institutions, the University of Michigan has relied much more heavily on the social science evidence to defend its race-conscious admissions policies.

Although many questions still need to be addressed by future research, as indicated throughout this book (researchers, of course, always want to conclude that more research is needed), the data supporting diversity and affirmative action are well and growing.[2] It is becoming increasingly clear that affirmative action policies work and that they are still very much needed in higher education, especially when framed in the broader organizing context we have presented in this book. We hope that our framework for examining the evidence around the themes of fairness, merit, and the benefits of diversity mirrors the way in which the public and the courts organize their beliefs around race and opportunity. The evidence to date offers not just a strong set of conclusions but also a way of building a coherent research agenda that tests these hypotheses in ever stronger form, and in ways that are demanded by the users of research.

HISTORICAL SUMMARY OF
AFFIRMATIVE ACTION

Daria Witt and Clara Shin

We have provided a brief historical summary of affirmative action not only to clarify some of the ambiguities in popular concepts surrounding it, but also to place these policies and their related debates in their appropriate historical context. Although the summary is far from comprehensive, in it we emphasize that affirmative action policies arose from the ineffectiveness of simple policies of nondiscrimination in combating inequalities that existed in employment and education. We have divided this summary into six different periods—the 1860s to the 1890s, the 1900s to the 1940s, the 1950s to the 1960s, and each decade thereafter—because each of these periods reflects important shifts surrounding notions of achieving equality and redressing discrimination that are linked to the evolution of affirmative action.

1860s–1890s

The Origins and Decline of Civil Rights
Protection for Blacks

It is difficult to pinpoint exactly when affirmative action began in the United States. Indeed, there are varied opinions on its actual origins. It can be said that affirmative remedies for past racial discrimination in the United States occurred as early as the post–Civil War Reconstruction period when constitutional amendments and other federal initiatives were created to establish equal opportunity for former slaves (Citizens' Commission on Civil Rights [CCCR] 1984). Although these remedies led to increased voter participation among blacks and to a number of blacks holding elected offices, most of the gains were lost by the late nineteenth century, when the federal government's support of civil rights for African Americans began to diminish (CCCR 1984).

1866   The Civil Rights Act of 1866, the first civil rights legislation passed in American history, declared that all persons in the United States had the same right to make and enforce contracts, to sue, and to have the equal protection of all laws and proceedings.

1868   The fourteenth amendment to the Constitution was ratified. This amendment applied the Bill of Rights to actions of state and local government, conferred citizenship on all persons born in the United States, and granted all persons equal protection of law and due process before removing life, liberty, or property.

1877   As a reflection of diminishing support for the rights of blacks, newly elected President Rutherford B. Hayes enacted the Compromise of 1877, which dismantled Reconstruction programs and removed the remaining federal troops from the South.

1883   The Supreme Court struck down the Civil Rights Act of 1875, which had prohibited discrimination by nongovernmental agencies. The emergence of Jim Crow laws in the South ensued.

1896   *Plessy v. Ferguson*, the Supreme Court decision that upheld the constitutionality of racial segregation ("separate but equal"), completed the removal of federal protection for racial minorities. The great migration of southern blacks to the North began.

1900s–1940s

The Origins of Affirmative Action

1909   National Association for the Advancement of Colored People (NAACP) was created by W. E. B. Du Bois, other African American intellectuals, and white reformers.

1932   The Great Depression gave rise to unemployment that often exceeded 50 percent among urban blacks. The disproportionate negative impact of the Depression on blacks helped focus African Americans' political activity (Weiss 1997).

1934   President Franklin Roosevelt's secretary of the interior, Harold Ickes, ordered that "there be no discrimination exercised against any person because of color or religious affiliation" on Public Works Administration (PWA) projects (quoted in Weiss 1997, 34). It was soon clear, however, that because this order did not define discrimination, and because so many African American workers had already been displaced, such a policy of passive nondiscrimination would accomplish little (Weiss 1997). Seeking a more effective mechanism, Ickes went to the PWA housing division, which constructed housing for urban blacks. Instead of giving a general nondiscrimination mandate, Ickes ordered that all PWA housing contractors direct a specified proportion to African American workers. Failure to achieve a certain percentage of contracts with African Americans would be interpreted as evidence of discrimination. This transfer of the burden of proof—from the employee's having to prove discrimination to the employer's having to prove nondiscrimination—became a standard feature of all PWA projects (Weiss 1997). Although it was not referred to as such, this directive was essentially the first federal affirmative action program.

1941   Roosevelt issued Executive Order 8802, which established the Fair Employment Practices Committee (FEPC) and ordered that all training and vocational programs for jobs with government defense contractors be administered without discrimination because of race, creed, color, or national origin (Weiss 1997). The purpose of the FEPC was to investigate complaints of discrimination and to redress grievances. The executive order did not provide a mechanism for actually enforcing the equal employment opportunity requirement (CCCR 1984).

1945   The Ives-Quinn Act of New York state—the first state FEPC law to pass—barred discrimination by employers and labor unions. More powerful than Roosevelt's FEPC, the New York FEPC was authorized to investigate charges of discrimination and to issue a "cease and desist" order if charges by the employee were confirmed (Weiss 1997). More significantly, when the commission found discrimination, it had the authority to require the employer to "take such affirmative action, including (but not limited to) hiring, reinstatement or upgrading of employees, with or without back pay, restoration to membership in any respondent labor organization" (quoted in Weiss 1997, 40–41). Although the New York law defined affirmative action differently than current legal interpretations do (concrete steps taken in response to individual acts of discrimination as opposed to class action suits or proportional hiring), it emphasized the inability of passive nondiscrimination to bring about equal opportunity for nonwhites (Weiss 1997).

Several states followed New York's lead and adopted FEPC laws that had varying strength and effectiveness (Weiss 1997). Very few discrimination charges were filed at the state level, however. Even when charges were filed, it was difficult to prove discrimination because employers could always claim that few qualified minorities had applied. Although the state FEPCs helped many individuals, they did not significantly alter hiring practices with regard to race (Weiss 1997).

1950s and 1960s

Federal Affirmative Action Takes Shape

1950   In *Sweatt v. Painter*, the U.S. Supreme Court struck down racial segregation in state-run law schools. In the decision handed down, the Court laid out its reasons why admission to selective institutions is important to minority applicants.

1954   In *Brown v. Board of Education*, the Supreme Court overruled *Plessy v. Fergusson*, thus dismantling all local, state, and federal laws that enforce segregation in the public schools. In subsequent opinions, the Supreme Court dismantled the notion of "separate but equal" in public libraries, parks, beaches, hospitals, and other publicly funded facilities. Because segregation continued in the South, however, the Supreme Court approved a number of race-conscious remedies (Americans United for Affirmative Action 1997).

1957   The U.S. Commission on Civil Rights was established under the Civil Rights Act of 1957 to investigate violations of civil rights and to recommend legislative actions and other measures that should be undertaken to eradicate discrimination (CCCR 1984).

1960s   Colleges begin to make proactive efforts to recruit and admit substantial numbers of African American students. The numbers of African American students enrolled at selective institutions remained very small at this time because no adjustments in admissions standards or financial aid were made. For example, at selective New England colleges, African Americans represented only 1 percent of the student body (Bowen and Bok 1998).

1961   The Presidential Commission on Government Contracts, headed by Richard Nixon (and established in 1953 by President Dwight Eisenhower), issued its final report, which stated, "Overt discrimination, in the sense that an employer actually refuses to hire solely because of race, religion, color, or national origin, is not as prevalent as is generally believed. To a greater degree, the indifference of employers to establish a positive policy of nondiscrimination hinders qualified applicants and employees from being hired and promoted on the basis of equality" (quoted in Weiss 1997, 44). This statement, without using the phrase *affirmative action*, nevertheless underscored the need for employers to do more than simply wait for qualified nonwhite job applicants to appear when an opening arises.

President Kennedy issued Executive Order 10925 and directed contractors on projects with federal funds to "take affirmative action to ensure that applicants are employed, and employees are treated fairly during their employment without regard to race, creed, color or national origin" (Executive Order 10925, sec. 201, quoted in CCCR 1984). The order also encouraged Congress to expand educational and employment opportunities for minorities and to move beyond merely prohibiting discrimination (Americans United for Affirmative Action 1997). This executive order marked the first time that actual penalties were prescribed for failure to comply with contractual obligations. It also marked the first time that the term *affirmative action* was used in federal law (CCCR 1984). Although it holds a significant place in affirmative action history, Executive Order 10925 when it was passed went virtually unnoticed and therefore engendered little backlash (Lemann 1995).

1963   The Southern Christian Leadership Conference launched Project C with the goals of persuading businesses to adopt fair hiring practices, achieving equal opportunities for blacks within city government agencies, and desegregating store facilities (Weiss 1997). Various peaceful demonstrations resulted in brutal police attacks, several bomb explosions, and riots throughout Birmingham, Alabama. The events in Birmingham awakened a national consciousness, and between May 13 and June 20 alone, 127 civil rights bills were introduced into the U.S. Congress (Weiss 1997).

1964   The Civil Rights Act of 1964 passed both houses of Congress and was signed into law (by President Lyndon Johnson) after many compromises, including a weakening of the FEPC, and assurances that the measure would only require nondiscrimination as opposed to preferential treatment policies (Weiss 1997; Lemann 1995). The Civil Rights Act contained eleven sections or "titles." In terms of affirmative action, the Civil Rights Act, and specifically Title VII, was open to interpretation. Although Title VII specifically stated that it did not "require" employers to "grant preferential treatment to any individual or to any group" in order to remedy an imbalance in "race, color, religion, sex, or national origin," it also recognized the authority of the courts to "order such affirmative action as may be appropriate, which may include reinstatement or hiring of employees, with or without back pay" (quoted in Weiss 1997, 71). The goal of Title VII was to end discrimination by large private employers regardless of whether they held government contracts (White House 1999). This act also established the Equal Employment Opportunity Commission (EEOC).

1965   A year after passage of the Civil Rights Act, President Johnson argued that to achieve fairness, policies must go beyond a mere commitment to impartial treatment (Cahn 1999). Operating on this belief, Johnson issued Executive Order 11246, which preserved the antidiscrimination/affirmative action requirements of President Kennedy's Executive Order 10925 but added new requirements. Under this order, all federal nonconstruction contractors and subcontractors (including colleges and universities that had contracts with the federal government) with more than fifty employees and contracts of more than $50,000 would be required periodically to submit written compliance reports that described the proportion of minority participation on their projects and written affirmative action plans (Weiss 1997; Murry 1998; CCCR 1984). Timetables and goals that were "significant, attainable, and measurable" needed to be established to remedy identifiable deficiencies in the hiring of minorities (and later women, in 1968), but no inflexible quotas were permitted (Murry 1998). Nevertheless, like its predecessor, Executive Order 11246 failed to define affirmative action and to provide specific criteria by which to determine compliance, which significantly weakened its enforcement capacity (Weiss 1997).

1967   The EEOC issued a report showing that "pure" affirmative actions (job training and recruiting of underrepresented groups) "may not produce affirmative results" (quoted in Weiss 1997, 92). One study of more than six hundred companies during the late 1960s by Frances Reissman Cousens, titled *Public Civil*

Rights Agencies and Fair Employment: Promise v. Performance (cited in Weiss 1997), found that 60 percent of executives felt the FEPC laws had "no effect" on their business practices. In fact, the study found that 50 percent of the respondents did not even know that public antidiscrimination agencies existed.

Acknowledging the need for more concrete and powerful remedies to problems of discrimination within the construction industry, the federal government shifted antidiscrimination/affirmative action enforcement to "special area" plans in given metropolitan areas (Weiss 1997). Introducing actions such as the Cleveland Plan and the Philadelphia Plan, the federal government required employers in these areas to develop a viable affirmative action program in which they created specific hiring goals that were flexible goals and not quotas. Except for that of Cleveland, most of these plans were unsuccessful. Nevertheless, they went on to become a staple of federal antidiscrimination efforts in the 1970s and signaled an increasing acceptance of using numerical goals to solve problems of discrimination (Weiss 1997).

Johnson issued Executive Order 11375, which extended affirmative action provisions of Executive Order 11246 to include sex discrimination.

1969   A revised Philadelphia Plan was issued, which required all federal contractors on projects of more than $500,000 to submit a written affirmative action plan that was to include "specific goals of minority manpower utilization" (quoted in Weiss 1997). A second Department of Labor order specified the ranges of minority hiring that were to serve as the basis for contractors' developing their goals and timetables. Black participation was to increase in construction projects from 5 percent in 1969 to between 19 and 26 percent by 1973 (Weiss 1997).

Despite many allegations that the Philadelphia Plan was a "quota system" and a misinterpretation of the Civil Rights Act of 1964 and of Executive Order 11246, the Nixon administration stood its ground in defense of it (Weiss 1997). In response to a complaint by the comptroller general, Attorney General John Mitchell rebutted:

> But it is now well recognized in judicial opinions that the obligation of
> nondiscrimination, whether imposed by statute or by the Constitution, does
> not require and, in some circumstances, may not permit obliviousness or
> indifference to the racial consequences of alternate courses of action which
> involve the application of outwardly neutral criteria. . . . There is no incon-
> sistency between a requirement that each qualified employee and applicant
> be individually treated without regard to race, and a requirement that an
> employer make every good faith effort to achieve a certain range of minor-
> ity employment. (Weiss 1997, 131)

Within two years, plans similar to the Philadelphia Plan were implemented by the federal government in Washington, D.C., Seattle, St. Louis, Atlanta, and San Francisco. After significant protests from labor unions and blue-collar workers (who had become increasingly important to Nixon's re-election hopes), the Nixon administration rejected the continued creation of more government-imposed plans, opting instead for "hometown solutions" under which community officials, contractors, and unions made agreements.

1970s

Affirmative Action Is Further Defined

During the late 1960s and early 1970s, the courts began increasingly to apply numerical formulas to job discrimination cases (Weiss 1997). In several cases during this time period (e.g., *Quarles v. Phillip Morris* and *Carter v. Gallagher*) in which there was a finding of job discrimination, the courts ordered the companies to hire a specific ratio of minorities to whites until they had achieved a certain number. In each of these cases, the courts were careful to distinguish between a temporary preference for qualified minority workers, which adhered to Title VII requirements, and quotas, which did not (*Carter v. Gallagher* 452 F.2d 315, 1971, in Weiss 1997). The ordered use of these numerical remedies acknowledged the failure of nonquantitative remedies for creating equal opportunity (Weiss 1997).

1971   Recognizing that the lack of guidance on affirmative action requirements of Executive Order 11246 had resulted in ineffectiveness, the Labor Department released new regulations in a policy directive titled Order #4, and later that year as Revised Order #4 (Weiss 1997). This memo removed all references to proportional hiring and established the requirement that all contractors with fifty or more employees and contracts of more than $50,000 create a written affirmative action compliance program within 120 days from the beginning of a contract (Weiss 1997). The order specified that the "minority groups" toward which contractors must direct their good faith efforts were "Negroes, American Indians, Orientals, and Spanish-surnamed Americans" (Cahn 1999). Acceptable levels of minority and female hiring were determined by the number of minorities and females in the local workforce and the extent of unemployment among those groups (Weiss 1997; Cahn 1999). Although Revised Order #4 provided a more detailed and precise directive on federal affirmative action than any previous order had, too many definitions were still left up to the discretion of the employer, which maintained the ambiguity of affirmative action and preventing effective compliance efforts (Weiss 1997).

In the landmark decision *Griggs v. Duke Power Company*, the U.S. Supreme Court held that it was a violation of Title VII of the Civil Rights Act of 1964 for an employer to use a paper-and-pencil test as the criterion for hiring new employees if use of the test had an adverse impact on minority applicants and the employer could not demonstrate that its use was dictated by business necessity.

Chief Justice Warren Burger reasoned that requirements such as a high school diploma and test scores were inherently discriminatory because they were not equally attainable across racial groups as a result of the racist educational system in the South (Weiss 1997). If, however, employers could prove that a test had strong predictive validity for job-related skills, then a test could be used, even if it disproportionately affected different racial groups. In this case and in many others, the Court was less concerned with the difficult task of allocating responsibility for what may have been multiple wrongs than with taking a practical approach to finding workable solutions (Weiss 1997).

In explicating the decision in another opinion two years later, the Court said: "*Griggs* was rightly concerned that childhood deficiencies in the education and background of minority citizens, resulting from forces beyond their control, not be allowed to work a cumulative and invidious burden on such citizens for the remainder of their lives" (*McDonnell Douglas v. Green* 411 U.S. 792, 806, 1973).

1972   Congress passed several comprehensive amendments to Title VII of the Civil Rights Act of 1964 that resulted in the expansion of Title VII to cover federal, state, and local employment (CCCR 1984). Among these amendments was the Equal Employment Opportunity Act, which expanded the resources and power of the EEOC to initiate civil suits (instead of relying on the Justice Department to do so). This act also made educational institutions and state and local employees subject to Title VII requirements for the first time, which meant that the EEOC could now be involved in any employment-related cases that involved discrimination within the education system. Passage of this act launched a more activist role for the EEOC (Weiss 1997). Significantly, during the debates on the Title VII amendments, Congress rejected many proposed amendments that would have severely limited the contract compliance program and prevented the use of goals and timetables, thereby reaffirming the federal government's support for these programs and processes (CCCR 1984).

1973   Two important statements on affirmative action policy were issued by government agencies:

The Statement on Affirmative Action for Equal Employment Opportunities was issued by the U.S. Commission on Civil Rights. Endorsing affirmative action and the continued use of numerical remedies, the commission concluded in its report that not only did "intentional and widespread discrimination remain widespread" but that, of even "greater significance," the "consequences of years of discrimination in the past remain" (U.S. Commission on Civil Rights, Publication No. 41-1973, quoted in CCCR 1984).

The chairmen of the Civil Service and Equal Employment Opportunity Commissions, the assistant attorney general for civil rights, and the acting director of the Office of Federal Contract Compliance issued a landmark joint memorandum on affirmative action policy. This memorandum asserted the continuing need for goals and timetables and drew a sharp distinction between these "proper" remedies and "impermissible" quotas and preferences (CCCR 1984). Goals were described as "numerical objectives" that were determined realistically by looking at the number of vacancies expected and the number of qualified applicants in the job market. Therefore, an employer was not to be penalized if he/she had fewer vacancies available than expected, or if he/she had made "every good faith effort" to include in the hiring process persons from the group that had been the target of discrimination but was still unable to meet the goal. According to this memo, employers were not asked or expected to displace current employees or to create unnecessary positions to meet their goals. In contrast, a quota system would disregard the number of qualified potential applicants and would impose a set number of positions that had to be filled in order to avoid sanction. This joint policy statement therefore reiterated the federal government's position that race-conscious numerical remedies had to be flexible, realistically attainable, and not involve the displacement of current employees or the hiring of unqualified ones (CCCR 1984).

1977   Eleanor Holmes Norton, nominated by President Jimmy Carter, became chair of the EEOC. In an effort to reduce the backlog of 130,000 unaddressed discrimination complaints, Norton implemented many reforms at the agency. Most significantly, Norton reoriented the agency's enforcement efforts from individual complaints toward broader "patterns and practices." This reorientation reflected the belief of Norton and many others that discrimination was not limited to isolated individual acts but was part of a deeply entrenched systemic discrimination (Weiss 1997). An aggressive affirmative action campaign ensued.

1978   *Regents of the University of California v. Bakke* was handed down by the U.S. Supreme Court. The University of California at Davis (UC Davis) medical school reserved sixteen spots in each entering class of one hundred for African American, Latino, and Asian American students who had experienced racial discrimination. Allan Bakke, a white applicant, sued UC Davis claiming that the admissions process violated the Equal Protection Clause as well as Title VI of the 1964 Civil Rights Act, which bars racial discrimination by federally assisted institutions. There was no majority opinion. The nine justices wrote six separate opinions, with four justices believing that the plan was constitutional and another four justices believing that the plan violated Title VI of the 1964 Civil Rights Act. Justice Powell, writing for the Court, held that racial quotas were unconstitutional but that a university should be permitted to take into account an applicant's race as part of the admissions process. Powell wrote that any racial or ethnic classifications must be subjected to strict scrutiny because such classifications are always suspect, regardless of their purpose.

Powell applied the strict scrutiny standard: the plan was permissible if (1) its objective was compelling and (2) the racial classification was necessary to achieve the objective. Powell wrote that diversity could be achieved by a plan similar to that of Harvard's in which, all things being equal, race could be a "plus" factor.

Powell stressed that this process treated each applicant as an individual. He rejected other proposed objectives, including the need to reduce the shortage of minority medical students and doctors, the need to cure the results of past discrimination by society, and the need to increase the number of doctors who will practice in currently underserved communities. Finally, Powell found that the Davis plan was not narrowly tailored because it was not related to any prior discrimination by the medical school.

1979   The EEOC issued "Guidelines on Affirmative Action Programs Appropriate under Title VII," which not only established standards for the implementation of affirmative action programs but also described the actions the commission would take if whites or males filed charges against a properly implemented affirmative action plan (CCCR 1984).

1980s

The Reagan Administration Curtails Affirmative Action and the Supreme Court Moves to the Right

1980   Ronald Reagan, who placed affirmative action at the center of his presidential campaign, appointed to key positions persons who were open opponents of affirmative action (e.g., Clarence Thomas to the EEOC and Antonin Scalia and Anthony Kennedy to the Supreme Court). In addition, funding for the Office of Federal Contract Compliance Programs (OFCCP) and EEOC was cut. Unlike the Carter administration, the Reagan administration rejected the idea of "systemic discrimination" that had formed the basis of so many affirmative action programs. Instead, discrimination was defined more in terms of acts against individuals. This philosophy undermined the legitimacy of class action suits and the need for numerical formulas to remedy past discrimination. Although many Reagan administration officials supported affirmative action, policies developed when Reagan was in the White House can be characterized in general as hostile to affirmative action (Weiss 1997).

Although the Department of Justice throughout most of the 1960s and 1970s supported the use of race-conscious numerical remedies to combat employment discrimination, under Ronald Reagan in the 1980s it began to oppose numerical remedies (CCCR 1984). The courts, however, maintained their support for numerical remedies.

1982   Clarence Thomas became the chair of the EEOC and reverted the agency's orientation from pursuing systemic patterns and practices back to pursuing individual complaints. Like many others in the Reagan administration, Thomas became increasingly anti–affirmative action as Reagan's tenure and popularity progressed (Weiss 1997). Goals and timetables were gradually eliminated.

1984   President Reagan replaced four of the six incumbent members of the U.S. Commission on Civil Rights with his own appointees. After a one-day meeting, the new commission reversed the old commission's endorsement of numerical race-conscious remedies (CCCR 1984).

1986   William Rehnquist replaced Warren Burger as chief justice of the Supreme Court. Rehnquist, a Nixon appointee, was generally known as the most conservative member of the court and highly opposed to affirmative action. Conservative justices Antonin Scalia and Anthony Kennedy were confirmed as justices at that time, moving the Court significantly to the right.

Wygant v. Jackson Board of Education was handed down by the Supreme Court. The Jackson board of education had affirmatively increased the number of African American teachers in its school system because they were disproportionately represented. However, when layoffs became necessary, rather than using the existing layoff policy based on seniority, the board and the teacher's union agreed to a modified policy whereby each of the teacher groups, black and white, would have the same percentage of members laid off. The purpose was to maintain the overall percentages of minorities on the faculty. White teachers who were laid off claimed that the scheme violated the Equal Protection Clause.

The Court stuck down the scheme although there was no majority opinion. Five justices held that societal discrimination did not furnish a sufficiently compelling objective and rejected the school board's argument that a certain percentage of African American teachers must be maintained as role models. Five justices also agreed that the policy was an unconstitutional means to achieve even permissible goals. The plurality distinguished between racial preferences in hiring and those in layoffs, explaining that denial of a future opportunity was less intrusive than the loss of an existing job.

1987   *U.S. v. Paradise* was handed down by the U.S. Supreme Court. A federal district court found that Alabama had for decades discriminated against African Americans in its hiring for state trooper positions. The court ordered that for every white promoted to corporal, an African American must also be promoted so long as there were qualified applicants. This plan was to exist only until the department developed its own procedures.

In a five–four decision, the Supreme Court upheld this numerically based remedy. *Paradise* is the closest the Court has come to approving a racially oriented quota scheme in the context of employment. The Court supported the proposition that quotas may be used in some circumstances to eradicate past proven discrimination. This case also suggests that affirmative action plans involving promotions may be more acceptable than those involving hiring or layoffs.

1989   *Wards Cove v. Atonio* was handed down by the U.S. Supreme Court. In this case, the Court moved the burden of proof in "discriminatory impact" cases from the employer (as directed by the Civil Rights Act of 1964) to the plaintiff.

City of Richmond v. Croson was handed down by the U.S. Supreme Court. The city of Richmond, Virginia, enacted a Minority Business Utilization Plan, which required prime contractors on construction contracts funded by the city to sub-contract at least 30 percent of the dollar amount of the contract to one or more Minority Business Enterprises (MBEs). An MBE was a business that was at least 51 percent owned by minority group members.

The Court ruled that any race-based governmental programs must be sub-jected to the same strict scrutiny as governmental actions that intentionally dis-criminated against racial minorities. The Court provided three reasons for this ruling: (1) there is no easy way to tell which racial classifications are "benign" and which are racist; (2) classifications based on race could cause stigmatic harm; and (3) unless race-conscious plans are strictly scrutinized, the goal of becoming truly race-neutral will never be achieved.

The Court found that although Richmond claimed to be pursuing the objec-tive of overcoming past racial discrimination in construction, there was no such evidence of this discrimination. The Court noted that there was no evidence of discrimination by anyone in the local construction industry, no direct evidence that there would be more minority contracting firms had there not been societal discrimination, and no showing of how many MBEs in the local market could have done the work. The Court thus required state entities to identify the dis-crimination with some specificity before using race-conscious relief. The idea was to have the state or city admit to some complicity in past racial discrimination in order to justify the plan. Finally, the Court ruled that the plan was not narrowly tailored. For instance, it was unable to show that race-neutral means would not increase minority participation.

The Court wrote that not all race-conscious remedial plans failed strict scru-tiny. If there was evidence of discrimination, its eradication might be a compelling objective. Moreover, Justice Sandra O'Connor stated that if there was a significant statistical disparity between the number of qualified minority contractors willing and able to perform a service and the number of such contractors working, then an inference of discrimination can be made—even without direct proof.

1990s

Despite a Supportive Presidential Administration, the Existence of Affirmative Action Is Threatened

1990   *Metro Broadcasting, Inc. v. FCC* was handed down by the U.S. Supreme Court. The FCC had implemented policies that favored minority applicants for broadcast licenses. For instance, in awarding new radio or television licenses, the FCC would consider minority ownership as one positive factor among several. The Court decided to apply intermediate scrutiny rather than strict scrutiny in judging whether race-conscious action by Congress violated the equal protection rights of nonminorities. Thus, the FCC's policies only had to be "substantially related" to the achievement of "important" governmental objectives. The Court also stated that Congress may enact such programs even if they are not remedial in the sense of compensating victims of past governmental or societal discrimination.

The Court ruled that enhancing broadcast diversity—by reducing the broadcast industry's 98 percent white ownership—was an important governmental objective; the interest protected was ensuring diverse viewpoints on the airwaves. Thus, the Court's focus was on obtaining the future benefit of broadcast diversity rather than on remedial benefits.

1991   Passage of the Civil Rights Act of 1991 helped individual victims of race discrimination to seek redress through the courts (Americans United for Affirmative Action 1997).

1994   *Podberesky v. Kirwan* was handed down by the Fourth Circuit Court of Appeals. The University of Maryland at College Park (UMCP) spent 1 percent of its financial aid budget to provide scholarships to approximately thirty high-achieving African American students. A Latino student sued UMCP claiming that the Banneker Scholarship Program was unconstitutional. The Fourth Circuit applied a two-step analysis: (1) the proponent of the measure must demonstrate a strong basis in evidence for its conclusion that remedial action is necessary; and (2) the remedial measure must be narrowly tailored to meet the remedial goal. Moreover, to make a finding of a present effect of past discrimination, the court required the proponent of the program to prove that the present effect was caused by past discrimination and that the effect was of a sufficient magnitude to justify the program.

The court suggested that the line between past discrimination and present effects must be extremely direct. It ruled that UMCP's poor reputation in the African American community and that a racially hostile campus climate were nexus to past discrimination. In addition, the court found that the evidence of underrepresentation of African American students as well as their low retention and graduation rates was inconclusive or questionable. The court also ruled that societal discrimination could not justify an affirmative action program. Finally, the court held that even assuming that African Americans were underrepresented at UMCP and that the higher attrition rate was related to past discrimination, the Banneker program was not narrowly tailored to remedy these problems.

1995   *Adarand Constructors Inc. v. Peña* was handed down by the U.S. Supreme Court. Adarand, a white-owned construction company, submitted the lowest bid for a subcontract to supply guardrails to a federal highway project in Colorado. The general contractor took a bid from a minority-owned firm that qualified under federal regulations as a Disadvantaged Business Enterprise (DBE). A small white-owned firm could qualify to be a DBE, but a firm owned by an ethnic minority or one owned by a woman was presumed to be disadvantaged. The prime contractor was not required to award the subcontract to a minority-owned DBE, but it received a financial incentive for doing so.

The Court overruled *Metro Broadcasting* and held that race-conscious affirmative action programs enacted by federal, state, or local government entities must be subject to strict scrutiny. In other words, such programs may be upheld only if necessary to achieve a compelling government interest.

The Court emphasized that the use of strict scrutiny did not necessarily mean that the governmental action being reviewed would be struck down. Justice O'Connor, writing for the Court, suggested that if government is responding to the "lingering effects of racial discrimination against minority groups," and does so in a "narrowly tailored way," race-conscious methods may survive.

The Court did not decide whether the regulations at issue could survive strict scrutiny but instead remanded the case to the lower courts. The Court suggested that on remand, the lower courts should consider whether the governmental interest being served was "compelling," whether the race-neutral means might have been effective to achieve that interest, and whether the remedy was appropriately short-lived so as not to "last longer than the discriminatory effects it is designed to eliminate."

The Dole-Canady Bill was introduced. Senate Majority Leader Bob Dole and Congressman Charles Canady introduced the Equal Opportunity Act, legislation that would end all "preference" for women and minorities in federal programs. Race and gender preferences were broadly defined and were not confined to numerical goals and timetables, but they would eliminate remedies that addressed specific and identifiable discrimination and court-approved settlements if the settlement included a "preference" (CCCR 1996).

President Bill Clinton reaffirmed his support of affirmative action. In the speech in which he coined the phrase "mend it don't end it," President Clinton established four criteria for programs: (1) no quotas; (2) no hiring of unqualified individuals; (3) no reverse discrimination; and (4) termination of programs once goals are achieved (in Weiss 1997). In response to the president's speech, the Justice Department investigated federal affirmative action programs to confirm their compliance both with the *Adarand* decision and with the directives of the president (CCCR 1996).

1996   By mid-1996, Republican congressional leaders replaced the Dole-Canady Bill and the all-encompassing attack on affirmative action with a narrower focus on eliminating programs designed to assist socially and economically disadvantaged businesses (CCCR 1996).

Proposition 209 was passed. California voters by a margin of 54 percent to 46 percent passed the ballot initiative Proposition 209 supported by Governor Pete Wilson. This initiative prohibited the state from discriminating against or giving "preferential treatment to any individual group on account of sex, color, ethnicity, or national origin in the operation of public employment, public education, or public contracting." Minority enrollments at the flagship universities in the University of California system dropped dramatically.

Hopwood v. Texas was handed down by the Fifth Circuit Court of Appeals. The University of Texas at Austin law school had implemented an affirmative action admissions program in response to a finding by the Office of Civil Rights that the Texas public higher education system had failed to eliminate vestiges of its former *de jure* racially dual system. The admissions process involved a presumptive admit band, a presumptive denial band, and a discretionary zone. The standards applied to assess applicants differed on the basis of race and national origin in two ways: (1) the standards for the presumptive admission and denial bands varied between minorities and nonminorities; and (2) the admissions committee used different procedures for reviewing minority and nonminority applicants in the discretionary zone.

The Fifth Circuit stated that *Bakke* was not binding because it had not received a majority vote. Thus, any consideration of race for the purpose of achieving a diverse student body was an impermissible interest. The court held that the only compelling interest that could justify racial classification was a remedy for past wrongs by the government unit at issue. With regard to the plan's remedial objectives, the court ruled that the institution's bad reputation and racially hostile environment could not sustain the use of race in the admissions process. Moreover, the court stated that for the purposes of determining whether the admission plan could act as a remedy for the present effects of past discrimination, the law school must be evaluated as the relevant alleged past discriminator. As a result of this decision, which the Supreme Court refused to hear, affirmative action programs in public institutions of higher education in Texas, Louisiana, and Mississippi were outlawed.

Taxman v. Piscataway was handed down by the Third Circuit Court of Appeals. Although accepted for review by the Supreme Court, this case was settled out of court. The Piscataway board of education had to lay off a teacher in the business department of a high school. The department was composed of ten whites and one African American woman. The board's layoff policy was based on seniority. The two individuals with the lowest seniority, however, were equal in classroom performance, evaluations, volunteerism, and certifications. The board thus voted to invoke the state's affirmative action policy whereby race could be considered. The white teacher who was laid off claimed that that policy violated Title VII of the Civil Rights Act. The court held that diversity is not a Title VII objective requiring accommodation. Moreover, the court found that the board failed to show that its plan was adopted to remedy past discrimination or to fix the manifest imbalance in the employment of minorities. Finally, the court held that the program lacked the requisite definition and structure. It stated that other plans affirmed by the Supreme Court under a Title VII analysis had the following features: (1) objectives; (2) benchmarks to evaluate progress, guide employment decisions, and ensure that racial preferences were used only when necessary to further the plan's purpose; and (3) measures that were temporary and that sought to attain, not maintain, a permanent racial balance.

1997   President Clinton launches a yearlong initiative on race called One America, which culminated in a report issued in the summer of 1998. Historian John Hope Franklin led the initiative. In reaction to the *Hopwood* decision, the University of Texas implemented a policy in which the top 10 percent of every high school graduating class would be admitted to the public colleges and universities in the state.

Two lawsuits challenging the University of Michigan's use of race in admission to the undergraduate program (*Gratz v. Bollinger*) and the law school (*Grutter v. Bollinger*) were filed. On May 14, 2002, the U.S. Court of Appeals for the Sixth Circuit overturned a lower court's ruling that the admissions policy used by the law school illegally discriminated against white applicants. A decision on the undergraduate case by the same court of appeals was still pending as of July 2002. The U.S. Supreme Court refused to hear a challenge to California's Proposition 209.

1998   Washington state voters passed I-200, a state referendum that does away with affirmative action in state hiring, contracting, and admissions.

Conclusion

Support for affirmative action policies has shifted along with changes in the social and political climate. It is clear that previous and existing policies have not achieved their intended goals and that much remains to be done. That new affirmative action policies are regularly introduced, especially after periods of "benign neglect," suggests that inequities persist. Although systematic discrimination and institutional racism cannot be eradicated by affirmative action alone, they also cannot be eradicated without affirmative action. Surely, minority students are better represented in our nation's universities than they once were, but the numbers are nowhere near a level proportional to their percentages of the population. In employment, whites continue to earn significantly more than do their minority counterparts performing the same job, regardless of educational background and skill levels. Men continue to earn more than women do when performing the same job, also holding constant educational preparation. Hiring practices have become less discriminatory, and notions of merit and qualifications have been broadened, but there continues to be evidence of employers relying on "old boy networks" and hiring employees around whom they are comfortable and who remind them of themselves. Although widespread opportunity and access have not been achieved, it is also becoming increasingly clear that affirmative action policies have contributed to significant gains and that more gains are likely if such policies continue to be administered effectively and judiciously. As these improvements show, affirmative action has benefited more groups than just racial minorities. It has also helped women, European immigrants, religious exiles, the poor, and others who are not afforded certain privileges at birth.

As demonstrated by this historical summary, this country has long been engaged in resolving the problem of race and the powerful legacy of slavery. Many different efforts and policies that varied with the political whims and interests of the time have been implemented. Those policies that have been most effective recognize the significance of race in American society. Conversely, neutral, passive policies of nondiscrimination have done little to combat the inequalities left behind by slavery and racism because the issue of race is neither neutral nor passive. Certainly, laws neither can nor should legislate people's attitudes or thoughts, especially about the emotionally charged matter of race. Yet as long as certain members of a society have privilege, equal opportunity for all cannot exist without some type of broad-based extra consideration to balance out that privilege. As a result, contemporary laws or policies ought to recognize that racial differences continue to play a significant role in determining life opportunities. Most of us desire a time when the vestiges of past and current discrimination are eradicated so that affirmative action will no longer be necessary. Unfortunately, that time has not arrived and does not appear imminent.

DEFINITIONS

We have defined the following key words because in this volume they may carry meanings different from those commonly used in other texts.

CULTURE. Culture, and specifically its relationship to and distinction from race, is important to define. Borrowing heavily from anthropologists, psychologists, historians, and others, we define culture as similar to a blueprint or pattern from which individual beliefs, actions, and experiences are interpreted and give meaning to a larger social grouping. For example, the religions of particular cultures help to establish certain moral codes and norms that guide human interactions. Culture is not an inanimate, fixed, and predetermined force but one that is constantly evolving and adapting to the people it guides (as well as helping them to adapt). In his book *Prejudice and Racism*, James Jones points out the centrality of the role of race in a concept of culture and vice versa: "the meaning of race cannot be separated from the meaning of culture. Attempts to objectify blacks in the absence of what Americans of European descent think about blacks is not possible. Therefore, the so-called race problem is, at its core, a problem with U.S. culture" (Jones 1997, 363).

DIVERSITY. We use *diversity* in this book to refer to the effects that various points of view, customs, and thought processes have on negotiated meanings and understanding in a society. These differences usually stem from differences in how various groups (women/men, black/white, rich/poor, etc.) are socialized and their consequent disparate interpretations of and perspectives on the world around them. We consider diversity in higher education to go beyond the simplistic notions of celebrating differences and admitting a student body that is representative of the U.S. population, to looking at the multiple layers of diversity that exist on college and university campuses (students, faculty, administration, curriculum) and acknowledging the ways that the different perspectives affect intergroup relations and change the surrounding climate.

ETHNICITY.   In this book we use the term *ethnicity* in the way it is most commonly defined in this country. Ethnicity is usually perceived by Americans to be a more mutable and flexible force than race. Instead of being associated with physical traits as race commonly is, ethnicity is usually linked more to cultural traits that differ from those of the dominant population. The cultural traits that customarily identify a person as a member of an ethnic minority are foreign-born status, speech with a nonstandard dialect or accent, and identification with a religion that differs from that of the dominant population. Race and ethnicity are often intertwined. For example, although it is possible for white ethnic minorities and their offspring in the United States to shed their ethnic identification by acquiring fluent command of standard English and adopting mainstream religious and cultural practices, the ethnicity of a person of color is not so easily discarded.

MERIT.   In this book, we consider merit in the schooling context similar to the way in which most college admissions officers use the term. The primary criterion of merit in this context is academic achievement—that is, high levels of scholastic performance in relation to available opportunities and obstacles, and high potential for intellectual growth. This component of merit is typically measured by grade point average (and quality of the curriculum taken) and scores on standardized national tests. However, because of a variety of factors related to the opportunities and obstacles on the road to academic achievement, the validity and reliability of test scores as an indicator of intellectual potential vary across individuals and groups. Grade point average is a measure of the student's opportunity to learn as well as of his or her scholastic achievement. Thus, these numerical indexes are useful but fallible indexes of the primary criterion. Further, merit is incompletely assessed if it is equated with the numerical indexes of test scores and grade point averages, that is, if the other aspects of merit are ignored or given unduly low weight. A secondary but important criterion is achievement outside the classroom and evidence of curiosity, persistence, creativity, citizenship, community service, and leadership. Merit is thus defined by a broad range of talents.

MINORITY.   We use the terms *minority* and *majority* not as numerical references to representation in the broader population but as an indication of the extent to which a particular group has access to and is represented by the power structure of the larger society. Therefore, although white males may number fewer in certain communities or on certain college campuses, they would not be considered a minority because they are well represented in the general power structures of the United States (e.g., in government, employment, curricula). The term *minority* refers to people, who by virtue of their social categorization (race, ethnicity, class, gender) suffer some form of discrimination because a significant sector of the population overtly or covertly considers them to be less competent and less intelligent and, therefore, less deserving of truly equal treatment.

RACE.   For this project, race is considered a social and historical category that is not biologically based and that varies according to the context in which it is being defined. Despite the somewhat artificial nature of racial categories and their lack of scientific validity in the defining of human groups, race is an undeniably potent psychological force that has shaped and continues to shape societal structure and relationships. Because of the power the notion of race has had and its consequences in this country for the cultural, economic, political, and historical interactions and interpretations between groups and individuals of different backgrounds, the category of race, as defined above, is central to an understanding of diversity.

RACIAL DYNAMICS.   The meaning of this term overlaps with the meanings inherent in other terms more traditionally used to indicate interaction among different racial and ethnic groups: race relations, diversity, racial climates, multiculturalism, and so forth. This term captures the multiple dimensions of intergroup relationships better than these other descriptors because it emphasizes the ephemeral, constantly changing, and multifaceted nature of intergroup relations, particularly within the context of such complex and evolving organizations as colleges and universities.

CHAPTER ONE

1. Although the percentage of Asian Americans enrolled in higher education exceeds their percentage of the national population (see Chap. 2), the high rates are not shared by all Asian ethnic groups. Hune and Chan (1997) reported that Chinese, Japanese, Asian Indian, and Korean Americans were twice as likely as Hmong, Guamanian, Samoan, Hawaiian, and Lao Americans to be enrolled in college.

2. The UCLA law school experienced a similar drop in the enrollment of underrepresented students. The 1996 class that enrolled before Proposition 209 had 19 African American students and 45 Latinos. By contrast, the 1999 class included only 2 African American and 17 Latino students among a class of 286 incoming law students (Pool 2000).

3. According to this news release, 9 African American students, 16 Chicano students, 8 Latino students, and 2 Native American students entered Boalt in the fall of 1998. In 1997, one African American, 6 Chicanos, 8 Latinos, and no Native Americans were part of the first-year class.

4. In fact, in contrast to the common perception of affirmative action as a widespread university policy, studies using regression analysis have found that only the top 20 percent of colleges and universities have an admissions policy that employs a significant degree of racial preference (Kane 1998).

CHAPTER TWO

1. The 1994–95 recoded Carnegie categories are used for each year of enrollment data reported in this chapter. The top of the following page shows the category frequencies for the recoded classifications used in our analyses.

2. Johnson's 1965 speech at Howard University is the source of the often-cited metaphor about affirmative action; in this speech he focused on what must be done in the name of fairness to "level the playing field" for a previously shack-

Value Label	Value	Frequency	%	Valid %	Cumulative %
Research I	1	87	1.8	1.8	1.8
Research II	2	37	0.8	0.8	2.6
Doctoral	3	110	2.3	2.3	4.9
Master's/bachelor's	4	1,129	23.7	23.7	28.6
Associate of arts	5	1,360	28.6	28.6	57.2
Tribal	6	24	0.5	0.5	57.7
Other	7	596	12.5	12.5	70.2
Uncategorized	8	1,420	29.8	29.8	100.0
Total		4,763	100.0	100.0	

Valid cases: 4,763   Missing cases: 0

led runner, who, upon being freed, participates in a 100-yard dash. Johnson argued that such a race was not fair, that "something more" needed to be done.

3. Daniel Patrick Moynihan, in a note to then President Richard Nixon, suggested that, because black enrollment in higher education in the United States was as great as the total number of citizens enrolled in higher education in Great Britain, "wasn't it time for a little benign neglect."

4. We make a distinction between poverty and class because it appears that the operationalization of the two is different in the thinking of those who use the terms. On the one hand, there are the deserving poor, who, with a helping hand, can be rescued from most of the disadvantages of the absence of economic means. On the other hand, there is an "underclass," which, in the strict sociological sense, is a class unto itself with a unique set of "oppositional" values that reinforce their separation from full participation. Children from this latter category are apparently more difficult to rescue because of entrenched class values (see Ogbu 1991).

5. Not all colleges and universities are faced with heavy competition for limited spaces. Nettles and Hudgins (1995) report that approximately 320 four-year colleges and universities are faced with this challenge.

6. The IPEDS data are available electronically for more recent years at the U.S. Education Department on-line site, but these data have not completed the data cleaning process.

7. Crossland (1971) used this measure, as did the 1971 Newman Report (U.S. Department of Health, Education, and Welfare 1971).

8. See note 1 above.

CHAPTER THREE

1. In *Missouri ex rel. Gaines v. Canada*, the Supreme Court determined that the University of Missouri could not deny admission to a black student, despite the

university's willingness to send the student to any of the four adjoining states that would admit him. In *Sipeil v. the Board of Regents of the University of Oklahoma*, the Supreme Court responded to the university's refusal to admit black students by demanding that it provide a law school education to qualified applicants regardless of race. The rulings in *Sweatt v. Painter* and *McLaurin v. Oklahoma State Regents for Higher Education* came down on the same day in 1950. In each of those rulings, the Court again confirmed that students could not be excluded from educational opportunity on the basis of race. It further demanded that physically separating black students from white students after admitting them to the program did not provide equal educational opportunity and was not acceptable.

CHAPTER FIVE

1. This argument is clearly articulated in the following statement by the American Council on Education and endorsed by forty-nine national education associations:

Many colleges and universities share a common belief, born of experience, that diversity in their student bodies, faculties, and staff is important for them to fulfill their primary mission: providing a quality education. The public is entitled to know why these institutions believe so strongly that racial and ethnic diversity should be one factor among the many considered in admissions and hiring. The reasons include:

It enriches the educational experience. We learn from those whose experiences, beliefs, and perspectives are different from our own, and these lessons can be taught best in a richly diverse intellectual and social environment.

It promotes personal growth—and a healthy society. Diversity challenges stereotyped preconceptions; it encourages critical thinking; and it helps students learn to communicate effectively with people of varied backgrounds.

It strengthens communities and the workplace. Education within a diverse setting prepares students to become good citizens in an increasingly complex, pluralistic society; it fosters mutual respect and teamwork; and it helps build communities whose members are judged by the quality of their character and their contributions.

It enhances America's economic competitiveness. Sustaining the nation's prosperity in the 21st century will require us to make effective use of the talents and abilities of all our citizens, in work settings that bring together individuals from diverse backgrounds and cultures. (American Council on Education 1998)

2. Examples of complex social structures include "situations where we encounter many rather than few people, when some of these people are unfamiliar to us, when some of them challenge us to think or act in new ways, when peo-

ple and relationships change and thus produce some unpredictability, and, especially, when people we encounter hold different kinds of expectations of us" (Gurin 1999, 105).

3. In this study, openness to diversity and challenge is represented by an eight-item scale that was created based on the results of an exploratory factor analysis of items derived from survey data. The eight items that comprise this scale include the following statements: (1) I enjoy having discussions with people whose ideas and values are different from my own; (2) The real value of a college education is being introduced to different values; (3) I enjoy talking with people who have values different from mine because it helps me understand myself and my values better; (4) Learning about people from different cultures is a very important part of my college education; (5) I enjoy taking courses that challenge my beliefs and values; (6) The courses I enjoy the most are those that make me think about things from a different perspective; (7) Contact with individuals whose background (e.g., race, national origin, sexual orientation) is different from my own is an essential part of my college education; and (8) I enjoy taking courses that are intellectually challenging.

4. These findings are from analyses of data gathered as part of the University of Michigan's Program on Intergroup Relations, Conflict, and Community (IGRCC). To test Gurin's hypothesis that the IGRCC program facilitates the development of learning outcomes and democracy outcomes, questionnaires were developed that assessed aspects of these constructs. Specifically, the complex thinking measure included items asking students to agree with whether they (a) enjoyed analyzing reasons for behavior, (b) preferred simple rather than complex explanations (reverse scaled), (c) did not enjoy discussions of causes of behavior (reverse scaled), and (d) took people's behavior at face value (reverse scaled). The measure of social/historical thinking asked students whether they agreed with statements that they (a) thought about the influence of society on other people, (b) thought causes of behavior often form a chain that goes back in time, and (c) thought about the influence of society on their own behavior and personality. The analyses performed with this data were longitudinal. In other words, seniors' scores on these indexes were compared with their scores on the same measures when they first entered Michigan as freshmen. The analyses indicated that differences in scores at these two time points were statistically significant and that participation in the IGRCC program had a significant effect on these outcomes.

5. Although black men and women who had attended selective institutions earned more than did blacks who had graduated from other institutions, the Bowen and Bok (1989) study replicates findings from other studies that indicate a persistent and troublesome earnings gap between black and white college graduates. The earnings of black men and women graduates were significantly less than those of their white peers. Multivariate analyses revealed that after control-

ling for the effects of grades, college majors, and socioeconomic status, blacks were likely to earn significantly less than their white colleagues.

6. Data for the analyses reported in this study came from information gathered from individual faculty members in the 1992–93 Survey of College and University Faculty conducted by the Higher Education Research Institute (HERI) at UCLA. The 1992–93 HERI faculty survey provided normative data for full-time faculty from across the nation who were employed at 344 institutions of higher education. The faculty included in this study reported that they had spent at least part of their time during the previous year teaching undergraduate students. The survey was sent to faculty at participating institutions during the fall of 1992. A second wave of surveys was sent to nonrespondents during the late fall of 1992 and early winter of 1993. The final response rate to the survey was 61 percent. Examination of the data gathered from faculty at these institutions indicates that every major type of institution was well represented in this data set (Dey et al. 1993).

7. In the studies cited by Cox (1993), *value congruence* refers to the degree of agreement between production workers and their supervisors in business settings. The findings of these studies indicate that higher levels of value congruence have a positive influence on individual outcomes (i.e., organizational commitment and worker satisfaction) *and* organizational outcomes (i.e., greater punctuality, lower turnover rates, higher levels of innovation).

8. Abelson and Levy (1985, 292) define groupthink as "a strong psychological drive for consensus within insular, cohesive decision-making groups such that disagreement is suppressed and the decision process becomes defective."

9. The label "Hispanics" for Latinos is used in this section of the chapter because it is the label used in Census Bureau reports.

10. This section on organizational forces relies heavily on the work of Astin (1985, 1991); Dey, Milem, and Berger (1997); Milem, Berger, and Dey (2000); and Berger and Milem (2000).

CHAPTER SIX

1. This is the first year for which scores for Hispanic students were disaggregated.

2. Even more evidence has since been compiled after the completion of this project. Some notable examples include the work of Orfield and Kurlaender (2001), Milem and Hakuta (2000), and the American Council on Education and the American Association of University Professors (2000).

Abelson, R., and A. Levy. 1985. Decision making and decision theory. In *Handbook of social psychology*, vol. 1, ed. G. Lindzey and E. Aronson. New York: Random House.

Abramowitz, E., ed. 1976. *Proceedings from the national invitational conference on racial and ethnic data*. Washington, D.C.: Institute for the Study of Educational Policy.

Alger, J. R. 1997. The educational value of diversity. *Academe* 20 (January/February).

Allalouf, A., and G. Ben-Shakhar. 1998. The effect of coaching on the predictive validity of scholastic aptitude tests. *Journal of Educational Measurement* 35:35–47.

Allen, W. R. 1992. The color of success: African American college student outcomes at predominantly white and historically black public colleges and universities. *Harvard Educational Review* 62:26–44.

Allport, G. W. 1954. *The nature of prejudice*. New York: Doubleday.

American Bar Association, Section of Legal Education and Admission to the Bar. 1993. *A review of legal education in the United States: Fall 1992 law schools and bar admission requirements*. Chicago.

American College Testing Program. 1973. *Assessing students on the way to college: Technical report for the ACT Assessment Program*. Iowa City, Iowa.

———. 1991. *Supplement to the preliminary technical manual for the Enhanced ACT Assessment*. Iowa City, Iowa.

———. 1997. *Supplement to the preliminary technical manual for the Enhanced ACT Assessment*. Iowa City, Iowa.

American Council on Education. 1998. Statement on diversity. *Chronicle of Higher Education*, February 13, A48.

American Council on Education and the American Association of University Professors. 2000. *Does diversity make a difference? Three research studies on diversity in college classrooms*. Washington, D.C.

Americans United for Affirmative Action. 1997. Affirmative action timeline 1776–1997. http://www.auaa.org/timeline.

Arbona, C., and D. Novy. 1990. Noncognitive dimensions as predictors of college success among black, Mexican-American, and white students. *Journal of College Development* 31:415–22.

Association of American Medical Colleges. 1994. Minority students in medical education: Facts and figures, No. 8. Washington, D.C.: AAMC.

Association of American Universities. 1997. On the importance of diversity in university admissions. *New York Times*, April 24, 27.

Astin, A. W. 1977. *Four critical years*. San Francisco: Jossey-Bass.

———. 1979. Testing in post secondary education: Some unresolved issues. *Educational Evaluation and Policy Analysis* 1(6): 21–28.

———. 1985. *Achieving educational excellence*. San Francisco: Jossey-Bass.

———. 1991. *Assessment for excellence: The philosophy and practice of assessment and evaluation in higher education*. New York: Macmillan.

———. 1993. *What matters in college: Four critical years revisited*. San Francisco: Jossey-Bass.

Astin, A. W., and J. W. Henson. 1977. New measures of college selectivity. *Research in Higher Education* 6(1): 1–9.

Astone, B., and E. Nuñes-Womak. 1990. *Pursuing diversity: Recruiting college minority students*. ASHE/ERIC Higher Education Report No. 7. Washington, D.C.: George Washington University Press.

Ayres, I. 1995. Further evidence of discrimination in new car negotiations and estimates of its cause. *Michigan Law Review* 94:109–47.

Ballard, A. B. 1973. *The education of black folk*. New York: Harper and Row.

Banaji, M. R., and A. G. Greenwald. 1994. Implicit stereotyping and prejudice. In *The psychology of prejudice: The Ontario symposium*, ed. M. P. Zanna and J. M. Olson, 7:55–76. Hillsdale, N.J.: Lawrence Erlbaum Associates.

Bates College. 1998. Bates College online / admissions. http://www.bates.edu/admissions/optional-testing.html.

Baydar, N. 1990. Effects of coaching on the validity of the SAT: Results of a simulation study. In *Predicting college grades: An analysis of institutional trends over two decades*, ed. W. W. Willingham, C. Lewis, R. Morgan, and L. Ramist, 213–24. Princeton, N.J.: Educational Testing Service.

Bendick, M., Jr. 1996. Discrimination against racial/ethnic minorities in access to employment in the United States: Empirical findings from situation testing. International Migration Papers 12. Geneva: Employment Department, International Labour Office.

Bennett, R. E. 1994. *An electronic infrastructure for a future generation of tests*. Princeton, N.J.: Educational Testing Service.

Berger, J. B., and J. F. Milem. 2000. Organizational behavior in higher education and student outcomes. In *Higher education: Handbook of theory and research*, ed. J. C. Smart. New York: Agathon Press.

Bikson, T. K., and S. A. Law. 1994. *Global preparedness and human resources: College and corporate perspectives*. Santa Monica, Calif.: RAND Corporation.

Blalock, J. M. 1967. *Toward a theory of minority-group relations.* New York: Wiley.

Bobo, L. 1983. Whites' opposition to busing: Symbolic racism or realistic group conflict? *Journal of Personality and Social Psychology* 45:1196–1210.

———. 1988. Group conflict, prejudice, and the paradox of contemporary racial attitudes. In *Eliminating racism: Profiles in controversy,* ed. P. A. Katz and D. A. Taylor, 85–116. New York: Plenum Press.

———. 2000. Race and beliefs about affirmative action: Assessing the effects of interests, group threat, ideology, and racism. In *Racialized politics: The debate about racism in America,* ed. D. O. Sears, J. Sidanius, and L. Bobo, 137–64. Chicago: University of Chicago Press.

Bok, D. 1990. *Universities and the future of America.* Durham and London: Duke University Press.

Bollinger, L. C. 1997. *Climate and character: Perspectives on diversity.* Ann Arbor: Office of the President, University of Michigan.

Bond, L. 1989. The effects of special preparation on measures of scholastic ability. In *Educational measurement,* 3d ed., ed. R. L. Linn, 429–44. New York: Macmillan.

Bowen, H. 1977. *Investment in learning.* San Francisco: Jossey-Bass.

Bowen, W. G., and D. Bok. 1998. *The shape of the river: Long term consequences of considering race in college and university admissions.* Princeton, N.J.: Princeton University Press.

Braddock, J. H. 1980. The perpetuation of segregation across levels of education: A behavioral assessment of the contact hypothesis. *Sociology of Education* 53:178–86.

———. 1985. School desegregation and black assimilation. *Journal of Social Issues* 41(3): 9–22.

———. 1993. Ability grouping, aspirations, and attainments: Evidence from the national longitudinal study of 1988. *Journal of Negro Education* 62(3): 324–36.

Braddock, J. H., and M. Dawkins. 1981. Predicting achievement in higher education. *Journal of Negro Education* 50:319–27.

Braddock, J. H., and J. M. McPartland. 1982. Assessing school desegregation effects: New directions in research. In *Research in sociology of education and socialization,* vol. 3. Greenwich, Conn.: JAI.

———. 1989. Social-psychological processes that perpetuate racial segregation: The relationship between school and employment desegregation. *Journal of Black Studies* 19:267–89.

Braddock, J. H., R. L. Crain, and J. M. McPartland. 1984. A long-term view of school desegregation: Some recent studies of graduates as adults. *Phi Delta Kappan,* December, 259–64.

Braddock, J. H., M. P. Dawkins, and W. Trent. 1994. Why desegregate? The effect of school desegregation on adult occupational segregation of African Americans, whites, and Hispanics. *International Journal of Contemporary Sociology* 31(2): 271–83.

Braddock, J. H., J. M. McPartland, and W. Trent. 1984. Desegregated schools
and desegregated work environments. Paper presented at the Annual
Meeting of the American Educational Research Association, New Orleans.

Braun, H., and D. Jones. 1981. *The Graduate Management Admission Test
prediction bias study*. Graduate Management Admission Council, Report
No. 81-04, and Educational Testing Service, RR-81-25. Princeton, N.J.:
Educational Testing Service.

Breland, H. M. 1979. *Population validity and college entrance measures*. College
Board Research Monograph No. 8. New York: College Entrance
Examination Board.

Brest, P., and M. Oshige. 1995. Affirmative action for whom? *Stanford Law
Review* 47(5): 855–900.

Bridgeman, B., and F. McHale. 1996. *Gender and ethnic group differences on the
GMAT Analytical Writing Assessment*. Graduate Management Admission
Council, Report No. 96-02, and Educational Testing Service, RR-96-02.
Princeton, N.J.: Educational Testing Service.

Brogan, D. W. 1944. *The American character*. New York: Alfred A. Knopf.

Brogden, H. E. 1946. On the interpretation of the correlation coefficient
as a measure of predictive efficiency. *Journal of Educational Psychology*
37:65–76.

Brown, J. L., and C. M. Steele. 1999. Creating trust vs. boosting confidence:
Contrasting approaches to reducing the effects of negative stereotypes on
intellectual performance. Manuscript. University of Washington, Seattle.

Cahn, S. 1999. Stephen Cahn on the history of affirmative action.
http://humanitas.ucsb.edu/projects/aa/docs/Cahn.html.

Campbell, F. A., and C. T. Ramey. 1994. Effect of early intervention on
intellectual and academic achievement: A follow-up study of children from
low-income families. *Child Development* 65:684–98.

Cantor, J. C., E. L. Miles, L. C. Baker, and D. C. Barker. 1996. Physician
service to the underserved: Implications for affirmative action in medical
education. *Inquiry* 33:167–80.

Carnoy, M. 1994. *Faded dreams: The politics and economics of race in America*. New
York: Cambridge University Press.

Carson, R. 1998. UW Regents show their displeasure with I-200; Unanimous
statement issued after hearing supports "diverse student body." *News Tribune*,
January 18.

Cassirer, N. R., and B. F. Reskin. 1998. The effect of organizational context on
women's and men's attachment to their jobs. Manuscript. Department of
Sociology, Notre Dame University, South Bend, Ind.

Chan, S., and L. Wang. 1991. Racism and the model minority: Asian-Americans
in higher education. In *The racial crisis in American higher education*, ed. P. G.
Altbach and K. Lomotey, 43–67. Albany, N.Y.: SUNY Press.

Chang, M. J. 1996. Racial diversity in higher education: Does a racially mixed student population affect educational outcomes? Ph.D. dissertation. University of California, Los Angeles.

―――. 1999a. Does diversity matter? The educational impact of a racially diverse undergraduate population. *Journal of College Student Development* 40(4): 377–95.

―――. 1999b. An examination of conceptual and empirical linkages between diversity initiatives and student learning in higher education. Paper presented at ACE Working Conference and Research Symposium on Diversity and Affirmative Action, Washington, D.C.

―――. 1999c. Expansion and its discontents: The formation of Asian American studies programs in the 1990s. *Journal of Asian American Studies* 2(2): 181–206.

―――. 2000. Improving campus racial dynamics: A balancing act among competing interests. *Review of Higher Education* 23(3): 153–75.

Chenoweth, K. 1996. SAT, ACT scores increase: Higher scores attributed to more rigorous coursework. *Black Issues in Higher Education* 13(14): 6–8.

Chronicle of Higher Education. 1999. Daily Internet news, October 27.

Citizens' Commission on Civil Rights [CCCR]. 1984. *Affirmative action to open the doors of job opportunity: A policy of compassion that has worked.* Washington, D.C.

―――. 1996. *Affirmative action: Working and learning together.* Washington, D.C.

Clayton, S. 1996. Reactions to social categorization: Evaluating one argument against affirmative action. *Journal of Applied Social Psychology* 26:1472–93.

Clayton, S. D., and S. S. Tangri. 1989. The justice of affirmative action. In *Affirmative action in perspective*, ed. F. A. Blanchard and F. J. Crosby, 177–92. New York: Springer-Verlag.

Cobb, D. L. 1998. Race and higher education at the University of Illinois, 1945 to 1955. Ph.D. dissertation. University of Illinois at Urbana-Champaign.

Coleman, J. S. 1964. *Equality of educational opportunity.* Washington, D.C.: U.S. Department of Health, Education, and Welfare, Office of Education.

College Entrance Examination Board. 1998. *SAT 1998 college bound seniors: National report.* New York.

Coser, R. 1975. The complexity of roses as a seedbed for individual autonomy. In *The idea of social structure: Papers in honor of Robert Merton*, ed. L. A. Coser. New York: Harcourt Brace Jovanovich.

Cox, T. H. 1993. *Cultural diversity in organizations: Theory, research and practice.* San Francisco: Berrett-Koehler.

Cronbach, L. J. 1975. Five decades of public controversy over mental testing. *American Psychologist* 30:1–14.

Cronbach, L. J., and G. C. Gleser. 1965. *Psychological tests and personnel decisions.* 2d ed. Urbana: University of Illinois Press.

Crosby, F. J. 1994. Understanding affirmative action. *Basic and Applied Social Psychology* 15(1/2): 13–41.

Crosby, F. J., and S. D. Clayton. 1990. Affirmative action and the issue of expectancies. *Journal of Social Issues* 46(2): 61–79.

Crossland, F. E. 1971. *Minority access to college; a Ford Foundation report.* New York: Schocken Books.

Crouse, J., and D. Trusheim. 1988. *The case against the SAT.* Chicago: University of Chicago Press.

Daniel, K., D. Black, and J. Smith. 1997. College quality and the wages of young men. Manuscript.

Davis, J. A., and T. R. Smith. 1994. *General social survey.* Chicago: National Opinion Research Center.

Devine, P. G. 1989. Stereotypes and prejudice: Their automatic and controlled components. *Journal of Personality and Social Psychology* 56:5–18.

Dey, E. L., J. F. Milem, and J. B. Berger. 1997. Changing patterns of publication productivity: Accumulative advantage or institutional isomorphism? *Sociology of Education* 70(4): 308–23.

Dey, E. L., C. Ramirez, W. S. Korn, and A. W. Astin. 1993. *The American college teacher: National norms for the 1992–93 HERI survey.* Los Angeles: UCLA, Higher Education Research Institute.

DiMaggio, P., and W. Powell. 1983. The iron cage revisited: Institutional isomorphism and collective rationality in organizational fields. *American Sociological Review* 48:147–60.

Donlon, T., ed. 1984. *The college board technical handbook for the Scholastic Aptitude Test and Achievement Tests.* New York: College Entrance Examination Board.

Dovidio, J. F. 1995. Bias in evaluative judgments and personnel selection: The role of ambiguity. Manuscript. Department of Psychology, Colgate University, Hamilton, N.Y.

Dovidio, J. F., and S. L. Gaertner. 1996. Affirmative action, unintentional racial biases, and intergroup relations. *Journal of Social Issues* 52(4): 51–75.

———. 1998. On the nature of contemporary prejudice: The causes, consequences, and challenges of aversive racism. In *Confronting racism: The problem and the response*, ed. J. L. Eberhardt and S. T. Fiske, 3–32. Thousand Oaks, Calif.: Sage Publications.

Dovidio, J. F., K. Kawakami, and S. L. Gaertner. 2000. Reducing contemporary prejudice: Combating explicit and implicit bias at the individual and intergroup level. In *Reducing prejudice and discrimination*, ed. S. Oskamp, 137–63. Hillsdale, N.J.: Lawrence Erlbaum Associates.

Dovidio, J. F., J. A. Mann, and S. L. Gaertner. 1989. Resistance to affirmative action: The implication of aversive racism. In *Affirmative action in perspective*, ed. F. A. Blanchard and F. J. Crosby, 83–102. New York: Springer-Verlag.

D'Souza, D. 1991. *Illiberal education*. New York: Free Press.

Duran, R. P. 1983. *Hispanics' education and background: Predictors of college achievement*. New York: College Entrance Examination Board.

Duster, T. 1993. The diversity of the University of California at Berkeley: An emerging reformulation of "competence" in an increasingly multicultural world. In *Beyond a dream deferred: Multicultural education and the politics of excellence*, ed. B. W. Thompson and Sangeeta Tyagi. Minneapolis: University of Minnesota Press.

Easton, J., and T. Guskey. 1983. Estimating the effects of college, department, course, and teacher on course completion rates. *Research in Higher Education* 19:153–58.

Eberhardt, J. L., and S. T. Fiske. 1994. Affirmative action in theory and practice: Issues of power, ambiguity, and gender versus race. *Basic and Applied Social Psychology* 15:201–20.

Edley, C., Jr. 1997. Why talk about race? President Clinton's initiative is more than a gabfest. *Washington Post*, final edition, December 7.

Elliott, R., and A. C. Strenta. 1988. Effects of improving the reliability of the GPA on prediction generally and on the comparative predictions for gender and race particularly. *Journal of Educational Measurement* 25:333–47.

Erickson, E. 1946. Ego development and historical change. *Psychoanalytic Study of the Child* 2:359–96.

———. 1956. The problem of ego identity. *Journal of American Psychoanalytical Association* 4:56–121.

Espanoza, L. G. 1993. The LSAT: Narratives and bias. *Journal of Gender and the Law* 1:121–64.

Evans, F. R. 1977. Applications and admission to ABA accredited law schools: An analysis of national data for the class entering in the fall of 1976. Report LSAC-77-1. In *Reports of LSAC sponsored research: 1975–1977*, vol. 3. Princeton, N.J.: Law School Admission Council.

Feldman, K. A., and T. M. Newcomb. 1969. *The impact of college on students*, vol. 1. San Francisco: Jossey-Bass.

Ferdman, B. M. 1989. Affirmative action and the challenge of the color-blind perspective. In *Affirmative action in perspective*, ed. F. A. Blanchard and F. J. Crosby, 169–76. New York: Springer-Verlag.

———. 1997. Values about fairness in the ethnically diverse workplace. *Business and the Contemporary World* 9:191–208.

Fields, C. D. 1997. An equation for equality: Maryland's Prince George's County puts Equity 2000 to the test. *Black Issues in Higher Education* 13(26): 24–30.

Fordham, S., and J. Ogbu. 1986. Black students' school success: Coping with the burden of acting white. *Urban Review* 18(3): 176–206.

Fuertes, J. N., and W. E. Sedlacek. 1995. Using noncognitive variables to predict the grades and retention of Hispanic students. *College Student Affairs Journal* 14(2): 30–36.

Gaertner, S. L., and J. F. Dovidio. 1986. The aversive form of racism. In *Prejudice, discrimination, and racism*, ed. J. F. Dovidio and S. L. Gaertner, 61–89. Orlando, Fla.: Academic Press.

Gaertner, S. L., M. C. Rust, J. F. Dovidio, B. A. Bachman, and P. A. Anastasio. 1994. The contact hypothesis: The role of a common ingroup identity on reducing intergroup bias. *Small Groups Research* 25:224–49.

Gallup Organization. 1997. *Black/white relations in the United States: A Gallup poll social audit*. Princeton, N.J.

Gamoran, A. 1998. Differentiation and opportunity in restructured schools. *American Journal of Education* 106(3): 385–415.

Garcia, M., and D. G. Smith. 1996. Reflecting inclusiveness in the college curriculum. In *Educating a new majority: Transforming America's educational system for diversity*, ed. Laura I. Rendon and Richard O. Hope. San Francisco: Jossey-Bass.

Globetti, E. C., G. Globetti, C. L. Brown, and R. E. Smith. 1993. Social interaction and multiculturalism. *NASPA Journal* 30(3): 209–18.

Green, K. C. 1982. The impact of neighborhood and secondary school integration on educational achievement and occupational attainment of college bound blacks. Ph.D. dissertation. University of California, Los Angeles.

Grissmer, D. W., S. N. Kirby, M. Berends, and S. Williamson. 1994. *Student achievement and the changing American family*. Santa Monica, Calif.: RAND Corporation.

Gumport, P. 1994. Graduate education: Changing conduct in changing contexts. In *Higher education in American society*, 3d ed., ed. P. G. Altbach, R. O. Berdahl, and P. J. Gumport, 307–31. Amherst, N.Y.: Prometheus Books.

Gurin, P. 1999. Expert report of Patricia Gurin. In *The compelling need for diversity in higher education*. Part of expert testimony prepared for *Gratz et al. v. Bollinger et al.*, no. 97-75321 (E.D. Mich.), and *Grutter et al. v. Bollinger et al.*, no. 97-75928 (E.D. Mich.). Ann Arbor: University of Michigan.

Hacker, A. 1992. *Two nations: Black and white, separate, hostile, unequal*. New York: Ballantine Books.

Hackett, E. J. 1990. Science as a vocation in the 1990s: The changing organizational culture of academic science. *Journal of Higher Education* 61:241–79.

Hanford, G. H. 1991. *Life with the SAT: Assessing our young people and our times*. New York: College Entrance Examination Board.

Health Resources and Services Administration. 1995. Selected statistics in health professional shortage areas of December 31, 1994. Rockville, Md.

Hebel, S. 2000. U. of Virginia sees its largest drop in black applicants. *Chronicle of Higher Education*, February 11. http://chronicle.com/daily/2000/2002/2000021105n.htm.

Heyns, B. 1974. Selection of stratification in schools. *American Journal of Sociology* 79:1434–51.

Hodgkinson, H. L. 1985. The changing pace of tomorrow's student. *Change* 17(3): 38–39.

Hood, D. W. 1992. Academic and noncognitive factors affecting the retention of black men at a predominantly white university. *Journal of Negro Education* 61(1): 12–23.

Hune, S., and K. S. Chan. 1997. Special focus: Asian Pacific American demographic and educational trends. In *Minorities in higher education*, ed. D. Carter and R. Wilson, 15:39–107. Washington, D.C: American Council on Education.

Huo, Y. J., H. J. Smith, T. R. Tyler, and E. A. Lind. 1996. Superordinate identification, subgroup identification, and justice concerns: Is separatism the problem; is assimilation the answer? *Psychological Science* 7:40–45.

Hurtado, S. 1993. The institutional climate for talented Latino students. *Research in Higher Education* 35(1): 21–41.

Hurtado, S., J. F. Milem, A. R. Clayton-Pedersen, and W. R. Allen. 1998. Enhancing campus climates for racial/ethnic diversity through educational policy and practice. *Review of Higher Education* 21(3): 279–302.

———. 1999. *Enacting diverse learning environments: Improving the campus climate for racial/ethnic diversity.* ASHE/ERIC Higher Education Reports Series 26 (8). Washington, D.C.: George Washington University.

Jacobs, J. A. 1989. Long-term trends in occupational segregation by sex. *American Journal of Sociology* 95:160–73.

Jencks, C., and M. Phillips, eds. 1998. *The black/white test score gap.* Washington, D.C.: Brookings Institute Press.

Jencks, C., and D. Riesman. 1968. *The academic revolution.* Garden City, N.Y.: Doubleday.

Johnson, S. T. 1984. Preparing black students for the SAT: Does it make a difference? An evaluation report for the NAAP test preparation project. Washington, D.C.: Howard University, School of Education.

Jones, J. N. 1997. *Prejudice and racism.* 2d ed. New York: McGraw-Hill.

Jones, R. F. 1986. A comparison of the predictive validity of the MCAT for coached and uncoached students. *Journal of Medical Education* 61:325–38.

Judy, R. W., and C. D'Amico. 1997. *Workforce 2020: Work and workers in the 21st century.* Indianapolis: Hudson Institute.

Kane, T. J. 1998. Misconceptions in the debate over affirmative action in college admissions. In *Chilling admissions: The affirmative action crisis and the search for alternatives*, ed. G. Orfield and E. Miller, 17–31. Cambridge: Harvard Education Publishing Group.

Kanter, R. M. 1977. Some effects of proportions on group life: Skewed sex ratios and responses to token women. *American Journal of Sociology* 82:965–89.

————. 1983. *The change masters*. New York: Simon and Schuster.

Karabel, J. 1999. Remarks at the conference Facing the courts of law and public opinion: Social science evidence on diversity in higher education. Stanford, Calif.: Stanford University.

Karen, D. 1990. Toward a political-organizational model of gate keeping: The case of elite colleges. *Sociology of Education* 63:227–40.

Keith, S. N., R. M. Bell, A. G. Swanson, and A. P. Williams. 1985. Effects of affirmative action in medical schools. A study of the class of 1975. *New England Journal of Medicine* 313(24):1519–25.

Kennedy, D. 1997. *Academic duty*. Cambridge: Harvard University Press.

King, P. 1978. William Perry's theory of intellectual and ethical development. In *Applying new developmental findings*, ed. L. Knefelkamp, C. Widick, and C. Parker. New Directions for Student Services, no. 4. San Francisco: Jossey-Bass.

Kline, B. B., and J. F. Dovidio. 1982. Effects of race, sex, and qualifications on predictions of a college applicant's performance. Paper presented at the annual meeting of the Eastern Psychological Association, Baltimore.

Kluegel, J. R., and E. R. Smith. 1986. *Beliefs about inequality: Americans' views of what is and what ought to be*. New York: Aldine de Gruyter.

Komaromy, M., K. Grumbach, M. Drake, K. Vranizan, N. Lurie, D. Keane, and A. B. Bindham. 1997. The role of black and Hispanic physicians in providing health care for underserved populations. *New England Journal of Medicine* 334(20): 1305–10.

Kramer, G. A., and J. Johnston. 1997. Validity of the optometry admission test in predicting performance in schools and colleges of optometry. *Optometric Education* 22(2): 53–59.

Kuh, G., J. S. Schuh, E. J. Whitt, R. E. Andreas, J. W. Lyons, C. C. Strange, L. E. Krehbiel, and K. A. MacKay. 1991. *Involving colleges: Successful approaches to fostering student learning and personal development outside the classroom*. San Francisco: Jossey-Bass.

Langer, E. J. 1978. Rethinking the role of thought in social interaction. In *New directions in attribution research*, vol. 2, ed. J. Harvey, W. Ickes, and R. Kidd, 35–58. Hillsdale, N.J.: Lawrence Erlbaum Associates.

Lawrence III, C. R., and M. J. Matsuda. 1997. *We won't go back: Making the case for affirmative action*. Boston: Houghton Mifflin.

Leary, L. F., and L. E. Wightman. 1983. *Estimating the relationship between use of test-preparation methods and scores on the Graduate Management Admission Test*. GMAC Research Report 83-1; ETS Research Report RR-83-22. Princeton, N.J.: Educational Testing Service.

Lemann, N. 1995. Taking affirmative action apart. *New York Times Magazine*, June 11.

Leo, J. 1997. Let's attack merit. *U.S. News and World Report*, November 24, 22.

Levinson, R. M. 1989. The faculty and institutional isomorphism. *Academe* 75(1): 23–27.

Lindquist, E. F. 1958. The nature of the problem of improving scholarship and college entrance examinations. In *1958 invitational conference on testing problems*. Princeton, N.J.: Educational Testing Service.

Linn, R. L. 1982a. Ability testing: Individual differences and differential prediction. In *Ability testing: Uses, consequences, and controversies*, ed. A. K. Wigdor and W. R. Garner, part 2, 335–88. Washington, D.C.: National Academy Press.

———. 1982b. Admissions testing on trial. *American Psychologist* 37(3): 279–91.

———. 1983. Predictive bias as an artifact of selection procedures. In *Principals of modern psychological measurement: A Festschrift for Frederic M. Lord*, ed. H. Wainer and S. Messick, 27–40. Hillsdale, N.J.: Lawrence Erlbaum Associates.

———. 1990. Admissions testing: Recommended uses, validity, differential prediction, and coaching. *Applied Measurement in Education* 3(4): 297–318.

———. 1994. Performance assessment: Policy promises and technical measurement standards. *Educational Researcher* 23(9): 4–14.

———. 1997. Evaluating the validity of assessments: The consequences of use. *Educational Measurement: Issues and Practice* 16(2): 14–16.

Linn, R. L., E. L. Baker, and S. B. Dunbar. 1991. Complex, performance-based assessment: Expectations and validation criteria. *Educational Researcher* 20(8): 15–21.

Linn, R. L., D. L. Harnisch, and S. B. Dunbar. 1981. Validity generalization and situation specificity: An analysis of the prediction of first year grades in law school. *Applied Psychological Measurement* 5:281–89.

Liu, G. 1998. Affirmative action in higher education: The diversity rationale and the compelling interest test. *Harvard Civil Rights–Civil Liberties Law Review* 33: 381–442.

Livingston, S. A., and N. J. Turner. 1982. *Effectiveness of the Graduate Record Examinations for predicting first-year grades: 1980–81 summary report of the Graduate Record Examinations Validity Study Service*. Princeton, N.J.: Educational Testing Service.

MacPhee, D., J. C. Kreutzer, and J. J. Fritz. 1994. Infusing a diversity perspective into human development courses. *Child Development* 65(2): 699–715.

Major, B., J. Feinstein, and J. Crocker. 1994. Attributional ambiguity of affirmative action. *Basic and Applied Social Psychology* 15:113–41.

Markham, W. T., S. L. Harlan, and E. J. Hackett. 1987. Promotion opportunity in organizations: Causes and consequences. *Research in Personnel and Human Resources Management* 5:223–87.

Marron, J. E. 1965. *Preparatory school test preparation: Special test preparation, its effect on College Board scores and the relationship of affected scores to subsequent college performance.* West Point, N.Y.: United States Military Academy.

Marx, D. M., J. L. Brown, and C. M. Steele. 1999. Allport's legacy and the situational press of stereotypes. *Journal of Social Issues* 55(3): 491–502.

Massey, D. S., and N. A. Denton. 1993. *American apartheid: Segregation and the making of the underclass.* Cambridge: Harvard University Press.

McConahay, J. B. 1986. Modern racism, ambivalence, and the modern racism scale. In *Prejudice, discrimination, and racism,* ed. J. F. Dovidio and S. L. Gaertner, 91–125. Orlando, Fla.: Academic Press.

McKinley, R. 1993. *Summary of self-reported methods of test preparation by LSAT takers for 1990–91 testing year.* Research Report 93-02. Newtown, Pa.: Law School Admission Council.

McLeod, P. L., S. A. Lobel, and T. H. Cox. 1993. Cultural diversity and creativity in small groups: A test of the value congruence process and its relationship to individual outcomes. Working paper. University of Michigan, Ann Arbor.

Mehrens, W. A. 1997. The consequences of consequential validity. *Educational Measurement: Issues and Practice* 16(2): 16–18.

Messick, S. 1980. *The effectiveness of coaching for the SAT: A review and reanalysis of research from the fifties to the FTC.* Princeton, N.J.: Educational Testing Service.

———. 1989. Validity. In *Educational measurement,* 3d ed., ed. R. L. Linn, 13–103. New York: Macmillan.

———. 1994. Foundations of validity: Meaning and consequence in psychological assessment. *European Journal of Psychological Assessment* 10(1): 1–9.

Messick, S., and A. Jungeblut. 1981. Time and method in coaching for the SAT. *Psychological Bulletin* 89:191–216.

Mickelson, R. A., and M. L. Oliver. 1991. Making the short list: Black candidates and the faculty recruitment process. In *The racial crisis in American higher education,* ed. P. B. Altback and K. Lomotey, 149–66. Ablany, N.Y.: SUNY Press.

Milem, J. F. 1992. The impact of college on students' racial attitudes and levels of racial awareness. Ph.D. dissertation. University of California, Los Angeles. Ann Arbor: University Microforms International, no. 9301968.

———. 1994. College, students, and racial understanding. *Thought and Action* 9(2): 51–92.

———. 1999. The importance of faculty diversity to student learning and to the mission of higher education. Paper presented at the American Council on Education Symposium and Working Research Meeting on Diversity and Affirmative Action.

———. 2001. Increasing diversity benefits: How campus climate and teaching methods affect student outcomes. In *Diversity challenged: Evidence on the impact of affirmative action*, ed. G. Orfield and M. Kurlaender, 233–46. Cambridge: Harvard Education Publishing Group.

Milem, J. F., J. B. Berger, and E. L. Dey. 2000. Faculty time allocation: A study of change over twenty years. *Journal of Higher Education* 71(4): 454–75.

Milem, J. F., and K. Hakuta. 2000. The benefits of racial and ethnic diversity in higher education. In D. Wilds, *Minorities in higher education: Seventeenth annual status report*, 39–67. Washington, D.C.: American Council on Education.

Miller, L. S. 1999. Promoting high academic achievement among non-Asian minorities. In *Promise and dilemma: Perspectives on racial diversity and higher education*, ed. E. Lowe, 47–91. Princeton, N.J.: Princeton University Press.

Moss, G. 1995. The effects of coaching on the ACT scores of African-American students. Paper presented at the Annual Meeting of the American Educational Research Association, San Francisco, Calif.

Moy, E., and B. A. Bartman. 1995. Physician race and care of minority and medically indigent patients. *Journal of the American Medical Association* 273(19): 1515–20.

Murrell, A. J., B. L. Dietz-Uhler, J. F. Dovidio, S. L. Gaertner, and C. Drout. 1994. Aversive racism and resistance to affirmative action: Perceptions of justice are not necessarily color blind. *Basic and Applied Social Psychology* 15:71–86.

Murry, J. 1998. *Affirmative action in higher education: A retrospective and prospective look at race-based preferences*. American Educational Research Association Affirmative Action Committee annual report. Washington, D.C.: American Educational Research Association.

Nacoste, R. W. 1989. Affirmative action and self-evaluation. In *Affirmative action in perspective*, ed. F. A. Blanchard and F. J. Crosby, 103–9. New York: Springer-Verlag.

———. 1990. Sources of stigma: Analyzing the psychology of affirmative action. *Law and Policy* 12:175–95.

———. 1994. If empowerment is the goal . . . : Affirmative action and social interaction. *Basic and Applied Social Psychology* 15:87–112.

———. 1996. How affirmative action can pass constitutional and social psychological muster. *Journal of Social Issues* 52(4):133–44.

Nairn, A., and Associates. 1980. *The reign of ETS: The corporation that makes up minds*. Washington, D.C.: Ralph Nader.

Nakanishi, D. 1989. A quota on excellence? The Asian-American admissions debate. *Change*, November/December, 39–47.

Natale, J. 1990. If not the SAT, What? The search is on. *American School Board Journal* 177(6): 32.

National Advisory Committee on Black Higher Education and Black Colleges and Universities. 1979. *Access of black Americans to higher education: How open is the door?* Washington, D.C.: Government Printing Office.

National Association for College Admission Counseling. 1995. *Trends in college admission*. Alexandria, Va.

Nemeth, C. J. 1985. Dissent, group process, and creativity. *Advances in Group Processes* 2:57–75.

———. 1986. Differential contributions of majority and minority influence. *Psychological Review* 93:23–32.

Nemeth, C. J., and J. Wachter. 1983. Creative problem solving as a result of majority versus minority influence. *European Journal of Social Psychology* 12:45–55.

Nettles, M. T., and C. Hudgins. 1995. Tolerance on campus: Establishing common ground. Colby College and Northern Illinois University. An evaluation by Philip Morris Companies, Inc.

Nickens, H. W., T. P. Ready, and R. G. Petersdorf. 1994. Project 3000 by 2000: Racial and ethnic diversity in U.S. medical schools. *New England Journal of Medicine* 331(7): 472.

Noble, J. 1996. *Differential prediction/impact in course placement for ethnic and gender groups*. ACT Research Report Series 96-8. Iowa City, Iowa: American College Testing Program.

Norton, E. H. 1996. Affirmative action in the workplace. In *The affirmative action debate*, ed. G. Curry. Reading, Mass.: Addison-Wesley.

Oakes, J. 1988. Tracking: Can schools take a different route? *NEA Today* 6(6): 41–47.

Ogbu, J. V. 1991. Immigrant and involuntary minorities in comparative perspective. In *Minority status and schooling: A comparative study of immigrant and involuntary minorities*, ed. M. A. Gibson and J. V. Ogbu, 3–33. New York: Garland Publishing.

Olivas, M. 1992. Legal norms in law school admissions: An essay on parallel universes. *Journal of Legal Education* 42(1): 103–17.

———, ed. 1986. *Latino college students*. New York: Teachers College Press.

Orfield, G. 1990. Public policy and college opportunity. *American Journal of Education* 98(4): 317–49.

———. 1992. Money, equity, and college access. *Harvard Educational Review* 62(3): 337–72.

Orfield, G., and S. E. Eaton. 1996. *Dismantling desegregation: The quiet reversal of Brown v. Board of Education*. New York: New Press.

Orfield, G., and M. Kurlaender, eds. 2001. *Diversity challenged: Evidence on the impact of affirmative action*. Cambridge, Mass.: Harvard University Publishing Group.

Orfield, G., and D. Whitla. 1999. *Diversity and legal education: Student experiences in leading law schools*. Cambridge: Harvard Civil Rights Project.

Pace, C. R. 1974. *The demise of diversity: A comparative profile of eight types of institutions*. Berkeley, Calif.: Carnegie Foundation for the Advancement of Teaching.

Pascarella, E. T., M. Edison, A. Nora, L. S. Hagedorn, and P. T. Terenzini. 1996. Influences on students' openness to diversity and challenge in the first year of college. *Journal of Higher Education* 67(2): 174–95.

Pascarella, E. T., and P. T. Terenzini. 1991. *How college affects students: Findings and insights from twenty years of research*. San Francisco: Jossey-Bass.

Pascarella, E. T., E. J. Whitt, A. Nora, M. Edison, L. S. Hagedorn, and P. T. Terenzini. 1996. What have we learned from the first year of the national study of student learning? *Journal of College Student Development* 37(2): 182–92.

Pennock-Roman, M. 1988. The status of research on the Scholastic Aptitude Test (SAT) and Hispanic students in post secondary education. Paper presented at a meeting organized by the Intercultural Development Research Association for the National Commission on Testing and Public Policy, San Antonio, Tex., February 26.

Perry, W. G. 1970. *Forms of intellectual and ethical development in the college years: A scheme*. New York: Holt, Rinehart and Winston.

———. 1981. Cognitive and ethical growth. In *The modern American college: Responding to the new realities of diverse students and a changing society*, ed. A. Chickering and Associates. San Francisco: Jossey-Bass.

Pettigrew, T. 1979. The ultimate attribution error: Extending Allport's cognitive analysis of prejudice. *Personality and Social Psychology Bulletin* 5:461–76.

Pharr, S., J. Bailey, and B. Dangerfield. 1993. Admission/continuance standards as predictors of academic performance of business students. *Journal of Education for Business* 69(2): 69–74.

Piaget, J. 1971. The theory of stages in cognitive development. In *Measurement and Piaget*, ed. D. R. Green, M. P. Ford, and G. B. Flamer, 1–11. New York: McGraw Hill.

———. 1985. *The equilibrium of cognitive structures: The central problem of intellectual development*. 1975. Reprint, Chicago: University of Chicago Press.

Pickering, J. W., J. A. Calliotte, and G. J. McAuliffe. 1992. The effect of noncognitive factors on freshman academic performance and retention. *Journal of the Freshman Year Experience* 4(2): 7–30.

Plumer, G. 1997. A review of the LSAT using literature on legal reasoning. LSAC Research Report. Newtown, Pa.: Law School Admission Council.

Pool, B. 2000. UCLA students arrested in admissions policy protest. *Los Angeles Times*, February 25, B4.

Popham, W. J. 1997. Consequential validity: Right concern (wrong concept). *Educational Measurement: Issues and Practice* 16(2): 9–13.

Powers, D. E. 1977. *Comparing predictions of law school performance for black, Chicano, and white law students*. Report No. LSAC-77-3. Newtown, Pa.: Law School Admission Council.

————. 1982. Long-term predictive and construct validity of two traditional predictors of law school performance. *Journal of Educational Psychology* 74(4): 568–76.

————. 1985. Effects of test preparation on the validity of a graduate admissions test. *Applied Psychological Measurement* 9(2): 179–90.

————. 1987. Who benefits most from preparing from a "coachable" admissions test? *Journal of Educational Measurement* 24(3): 247–62.

————. 1993. Coaching for the SAT: Summary of the summaries and an update. *Educational Measurement: Issues and Practice* 12(2): 24–30.

Powers, D. E., and M. K. Enright. 1987. Analytical reasoning skills in graduate study: Perceptions of faculty in six fields. *Journal of Higher Education* 58:658–82.

Ramist, L. 1984. Predictive validity of the ATP tests. In *The college board technical handbook for the Scholastic Aptitude Test and Achievement Tests*, ed. T. F. Donlon. New York: College Entrance Examination Board.

Ramphele, M. 1999. Equity and excellence—Strange bedfellows? A case study of South African higher education. In *Promise and dilemma: Perspectives on racial diversity and higher education*, ed. E. Lowe, 145–61. Princeton, N.J.: Princeton University Press.

Reskin, B. F. 1998. *The realities of affirmative action in employment*. Washington, D.C.: American Sociological Association.

Reskin, B. F., and H. Hartmann. 1986. *Women's work, men's work: Sex segregation on the job*. Washington, D.C.: National Academy Press.

Reskin, B. F., and P. Roos. 1990. *Job queues, gender queues*. Philadelphia: Temple University Press.

Riesman, D. 1956. *The academic procession. Constraint and variety in American higher education*. Lincoln: University of Nebraska Press.

Rodriguez, R. 1996. Life after *Hopwood*: Standardized tests may be the first to go. *Black Issues in Higher Education* 13(12): 8–10.

Rogers, B. H. 1984. The use of non-cognitive variables in the prediction of black freshmen's academic performance. Paper presented at the Annual Meeting of the Southern Association for Institutional Research, Little Rock, Ark., October 24–26.

Rothbart, M. 1981. Memory processes and social beliefs. In *Cognitive processes in stereotyping and intergroup relations*, ed. D. L. Hamilton, 145–81. Hillsdale, N.J.: Lawrence Erlbaum Associates.

Rudenstine, N. L. 1997. The uses of diversity. *Harvard Magazine* 98(4): 49–62.

Sax, L. J., and A. W. Astin. 1997. The development of "civic virtue" among college students. In *The senior year experience: Facilitating integration, reflection, closure, and transition*, ed. J. N. Gardner and G. Van der Veer. San Francisco: Jossey-Bass.

Sax, L. J., A. W. Astin, W. S. Korn, and S. K. Gilmartin. 1999. *The American college teacher: National norms for the 1998–1999 HERI faculty survey*. Los Angeles: Higher Education Research Institute, UCLA.

Scheuneman, J. D., and C. Slaughter. 1991. Issues of test bias, item bias, and group differences and what to do while waiting for the answers. ERIC Document Reproduction Service, no. ED400294.

Schuman, H., C. Steeh, L. Bobo, and M. Krysan. 1997. *Racial attitudes in America: Trends and interpretations*. Rev. ed. Cambridge: Harvard University Press.

Schweinhart, L. J., H. V. Barnes, and D. P. Weikart. 1993. *Significant benefits: The High/Scope Perry Preschool study through age 27*. Monographs of the High/Scope Educational Research Foundation, no. 10. Ypsilanti, Mich.: High/Scope Press.

Scott, W. R. 1995. *Institutions and organizations*. Thousand Oaks, Calif.: Sage.

Sears, D. O. 1988. Symbolic racism. In *Eliminating racism: Profiles in controversy*, ed. P. A. Katz and D. A. Taylor, 53–84. New York: Plenum Press.

———. 1998. Racism and politics in the United States. In *Confronting racism: The problem and the response*, ed. J. L. Eberhardt and S. T. Fiske, 76–100. Thousand Oaks, Calif.: Sage Publications.

Sears, D. O., C. van Laar, M. Carrillo, and R. Kosterman. 1997. Is it really racism? The origins of white Americans' opposition to race-targeted policies. *Public Opinion Quarterly* 61:16–53.

Sedlacek, W. E., and S. H. Kim. 1995. Multicultural assessment. ERIC Document Reproduction Service, no. ED391112.

Shapiro, H. T. 1995. Affirmative action: A continuing discussion—A continuing commitment. *Princeton Weekly Bulletin*, October 16.

Shepard, L. S. 1997. The centrality of test use and consequences for test validity. *Educational Measurement: Issues and Practice* 16(2): 5–8, 13.

Sidanius, J. 1993. The psychology of group conflict and the dynamics of oppression: A social dominance perspective. In *Explorations in political psychology*, ed. S. Iyengar and W. McGuire, 183–219. Durham, N.C.: Duke University Press.

Sidanius, J., S. Levin, and F. Pratto. 1998. Hierarchical group relations, institutional terror, and the dynamics of the criminal justice system. In *Confronting racism: The problem and the response*, ed. J. L. Eberhardt and S. T. Fiske, 136–65. Thousand Oaks, Calif.: Sage.

Sidanius, J., S. Levin, J. L. Rabinowitz, and C. M. Federico. 1999. Peering into the jaws of the beast: The integrative dynamics of social identity, symbolic racism, and social dominance. In *Cultural divides: Understanding and overcoming group conflict*, ed. D. A. Prentice and D. T. Miller, 80–132. New York: Russell Sage.

Sidanius, J., and F. Pratto. 1999. *Social dominance: An intergroup theory of social hierarchy and oppression*. Cambridge: Cambridge University Press.

Sidanius, J., P. Singh, J. J. Hetts, and C. Federico. 2000. It's not affirmative action, it's the blacks: The continuing relevance of race in American politics. In *Racialized politics: The debate about racism in America*, ed. D. O. Sears, J. Sidanius, and L. Bobo, 191–235. Chicago: University of Chicago Press.

Slavin, R. 1990. Achievement effects of ability grouping in secondary schools: A best-evidence synthesis. Madison, Wis.: National Center on Effective Secondary Schools.

Smith, D. G. 1995a. *The drama of diversity and democracy*. Washington, D.C.: Association of American Colleges and Universities.

―――. 1995b. Organizational implications of diversity in higher education. In *Diversity in organizations: New perspectives for a changing workplace*, ed. M. M. Chemers, S. Oskamp, and M. A. Costanzo, 220–44. Thousand Oaks, Calif.: Sage.

Smith, D. G., G. L. Gerbick, M. A. Figueroa, G. H. Watkins, T. Levitan, C. M. Leeshawn, P. A. Merchant, H. D. Beliak, and B. Figueroa. 1997. *Diversity works: The emerging picture of how students benefit*. Washington, D.C.: Association of American Colleges and Universities.

Smith, H. J., and T. R. Tyler. 1996. Justice and power: When will justice concerns encourage the advantaged to support policies which redistribute economic resources and the disadvantaged to willingly obey the law? *European Journal of Social Psychology* 26:171–200.

Springer, L., B. Palmer, P. Terenzini, E. Pascarella, and A. Nora. 1996. Attitudes toward campus diversity: Participation in a racial or cultural workshop. *Review of Higher Education* 20(1): 53–68.

Stanley, J. C. 1977–78. The predictive value of the SAT for brilliant seventh- and eighth-graders. *College Board Review* 106:31–37.

Steeh, C., and M. Krysan. 1996. The polls-trends: Affirmative action and the public, 1970–1995. *Public Opinion Quarterly* 60:128–58.

Steele, C. M. 1997. A threat in the air: How stereotypes shape intellectual identity and performance. *American Psychologist* 52:613–29.

Steele, C. M., and J. Aronson. 1995. Stereotype threat and the intellectual test performance of African Americans. *Journal of Personality and Social Psychology* 69:797–811.

Steele, S. 1990. *The content of our character*. New York: Basic Books.

Sugrue, T. J. 1999. Expert report of Thomas J. Sugrue. In *The compelling need for diversity in higher education*. Part of expert testimony prepared for *Gratz et al. v. Bollinger et al.*, no. 97-75231 (E.D. Mich.), and *Grutter et al. v. Bollinger et al.*, no. 97-75928 (E.D. Mich.). Washington, D.C.: Wilmer, Cutler, and Pickering Law Firm.

Tajfel, H. 1981. *Human groups and social categories*. Cambridge: Cambridge University Press.

Tajfel, H., and J. Turner. 1986. The social identity theory of intergroup behavior. In *Psychology of intergroup relations*, ed. S. Worchel and W. G. Austin, 7–24. Chicago: Nelson-Hall.

Tanaka, G. K. 1996. The impact of multiculturalism on white students. Ph.D. dissertation. University of California, Los Angeles. *Dissertation Abstracts International* 57(05): 1980A.

Taylor, M. C. 1994. Impact of affirmative action on beneficiary groups: Evidence from the 1990 general social survey. *Basic and Applied Psychology* 15:143–78.

Taylor, W. L. 1998. Racism and the poor: Integration and affirmative action as mobility strategies. In *Locked in the poorhouse: Cities, race, and poverty in the United States*, ed. F. R. Harris and L. A. Curtis. Lanham, Md.: Rowman and Littlefield.

———. 1999. Remarks at the conference on Facing the Courts of Law and Public Opinion: Social Science Evidence on Diversity in Higher Education. Stanford University, Stanford, Calif.

Thernstrom, S., and A. Thernstrom. 1997. *America in black and white: One nation indivisible*. New York: Simon and Shuster.

Thomas, B. 1990. Women's gains in insurance sales. In *Job queues, gender queues*, ed. B. F. Reskin and P. A. Roos. Philadelphia: Temple University Press.

Tierney, W. G. 1993. *Building communities of difference: Higher education in the twenty-first century*. Westport, Conn.: Bergin and Garvey.

———. 1997. The parameters of affirmative action: Equity and excellence in the academy. *Review of Educational Research* 67(2): 165–96.

Tracey, T. J., and W. E. Sedlacek. 1984. Noncognitive variables in predicting academic success by race. *Measurement and Evaluation in Guidance* 16(4): 171–78.

———. 1985. The relationship of noncognitive variables to academic success: A longitudinal comparison by race. *Journal of College Student Personnel* 26(5): 405–10.

———. 1987a. A comparison of white and black student academic success using noncognitive variables: A LISREL analysis. *Research in Higher Education* 27(4): 333–48.

———.1987b. Prediction of college graduation using noncognitive variables by race. *Measurement and Evaluation in Counseling and Development* 19(4): 177–84.

Traub, J. 1999. The end of affirmative action (and the beginning of something better): How diversity survived Prop. 209 in California. *New York Times Magazine*, May 2, 44–51, 76–79.

Trent, W. T. 1991. Student affirmative action in higher education: Addressing underrepresentation. In *The racial crisis in American higher education*, ed. P. B. Altbach and K. Lomotey, 107–32. Albany, N.Y.: SUNY Press.

Triandis, H. C., E. R. Hall, and R. B. Ewen. 1965. Member heterogeneity and dyadic creativity. *Human Relations* 18:33–55.

U.S. Bureau of the Census. 1980. *Major field of study of college students: October 1978.* Current population reports, P20-351. Washington, D.C.: Government Printing Office.

———. 1990. *Decennial census school district special tabulation, 1990.* SDAB tabulation reference RQ2H10R. Washington, D.C.: Government Printing Office.

———. 1997. *Statistical abstract of the United States: 1997.* 11th ed. Washington, D.C.: Government Printing Office.

———. 1998. Current population reports, P60-198. Washington, D.C.: Government Printing Office.

U.S. Department of Education, National Center for Education Statistics. 1986–92. Common core of data surveys. Washington, D.C.: Government Printing Office.

———. 1978. *The condition of education.* Washington, D.C.: Government Printing Office.

———. 1990. *Trends in racial/ethnic enrollment, fall 1978 through 1988.* Washington, D.C.: Government Printing Office.

———. 1992. *Race/ethnicity trends in degrees conferred by institutions of higher education, 1980–81 through 1989–90.* Washington, D.C.: Government Printing Office.

———. 1994. *School district data book.* Version 1.0. Washington, D.C.: Government Printing Office.

———. 1995. *Digest of education statistics, 1995.* Washington, D.C.: Government Printing Office.

———. 1996. *Digest of education statistics, 1996.* Washington, D.C.: Government Printing Office.

———. 1997a. *Digest of education statistics, 1997.* Washington, D.C.: Government Printing Office.

———. 1997b. *NAEP 1996 trends in academic progress.* Washington, D.C.: Government Printing Office.

———, Office for Civil Rights. 1976, 1984, 1988, and 1990. *Elementary and secondary school civil rights survey.* Washington, D.C.: Government Printing Office.

U.S. Department of Health, Education, and Welfare. 1971. *Report on higher education.* Washington, D.C.: Government Printing Office.

U.S. News Online. 1997. How important is the SAT? Interview with William Hiss and John Blackburn. http://www.usnews.com/usnews/edu.

Valencia, R., ed. 1991. *Chicano school failure and success.* Bristol, Pa.: Taylor and Francis.

Villalpando, O. 1994. Comparing the effects of multiculturalism and diversity on minority and white students' satisfaction with college. Paper presented at the Annual Meeting of the Association for the Study of Higher Education, Tucson, Ariz. ERIC Document Reproduction Service, no. ED375721.

Weiner, B. 1985. An attributional theory of achievement motivation and emotion. *Psychological Review* 92:548–73.

Weiss, R. 1997. *"We want jobs": A history of affirmative action.* New York and London: Garland Publishing.

White House. 1999. Affirmative action history and rationale. http://www.whitehouse.gov/WH/EOP/OP/html/aa/aa02.html.

White, T. J., and W. E. Sedlacek. 1986. Noncognitive predictors: Grades and retention of specially-admitted students. *Journal of College Admissions* 111:20–23.

Whitt, E. J., M. I. Edison, E. T. Pascarella, P.T. Terenzini, and A. Nora. 1998. Influences on students' openness to diversity and challenge in the second and third years of college. Paper presented at the annual meeting of the Association for the Study of Higher Education.

Wightman, L. F. 1993. *Predictive validity of the LSAT: A national summary of the 1990–92 correlation studies.* Research Report 93-05. Newtown, Pa.: Law School Admission Council.

———. 1997. The threat to diversity in legal education: An empirical investigation. *New York University Law Review* 72(1): 1–53.

———. 1998a. Are other things essentially equal? An empirical investigation of the consequences of including race as a factor in law school admission decisions. *Southwestern Law Review* 28(1): 1–43.

———. 1998b. LSAC national longitudinal bar passage study. Newtown, Pa.: Law School Admission Council.

Wightman, L. F., and L. F. Leary. 1985. *GMAC validity study service: A three-year summary.* Princeton, N.J.: Graduate Management Admission Council.

Wightman, L. F., and D. G. Muller. 1990. *An analysis of differential validity and differential prediction for black, Mexican American, Hispanic, and white law school students.* Research Report 90-03. Newtown, Pa.: Law School Admission Council.

Wilder, D. A. 1981. Perceiving persons as a group: Categorization and intergroup relations. In *Cognitive processes in stereotyping and intergroup relations,* ed. D. L. Hamilton, 213–57. Hillsdale, N.J.: Lawrence Erlbaum Associates.

Williams, T. M., and M. M. Leonard. 1988. Graduating black undergraduates: The step beyond retention. *Journal of College Student Development* 29(1): 69–75.

Willingham, W. W. 1988. Admission decisions. In *Testing handicapped people,* ed. W. W. Willingham, M. Ragosta, R. E. Bennett, H. Braun, D. A. Rock, and D. E. Powers, 71–81. Boston: Allyn and Bacon.

Willingham, W. W., and H. M. Breland. 1977. The status of selective admissions. In *Selective admissions in higher education,* ed. Carnegie Council on Policy Studies in Higher Education. San Francisco: Jossey-Bass.

Wilson, W. J. 1980. *The declining significance of race.* 2d ed. Chicago: University of Chicago Press.

————. 1987. *The truly disadvantaged*. Chicago: University of Chicago Press.

Xu, G., S. K. Fields, C. Laine, J. J. Veloski, B. Barzansky, and C. J. Martini. 1997. The relationship between the race/ethnicity of generalist physicians and their care for underserved populations. *American Journal of Public Health* 87(5): 817–22.

Young, J. W. 1994. Differential prediction of college grades by gender and ethnicity: A replication study. *Educational and Psychological Measurement* 54(4): 1022–29.

Zurayk, C. K. 1968. Universities and the making of tomorrow's world. In *Higher education in tomorrow's world*, ed. A. D. Henderson. Ann Arbor: University of Michigan.

Zwick, R. 1993. The validity of the GMAT for the prediction of grades in doctoral study in business and management: An empirical Bayes approach. *Journal of Educational Statistics* 18(1): 91–110.